Inventories of Ruin

CATHOLIC PRACTICE IN THE AMERICAS

SERIES EDITORS:
John C. Seitz and Jessica Delgado

SERIES ADVISORY BOARD:
Emma Anderson, Ottawa University
Kathleen Sprows Cummings, University of Notre Dame
Jack Lee Downey, University of Rochester
Thomas Ferraro, Duke University
Jennifer Scheper Hughes, University of California, Riverside
Brianna Leavitt-Alcantara, University of Cincinnati
Mark Massa, Boston College
Kenneth Mills, University of Michigan
Paul Ramirez, Northwestern University
Thomas A. Tweed, University of Notre Dame
Pamela Voekel, Dartmouth University

Inventories of Ruin

THE DEMISE OF THE MEXICAN JESUITS,
IN THREE ACTS

J. Michelle Molina

FORDHAM UNIVERSITY PRESS
New York 2026

Copyright © 2026 Fordham University Press

All rights reserved. No part of this publication may be reproduced, stored in a retrieval system, or transmitted in any form or by any means—electronic, mechanical, photocopy, recording, or any other—except for brief quotations in printed reviews, without the prior permission of the publisher.

Fordham University Press has no responsibility for the persistence or accuracy of URLs for external or third-party Internet websites referred to in this publication and does not guarantee that any content on such websites is, or will remain, accurate or appropriate.

Fordham University Press also publishes its books in a variety of electronic formats. Some content that appears in print may not be available in electronic books.

Visit us online at www.fordhampress.com.

For EU safety / GPSR concerns: Mare Nostrum Group B.V., Mauritskade 21D, 1091 GC Amsterdam, The Netherlands, gpsr@mare-nostrum.co.uk

Library of Congress Cataloging-in-Publication Data available online at https://catalog.loc.gov.

Printed in the United States of America

28 27 26   5 4 3 2 1

First edition

Contents

Introduction: Disappearing Acts	1
ACT I. Arrest	**24**
SCENE I. *Notarial Observation at the Colegio Espíritu Santo*	31
SCENE II. *The Action of Subtraction*	37
SCENE III. *Departures and Returns, Replications and Excisions*	45
SCENE IV. *Aramburu's Desk*	50
SCENE V. *Madre Santísima de la Luz, Owner of the Means of Her Own Reproduction*	53
SCENE VI. *Counting the Silver*	62
SCENE VII. *Care for the Sacramental Silver on the Jesuit Hacienda*	75
SCENE VIII. *Charting Virtue, Enforcing Devotionalism*	79
SCENE IX. *Silver, Salvation, and Racialization*	88
ACT II. Possibility?	**98**
SCENE I. *The First Book*	101
SCENE II. *Shipboard Disputation*	103
SCENE III. *Off the Page, or, Things Thjülen Is Too Self-Absorbed to See*	107
SCENE IV. *Missing Books*	114
SCENE V. *The Virgin Mary Conquers Lutheran Heresy*	119
SCENE VI. *Chasing Spiritual Union across the Mediterranean*	123
SCENE VII. *Betrayal*	126

ACT III. Ruination   134

   SCENE I. *The Transatlantic Culling of the Mexican Province*   139

   SCENE II. *"True" Monuments: The Ruination of* el Verdadero Jesuita   149

   SCENE III. *Off the Page: Bologna*   161

   SCENE IV. *Displaced, or the Jesuit "College" in a New World*   163

   SCENE V. *The Hacienda, Another Model*   166

   SCENE VI. *"La América" and Nostalgia for Tepotzotlán*   170

   SCENE VII. *To Live Dying: Mourning in an Etiological Mode*   172

   SCENE VIII. *Necrocommunity, or a Mournful Mode of Sociability*   179

   SCENE IX. Verdadero *Anchorites*   182

Concluded: The Mexican Province   189

Acknowledgments   197
Notes   203
Bibliography   243
Index   259

Inventories of Ruin

Introduction
Disappearing Acts

Disappearance is not antithetical to remains.

Rebecca Schneider

This work stages the ruination of the Mexican Province of the Society of Jesus (the Jesuits) whose demise unfolds over a period of approximately fifty years in the eighteenth-century Spanish Atlantic world. Founded by Ignatius of Loyola in the sixteenth century, the Jesuits established a missionary presence around the globe and built an education system that shaped Catholic arts and humanities worldwide.[1] But after two and half centuries of global influence, the Society was forcibly removed from the stage of Catholic global evangelization when these missionary men were expelled in quick succession from Portugal (1759), France (1764), and Spain and the Spanish Americas (1767), only to be abolished by Pope Clement XIII in 1773.

To tell the story of the arrest, migration, and ultimate dissolution of this powerful organization of missionary men, I juxtapose three sets of "inventories." The first set of inventories is composed by notaries, who mark down the many objects left behind by the Jesuits at a college in Puebla de los Angeles when they were arrested at dawn on June 25, 1767. The second is an "inventory of the self"—a conversion narrative—composed by a Swedish convert who encounters the Mexican Jesuit refugees while shipboard on the Mediterranean Sea. The last is an inventory of the dead written by an exiled ex-Jesuit in Bologna, Italy, whose necrology memorializes the life and death of each of his brethren from the now defunct Mexican Province.

Two narrative arcs drive this book. The first emphasizes the story of the complete ruination of the Mexican Jesuits. In a "before-and-after" argument, I describe the breadth and depth of Jesuit power in New Spain

FIGURE 1. Anonymous, *The Society of Jesus Expelled from the Kingdom of Portugal by the Royal Decree of 3 September 1759*. The text reads "*Frons impia fulmina allicit*/The impious brow attracts lightning." The sword-wielding priest puts a torch to the globe, to the Church (miter), and to the Crown. The Jesuits are accused of accumulating wealth (a bag of gold at his feet) and offering nothing worth teaching (a book closed). Open access, courtesy of Museu de Lisboa, Portugal.

to make vivid how their power to act as "Jesuits" disintegrates as they move across space and through time in the Atlantic world in the years 1767 to 1815. This is an argument about the *disappearance* of Jesuit ways of being. Historians characterize the years from 1767–1814 as "the Suppression," a short-lived period of contraction for the Society of Jesus.[2] But this is to lean too heavily on the nineteenth-century Jesuit claim to have been "restored" by the papacy and "reestablished" in Mexico in 1814. Here I stage the tale differently, pointing first toward the complete demise of the Mexican Province of the Society of Jesus during the era of the abolition. The Society of Jesus has been removed from its former dominance not only as missionaries in the Americas but also across the global stage. I am well aware that after the Society is reestablished in 1814 there are some Jesuits in Mexico once again. In Europe, these religious men develop an ultramontane sensibility in the nineteenth century, found colleges in the United States, and take leading roles in more recent history both as defenders of liberation theology and, like other Catholic priests, authors of sexual abuse. Pope Francis was a Jesuit.[3]

But any measure of their ruination or restoration must account for the density of their material power in the Americas and on the world stage prior to 1773.[4] Any assessment of the Jesuit "return" must first come to terms with the way that religious power once pulsated along global Jesuit networks and colonial Mexico presents a prime example. I counter "reestablishment" histories with a description of the material density of Jesuit power in New Spain and ask, when was *this* ever reestablished? By comparison, postabolition Jesuits were compelled to operate under conditions of material scarcity within an Atlantic world whose ideological and institutional contours had changed dramatically.[5] "Restoration" arguments must first account for the complete denouement of their material network within a global order undergoing deep structural transformations.

A second tightly related but separate narrative arc of this book pertains to how this story of ruination *appears* in the archives. To tell it, I pay close attention to the epistemological drama of inventorying. These eighteenth-century writers are laboring, respectively, to uproot religious power, to locate and secure a religious self, and to capture religious histories. But while inventories can make items locatable, they also mark what should be disentangled, revalued, broken apart, and redistributed, all the while revealing obstacles that make this no easy task. As these authors attempt to secure unruly objects or inchoate human experiences, they are also restricted by genre: the notarial list with its necessary legalese, the conversion narrative leaning into its moment of authentic revelation, the memorial of each Jesuit life lived virtuously. Accordingly, I have read each of these inventories with an eye to the demands of these different genres.[6]

Yet the term "genre" has no feeling when, in fact, traces of embodied human experience weigh upon and mark these texts—sometimes subtly, at other times quite vividly. In other words, these texts exhibit a certain "aliveness." Among the varieties of felt experiences that weigh upon these texts is a profound sense of anxiety because the question—What will be found?—animates each of the authors of the inventories under study here. Their literary exertions appear as historiographical struggles to have a say over what appears and what vanishes, to have the last word before leaving the stage or before pushing others toward the exit.[7] These historiographical actors, often despite themselves, script traces of phenomenological perception as well as epistemological anxieties about recording appearance and disappearance into the resulting documents.[8] Suddenly, especially for the Jesuit writers, their "present" appears as naked exposure to an unknown future. This uncertainty transforms the inventories into scenes of apprehensive struggles with writing; the pages are rife with authorial tensions or worries about *what* they are authoring. There is drama in how writers navigate the tension between content and form, especially when their embodied repertoires are *intended* toward capturing history, toward what scholars call "the archive."[9] But the word "archive" conveys a sense of fait accompli that, in these inventories, was never quite attained. Each "master" of the genre performs a sense of inadequacy about his own inability to contain and constrain the intentional objects.

A mercurial mobility creates the uneasy context in which these writers take up the practice of scripting the appearances and disappearances of objects and people. Juxtaposed with one another, the inventories tell a moving transatlantic story. A dynamic mobility begins with the notary who paces around colleges and haciendas; the Jesuits march toward the sea, travel from port to port across the Atlantic and Mediterranean, find new shelter, again moving from town to town in Italy, then slowing to take shorter journeys—ambling through Bologna from temporary homes to local churches or to a friend's deathbed. This is epistemology in motion. Not only are all these men on the move, but their intentional objects— a locatable God, a stable self, a useable history—are also notorious shapeshifters. I use the phrase "locational anxieties" because locational pressures—to find, to be found, while in motion—lend urgency to these inventories. The weight of such locational anxieties inscribes a plot into what could otherwise be considered mere lists. Their textual problem-solving brings the writers themselves into being as "characters" on the page.[10]

But what should we do with such characters? There is a strong sense that they are performing roles. The notary! The convert! The necrologist! Yet I contend that these shadowy figures ought not be "fleshed out." In my own writing, I aim toward the sensibility captured by Rebecca Schneider's characterization of performative bodies as ghostly figures: "disappearing but resiliently eruptive, remaining through performance like so many ghosts at the door marked 'disappeared.'"[11] The only bodies with material density are the manuscripts. Yet we must keep these shadowy figures called "characters" in view because, as noted in the epilogue, "disappearance is not antithetical to remains." The story of Jesuit demise, told here, is how these writers' experiences of disappearance appear in the archives.

Stage Setting: Anti-Jesuitism in the Eighteenth Century

Why were the Jesuits expelled? While some of the most important controversies pertaining to Jesuit theology will be explored in Act I, here I paint the scene in broad strokes with a quick overview of how historians have approached this question. Most recently, Dale Van Kley has addressed how a centuries-old and very finely honed (and specifically French) anti-Jesuitism found new life in Iberian and Italian terrain, which culminated in the arrest, expulsion, and extinction of the Society of Jesus in both Europe and the Americas. Gallicanism and Jansenism were the twin pillars of eighteenth-century Reform Catholicism that supported the converging components of anti-Jesuitism.[12] Briefly, Gallicanism had been grounded in fourteenth- and fifteenth-century church/state politics, which resulted in an episcopacy that had greater control over decision making in France, a status that French bishops were keen to preserve. Jansenism was a seventeenth-century spiritual movement that was grounded in a "rigorist" theology that considered postlapsarian humans as radically fallen.[13] Critiqued by the Jesuits as "reboiled Calvinism" and squelched by both papacy and Crown in the seventeenth century, Jansenism nonetheless experienced a grass-roots resurgence in France in the eighteenth century, popular in Parisian parishes and closely covered in the press. The Society of Jesus was an international order of religious men with a hierarchical structure based upon obedience to the Jesuit general in Rome, and whose members, in making final vows, declared obedience to the pope. It is therefore not surprising that they often ran headlong against the keen Gallican desire to keep Rome at a distance. As to the Jansenists, Jesuit spirituality was distasteful to them. Ignatian spirituality was grounded in a relatively optimistic view that humans had free will that was inherently guided by what the Jesuit theologian Luís Molina (1535–1600) conceived of as "sufficient grace." Rigorist Jansenist theologians critiqued Jesuit penitential practices as exercises in moral laxity, made even more appalling by their deeply held view that shoddy Jesuit confessions had deluded fallen sinners into thinking they were worthy to take the Eucharist more frequently. As eighteenth-century anti-Jesuitism gained ground, the Gallican critique of Jesuit despotism and their affiliation with the papacy found common ground with Jansenist critiques of moral laxity. Eighteenth-century critics began to reexamine the writings of sixteenth- and seventeenth-century Jesuit theologians, not only Molina's work on free will and divine foreknowledge, but also Robert Bellarmine's (1542–1621) advocacy of *Molinismo*, as well as the writings of Juan de Mariana (1536–1624), whose probabalist theological speculations included the possibility that it could be moral to overthrow a king.[14]

Van Kley draws upon a musical metaphor, the fugue, to describe the conditions in which heretofore unrelated critiques of the Jesuits were mobilized to launch a movement against the Order. He explains how aspects of anti-Jesuitism that had been playing as singular phrases for almost as long as the Jesuits had existed (and especially in France) were "rather like themes seemingly left dangling in a Bach fugue only to be recalled and combined in a final crescendo, every theme ever sounded against Jesuits seemed to resonate and resound anew in the acoustics of contemporary events with the help of a little editorial orchestration and direction."[15]

But the how did such music play outside of France? Unlike the slow-building French anti-Jesuitism, its appearance on the Iberian Peninsula represented a radical shift from prior attitudes toward the Society of Jesus. In Spain, this new movement against the Order was largely top-down and orchestrated by Crown advisors (as opposed to the parish-based movement in France, which found a voice in the popular press). The Gallican arguments were most appealing to the Spanish as a means of wresting control over religious institutions from Rome, but the theological musings of "roguish" Jesuits so contentious in France until this moment had been easily published in the Iberian Peninsula, and even by the mid-eighteenth century Jansenism was never rooted deeply enough among the populace to be a causal factor for the expulsion of the Jesuits from Spanish holdings.[16]

Rather, the modernizing Bourbon state was keen to sideline all regular orders. Bourbon political thinkers wanted reforms. Although informed by Enlightenment trends, they did not reject Christianity so much as wish to maintain tighter control over institutional powers of the Catholic church, especially over the appointment of bishops. Accordingly, the Bourbon Crown asserted its primacy and control in the language of "regalism" and "nationalistic" priorities. But while the mendicants were lumped together as "backward," the Jesuits were distinguished as "dangerous."[17] The discourse about despotism and regicide played well on the Iberian Peninsula because the American Jesuits had been critiqued as operating as an independent state in the Paraguay missions. When the Paraguay missions were compelled to close, some indigenous Guaraní revolted and fought Crown militias. It was rumored that some Jesuits joined in the rebellion. This amplified the Jesuit reputation for exercising autonomy from both church *and* state. In the Americas the Jesuits had also successfully maneuvered against episcopal power in the battle against Juan de Palafox in Mexico in the seventeenth century. On the world stage, controversy arose surrounding Jesuit practices of accommodation to local cultural politics in India and China (respectively, the Malabar Rites and Chinese Rites controversies). Critique was transatlantic, with bishops in Europe and the Americas decrying this adaptation of Christianity as scandalous.[18] And of course the Jesuits in the Americas benefited from an exemption from tithing. Until the mid-eighteenth century they did not have to pay the ten percent tax on the earnings from their hacienda production. The Society's dogged fight to preserve this privilege fomented long-lasting resentments. Their predominance in education combined with their economic prosperity meant that the Jesuits had outsized influence in the Americas. When an assassination attempt was made on Portugal's King José I in 1758, the Jesuits' "regicidal theology" appeared to be a palpable and disturbing possibility. Finally, when a popular revolt took over the streets of Spain, the Crown swiftly blamed the Jesuits for supporting, even organizing, the uprising.

8   INTRODUCTION

Thus, if the "fugue" is a French export, then to describe its impact on the Iberian Peninsula Van Kley relies upon the language of tectonics. Accordingly, the adoption of Gallicanism, the sharpened critiques of probabilism, and a developing taste for Jansenist spirituality represented a seismic shift on the Iberian Peninsula.[19] Even so, Van Kley points out, Jansenism took root as an international movement largely as the *result* of deployment of its tenets by state agents eager to expel the Jesuits. Jansenism was, he might have said, an aftershock, and one that continued to be felt in the maneuvering of the combined efforts of diplomats from the French, Spanish, and some Italian states to compel the papacy to dismantle the Society of Jesus altogether, which it did in 1773.[20]

Textual Worries, Locational Anxieties

The specific historical details of the transatlantic story of the expulsion of the Jesuits from the Mexican Province have been very well presented by Eva St. Clair Segurado.[21] Indeed, her monograph has made possible my own exploration of how the archive of this history has come into being. Yet my take on the demise of the Mexican Jesuits is unique, first because each of the inventories discussed here remains completely unstudied in the historiography of Jesuit missionary movements in colonial Mexico and their subsequent expulsion. But more important, my staging of Jesuit demise is primarily concerned to present how these eighteenth-century humans engaged with textual practices to anchor themselves in a changing world. My work is grounded in archival research; my methods of interpretation are not strictly historical. In foregrounding movement and transformation, I bring an ethnographic eye to the study of texts, while my interpretations draw variously from the anthropology of religion, performance studies, existentialist phenomenology, and comparative literature. My aim is to locate writing practices spatially and materially. Note that I say "situated." I will insist that these writers were never "grounded," although they clearly sought to attain what Stephen Greenblatt calls a *sense* of rootedness.[22] Accordingly, in each inventory, these authors take account of the mobility of people, things, and of their God. And they also had to account for their changing senses of self as they moved through space and time.

Change. At the moment of their arrest, the Jesuits of the Mexican Province are abruptly taken away from their homes. Scholars often think about missionaries as foreigners, but the majority of the Jesuits of the Mexican Province are *naturales*—that is, in the parlance of the time, they are "native to" or born in New Spain.²³ Jesuits are not only pulled from beds to become migrants and refugees; they are wrenched away from the books, things, people, and practices that anchored them. As deeply embedded locals, they are occupied with the very concrete locational anxieties of the recently uprooted. Can they say farewell to family? Where will they next lay their heads?

My focus is on transformation and my primary investment, then, is with poiesis, or what Leo Cabranes-Grant calls the labors of becoming.²⁴ The *work* of transformation underwrites my tight focus on the unfolding human experience of writing to pare down self and/or other into the shape of an aesthetic object of remembrance. What is it to become a ruin? Using this framework, *becoming history* is a drama about how loss, anxiety, as well as nostalgia, are recorded in inventories. These authors try to document what is passing, but they do so under conditions of duress. For the Jesuit writers especially, epistemological struggle takes place on the page, in the writing itself, but against a very unclear horizon. Questions about emplacement in an unstable "now" become more urgent with a deepening sense of ambiguity about what is yet to come.²⁵ The shifting shapes of clouded futures color the way that time, space, and objects are captured on the pages of these inventories.

The Spanish state wants change, but it, too, has its locational burdens. Worries about religious power are at the root of the Spanish Crown's concerted efforts not only to arrest and evict approximately 2,500 Jesuits from the Americas, but also to name and contain all aspects of Jesuit influence that might persevere in their absence. Do these inventories successfully "work" to locate or contain intentional objects? Spoiler alert: The Spanish state is largely successful in locating and shutting down Jesuit power. Throughout, I define power in spatiotemporal terms, paying attention to the knots of relations among very mobile people and things. Marked for termination, their forced departure, their transatlantic journeys, and their general struggle to persist is staged here as a material and spatiotemporal crisis because the missionaries are removed from the people-thing density upon which their power and influence had depended. For the Jesuits, their efforts to collect themselves, to hang on to treasured books, to minister to new people is a losing battle. They forge but temporary resting points, islands of persistence that dwindle down to sandbars. That is, none of their efforts to persist add up to the former connected and thriving global missionary network of people and things.[26] Their institutions are being gutted and hollowed out from the inside, while the men are fragmented, dispersed and, in a word, ruined.

My argument about ruination depends upon developing a sense of the prior breadth and depth of Jesuit power and influence in this colonial setting. In Act I, we gain this understanding by analyzing the Spanish Crown's attempt to name, contain, and archive Jesuit material remains in New Spain. What had been the nature of Jesuit power in the colony? Given that the Society of Jesus was the target of state power, it follows that the way the Crown evaluated their material holdings can tell us much about the Jesuits among other competing sovereignties in the colony.

Power Objects and "Inventory" as the Machinery of Capture

Simultaneously across the Americas, the Jesuits had been awakened before dawn on June 25, 1767, and herded into the public spaces of their colleges, never to return to their reading, writing, teaching, confessing, and preaching, among other things, all of which had been activities central to their place among competing sovereignties in this colonial setting. Now notaries entered their rooms to write brief descriptions of the books and things that remained behind, providing a glimpse of each individual Jesuit's personal space. My initial encounter with the Crown's agenda to "capture" Jesuit religious authority on the page began with an inventory of books and furniture held at the Huntington Library. These included descriptions of posters or maps a missionary had pinned to his walls, or the utensils he might use to prepare chocolate or coffee. For a moment, the Huntington inventory struck me as a Vesuvius moment that concretizes a particular moment in time. As Alessandra Russo notes, "Even today, when the objects in question do not survive, the lists have the capacity to thrill, as if they were capable of materializing the items before the reader's eyes."[27] Lists of these kinds of things are, indeed, sacred matter to historians because they conjure "facts" and "things," which we nervously amass, anxious about the loss of even a single item that may help us locate ourselves in relation to past and future. But these inventories of objects, especially the books in the abandoned rooms, also illustrate how ideas move *through* time, as complex and fragile assemblages. A single Jesuit's desk is a sedimentary thoughtscape: The medieval Thomas Aquinas and the early modern Francisco Suárez are perched next to the latest guides to surgery and clock repair, and next to those, side by side, sit Ovid's *Metamorphosis* and Cervantes's *Quixote*. I imagined a Jesuit at his desk. What did he think about while sifting through these literary, practical, philosophical, and theological remains?[28]

But then there is that early morning knock on the door on June 25, 1767, and everything comes to a crashing halt. Jesuits. Exit, stage left. Enter the notary. In the Huntington document, the notary is unassuming. Making lists seems the relatively quiet activity of a scribe or two, working in colleges now empty of any hustle and bustle. There is little on the page to mark the notary's embodied individuality but for the drawings of flowers or birds that he makes to distinguish first drafts from final copies. But an inventory is not only a list of things; "to inventory" is a process that has a telos. The notary's labor is performative and profoundly so. The notary's listmaking and bird drawing is labor intended to *unfound* the Jesuits. His lovely doodles distract from the fact that he is an agent of a state power that has laid its weight against . . . what? Against books? Against maps?

The objects in these inventories are fascinating and varied. But to focus on the singular items is to miss the big picture: The seemingly disparate fragments listed in the inventories of Jesuit books and things index the accumulation of colonial power. The nature of this power came into sharper focus when I began to study another inventory, this document held at the Newberry Library. Ayer 1128 is an inventory of books and things found at the Colegio de Espíritu Santo in Puebla de los Angeles, the second most important city in New Spain. This gem of a manuscript put "inventory" center stage as a source of dramatic action unfolding in time. The manuscript opens approximately twenty-four hours prior to the arrest and within its pages, the hours are marked. The captain, who is charged with overseeing the arrest in Puebla, notes his hiring of notaries but also how they are swiftly locked into rooms so that news of the Jesuits' pending doom could not be leaked to the public. The notary documents how the militia circles the college at dawn and scribbles down even the short prayer invoked by the captain before knocking on the door

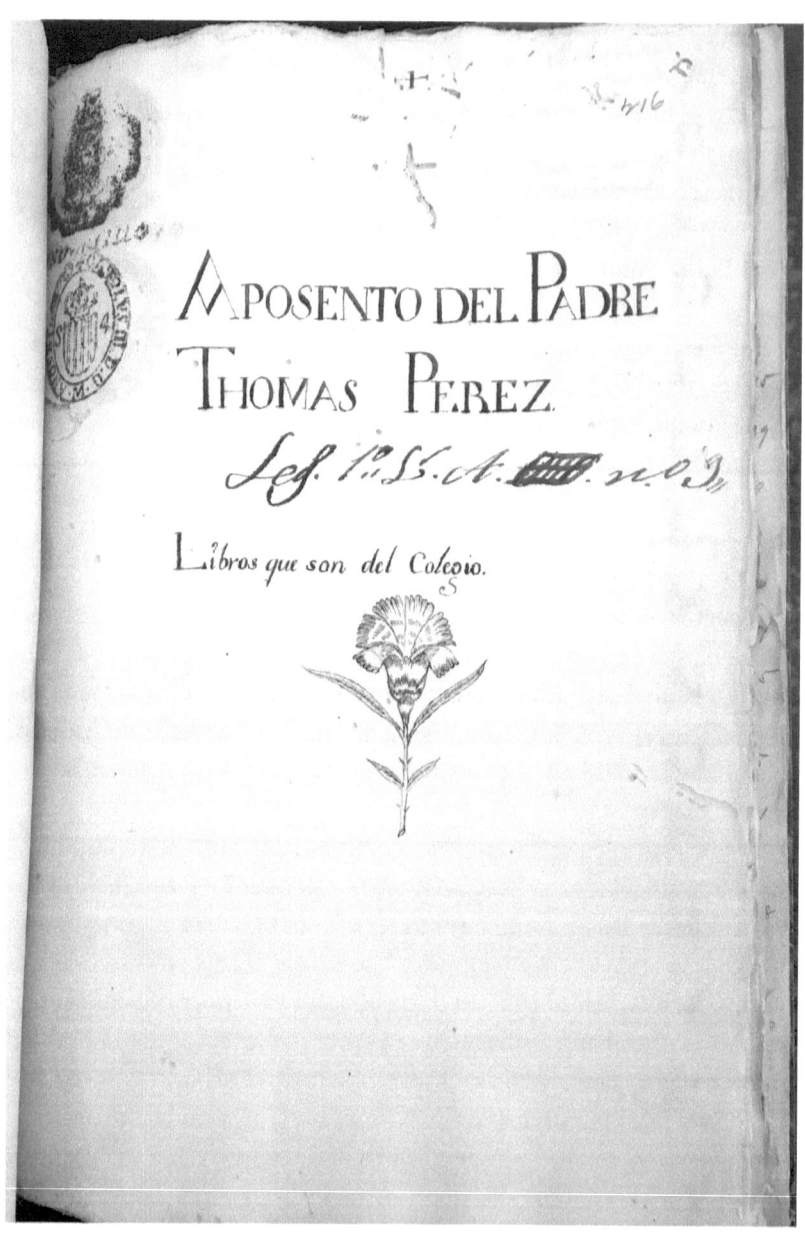

FIGURE 2. Front page of an inventory from the Jesuit college in Veracruz. Noted on the cover, Padre Tomás Pérez makes an appearance in Act III. HM 15000, Huntington Library, San Marino, California.

to arrest the sleeping Jesuits. We continue to track the notary through the day as he marks down the property that belongs to the Society, to the individual men, and to various people outside of the college walls.

I approach these eclectic materials as an assemblage and, rather than categorizing and sorting them, I trail after the notaries to understand how *they* are approaching the sorting process. In so doing, I have observed how these disparate items converge and cohere around the digestible body of the Catholic God-man, revealing a dense thicket of power embedded in sacramentally driven relationships. The sorting of silver altarware has been particularly eye-opening about how the social order of things in colonial Mexico moved around the Eucharist, not only indicating how Christ is a "distributed person" but also making clear how the decorative objects on the altar are, in Alfred Gell's words, "person-like" in that they are "sources of and targets for social agency."[29] Notarial observations about silver that had touched the body of Christ, as well as who had access to that silver, alerted me to the spatiotemporal flows of people and things around the altar. Subsequently, I reconfigured my thinking about how to theorize colonial power in this Catholic context and came to the firm conclusion that to cordon off this network with the label "religious" is just not sufficiently specific.

To more accurately articulate the terrain upon which sovereignties competed in this early modern colonial setting, I began to consider how *sacramentality* presented spatiotemporal problems. What will become clearer in Act I is how competition for power and authority in this Catholic colonial setting moves according "sacramental logics." Old and new arguments in the field of the anthropology of religion have informed how I make a new materialist argument that places Christ incarnate as a vitalist force at the center of flows of colonial power. I lean upon a venerable theorist of embodied religious power; the God-man is, in Durkheim's terms, *mana*, a religious force. Christ-as-*Mana* is at once structuring *and* unruly, a source of order and excess.[30] Thus, what I am calling *sacramental logics* names the way that incarnational theology both girds the scaffolding and propels the flow of power among competing colonial sovereignties in a very material way.[31] My work responds to Robert Orsi's call to write historical accounts that elucidate how a people's gods were experienced as "really present." Orsi contends that scholars ought "to withhold from absence the intellectual, ethical, and spiritual prestige modernity gives it, and to approach history and culture with the gods fully present to humans."[32] There are also affinities here with Amira Mittermaier's call for an "ethnography of God" as one that "makes space for alterity without containing it."[33] What both scholars make clear is that confronting God's presence *and* absence is not only an intellectual gambit, it also describes an existential experience. So too does the desire of colonial Mexicans to *contain* a divine alterity take many forms. I am deeply curious as to how the historical subjects I study in this book write "with God in the picture," using inventories to control or understand alterity, both human and divine. I trace this struggle most closely in Act I in which notaries labor to comprehend and constrain the *intermittent* appearances of the God-man. Their work highlights how the body of Christ is experienced as a shape-shifter and, accordingly, how the sacramental logics that underwrote colonial power relations could provoke a locational anxiety: Where is the god to be found; how does one get a piece?[34] Act I works with the idea that the Catholic altar served as a key nodal point in system of colonial power built upon a sacramental network. So, when I say that incarnational theology shapes the field in which colonial sovereignties compete, I understand this as a risky on-the-ground situation.

The scaffolding of Jesuit sovereignty is built upon this circuitry of exchange. Closer attention to sacramental logics illuminates how all colonial power seekers are compelled to account for the body of Christ. Ayer 1128, the inventory held in the Newberry library, stages a scene in which Jesuit mediation of the divine through sacramental practices shaped the way in which people, books, and things moved not only in and through a single Jesuit college, but also beyond its walls, into the streets of Puebla and out into the adjacent countryside. The notary's neatly delineated notes and lists show the Crown moving swiftly and purposefully to quickly shut down Jesuit power and influence by carefully marking, sequestering, and disassembling the items that comprised this network of activity that hummed around Jesuit colleges and haciendas. The Crown is documenting all possible conduits of Jesuit power, anxious to ensure that the Society of Jesus is "history." But as will become clear, such industry is pitched on unruly terrain because a God-present on the altar put limits on the Crown's power to fully impose its sovereign will. The latter becomes evident in another inventory, this one of silver altarware that shows how the Crown, too, is compelled to step back from the altar. While the altar would remain a lively and uncontested center of power in New Spain (at least for the next fifty years), in 1767 the Jesuits are abruptly and decisively severed from that peripatetic network of people and things anchored in the body of Christ.

Having set this scene in Act I, the "demise" of the Mexican Province unfolds as a story about their struggle to collect themselves as they are *distanced* in space and time from the dense thicket of sacramental power that was once lodged in the people and things that moved through its former institutions. The arrested missionaries are sent under armed guard to the coastal port town of Veracruz, where they await ships to take them first to Havana and then onward to Spain. They wait again in the port of Cádiz in southern Spain.

In Act II we move with them across the Atlantic and Mediterranean Sea by studying a very different genre, a conversion narrative written by Lorenzo Thjülen in 1771. This is an "inventory of self." This unlikely story of a young Swedish convert opens in the middle of the Mediterranean Sea. Thjülen left Gothenburg in 1768 because his love of Voltaire propelled him to seek answers about religion via "reasoned disputation" in the world. Thjülen arrives in southern Spain, and he finds this conversation with the "Gesuiti Messicani" when he takes a position on a ship he describes as "weighted down with Jesuits." Two hundred Mexican Jesuits, to be precise. His conversion narrative provides a vantage point on how these unmoored Jesuit migrants attempt to reshape shipboard routines, countering the absence of the buzzing activity of the college setting that had once anchored their daily lives. But if there is any material density to their story in this act, it is made up of the black-robed men themselves, crowded on deck. The Jesuits find few other souls on hand to which to minister. Yet even with a stripped-down arsenal of devotional tools at hand, they succeed in converting the curious young Lutheran to Catholicism.

Thjülen's conversion narrative provides an important site to continue to explore "inventorying," here as anguished epistemological struggle. Accordingly, Act II approaches the problems of mobility and knowledge production on a far more intimate and existential scale. Here the focus is on the convert; we see his struggle with transformation unfolding on the page. The intercultural scenario is key to how his emergent sense of self is taking shape.[35] He is entangled with the Jesuits, who are at sea. Their sense of loss modifies how Thjülen locates his own experience. His account of self is simultaneously an interior *and* locational exploration because

Jesuit spatiotemporal instability is the constraint that impacts Thjülen's decision making.

Accordingly, the conversion narrative is a sorting experience. This approach to inventorying and sorting as spiritual exercise—that now feels intuitive to me—had been shaped by prior study of the way that people experienced transformation when making the Ignatian Spiritual Exercises. In studying how this Jesuit mode of meditation encouraged Catholics in Europe and in New Spain to take stock of themselves, I learned from Mary Carruthers that the "craft of thought" depends upon a carefully curated *inventory*: Thought is "invention" cultivated by selectively moving the items in one's inventory.[36] In short, I was primed to read a process of "taking inventory" into Thjülen's spiritual self-formation and to interpret his conversion narrative as a memory exercise that entails intentional sifting and repatterning of memory to meet the genre's requirement of a clearly demarcated "before" and "after." Yet in Thjülen's text one finds an excess of "before/after" setups because he worries anew over each fresh encounter with Catholic books, things, and people. Most important, he chases after the stability that he finds in being with a Jesuit theologian named Iturriaga, a man on the move.

This makes Thjülen's inventory of self a high-stakes literary invention: He is grappling to find and then hang on to his sense self.[37] The work attempts to fulfill the conversion narrative's demand that he describe the emergence of a new self. Who is he now? I have to say, that answer is never clear! So how can we understand this as a story of his transformation? Thjülen's organizational labor, I contend, is best understood with an eye trained on the affective plotline. In following the tumultuous turning points, it becomes plain that his primary anxiety is about *loss* of self. Close reading reveals how disquiet compels Thjülen to rework his causal narrative, a task born of confusion, because although he clearly understands himself to be a rational Enlightenment subject, his *sense* of "self" appears to exist *outside of* himself. The narrative becomes a series of "findings" because he is chasing after stability in that moving target, Iturriaga, the father of his soul. The conversion narrative does not console or contain him, rather, we see how Thjülen becomes subject to external vectors, relays, mediators in people and things that make his transformation an anxious ride.[38] In locating "self" in an "other," I contend that Thjülen's religious desire is experienced as a form of "separation anxiety."

Additional textual tension resides in the way that Thjülen points toward Jesuit fragility within a story staged as one of triumph. More auspicious even than landing a convert to Catholicism is the Swedish youth's ultimate decision to take vows as a Jesuit. The General of the Society of Jesus asked Thjülen to write his conversion narrative to demonstrate that the Jesuits had kept their evangelical mission alive even in their diminished condition. Through Thjülen's conversion narrative, we glimpse how the Jesuits' journey across the Atlantic entails a continuous effort to reassemble their social world in the face of circumstances that continuously erode their sense of corporate connection. In the midst of hardship, Thjülen's conversion offers the thrill of success and captures a moment of possibility for the struggling Order. Yet his story offers an inadequate counterweight to what, in Act III, becomes a narrative of relentless ruination. Accordingly, even as the Jesuits encourage him to write *his* story as *their* triumph, his conversion narrative plants a seed of doubt about Jesuit futures. And what of his own future? Thjülen himself never completely *has* his Jesuits. Any possibility for a Jesuit future signaled in the conversion narrative gives way to complete demise when, as we see in Act III, the pope "cancels" the Society of Jesus, leaving both the new convert and the Mexican Jesuits scrambling.

In the final act, an ex-Jesuit named Felix de Sebastián enters the stage. He writes memorials for each of the Jesuits from the Mexican Province who died in exile from 1767 to 1796. Originally I had intended to explore Sebastián's memorials to pair his biographical entries with the items on a few of the Mexican desks described in the Huntington Library inventories. But when reading the obituaries one after the other, the manuscript began to read like a drama of disappearance. In Sebastián's memorials, the ex-Jesuits struggle to maintain some semblance of their former Order by creating ad-hoc routines mimicking those established in their former colleges and haciendas. These efforts fail. Here again, the story of Jesuit demise unfolds as a drama of spatial and temporal distance from a former mode of life which we see in Sebastián's nostalgic backward glance to a time in New Spain when Jesuits were energetic participants at the center of a densely material, sacramentally structured world.

I read the entire nine-hundred-page manuscript during the early months of Covid lockdown. Sebastián began to appear in my mind as "the Necrologist," whose memorialization of Mexican lives as virtuously busy to the point of exhaustion inadvertently calls attention to the fact that, in Italy, they minister largely to themselves. I was drawn toward the literary dimensions of this inventory of the dead. His *Memorias*, taken as a whole, describes men who struggle to persist as their form of life is hollowed out, as their prior ways of proceeding become fragmented, the men themselves dispersed and then dying. "They are so *finished*," I would comment to anyone who cared to listen (and there were people home during Covid, truly captive was my audience). Individual men may have found ways to survive and thrive, but Sebastián writes the stories of religious men who have no future because there are no longer any structuring institutions. Individually, ex-Jesuits move on, but "the Jesuits" are over. The overarching theme of "ruination" became crystal clear: For Sebastián, listing, inventorying, and archiving is a faith-based practice, collecting the dead for an unknowable future.[39]

Sebastián's inventory is comprised of small monuments to the dead that, taken in aggregate, pays homage to the vestiges of an entity that becomes more ghostly over the thirty years that he continues this project. The literary dimensions of listing and counting became clear to me. In the *Memorias*, the Province of Mexico is the well-rounded protagonist, a hyperpresence that, paradoxically, is hidden from view because its character-space is both shaped by *and* obscured by the large cast of minor characters who inhabit its many pages.[40] How does one find "the Jesuits" among these many dying individual ex-Jesuits? In fact, what Sebastián captures is the inability of these ex-Jesuits to measure up to the ghost of their idealized purposeful former selves in the Mexican Province. Despite what is unfolding in their everyday experiences in Italy, they live and die on Sebastián's pages in an ongoing state of futurelessness. Until 1796, that is, the year when Sebastián drops his pen and walks off stage, quitting well before all the dying is done. Ultimately, Sebastián's shifting modes of narration signal how his memorialization of the past is rooted in doubts about the future. Once again, inventorying is a future-oriented process. Here Sebastián seems to ask: *How will we be found?*

After I studied Sebastián's *Memorias*, this book fell into place. The two narrative arcs—the transregional history of the *disappearance* of the Mexican Jesuits, and the epistemological-existential struggles of inventorying as an attempt to capture *remains*—had to be told together, as an interrelated drama. If Act I is about arresting religious power by dismantling a network of people and things, I now had a view of Thjülen's inventory of self as a middle act, not only because it takes place halfway through their journey across the Mediterranean, but because it represents a moment of uplift, when the Mexican Jesuits can congratulate themselves on this conversion as a mission accomplished. I call this interlude "Possibility" to highlight how Thjülen imagines his own future with the Jesuits, but also how the members of the Society of Jesus latch on to the Lutheran's conversion to posit a "continuity" that is grounded in Catholic Reformation rhetoric. Their centuries-long global evangelical project is a show that must go on. But I discuss how, in Laurent Berlant's terms, this is a cruel optimism, indeed, as we see in Act III, titled "Ruination."[41] The crossing of various boundaries and borders delivers a shock to this formerly privileged group that finds itself in a state of unrelenting precarity. The curtain drops on Mexican ex-Jesuits who are compelled to adjust to their new place around the altar, that is, on the *other side*, no longer mediators of the divine but anchored now as parishioners in the pews and among the dead buried in and around Italian churches. This is where they find their end.

A final note about the anxiety of inventorying. All these authors find themselves dependent upon a cultural form, the inventory. Is it an adequate container? The inventory *form* offers a schema for organization, but inventorying as a *practice* is a space of encounter. This tale of demise traces the vicissitudes of a very resonant archive. Disquiet about an inventory's ability to hold its shape—that is, worries about the adequacy of the form—inform the scenes of struggle that unfold across all three acts.

In sum, if "inventorying" is a practice indicative of anxiety about whether power/self/meaning can be named and secured in space, in time, and on the page, then we can read these inventories like sets of worry beads.

The Notary: How to locate and extinguish Jesuit power?

The Convert: How to track down a sense of self after losing it in another?

The Necrologist: How to record the past when one's future is dissolving?

Staging Affective Epistemological Practices

> Our perceptual field is made of "things" and "gaps between things." . . . Were we to attempt to see the gaps between things as themselves things, the appearance of the world would be just as notably changed as that

of the visual puzzle at the moment when I discover in it "the rabbit" or "the hunter." This would not involve the same elements differently linked, the same sensations differently associated, the same test invested with a different sense, or the same matter in a different form, but a truly different world.[42]

This book, as I have stated, pays close attention to the labor of inventorying, and I have experimented with maintaining the *processes of writing* these inventories in view, while also allowing the resulting documents to tell a story. My action-oriented interpretation has some affinities with "archive tales."[43] But my primary goal is to draw our attention to the drama inherent in the very attempt to list important things. Drama, as deployed here, illustrates the irresolvable doubleness of the inventories under study. Accordingly, I do not invest in the quest for authentic representation; rather, I work with the idea of mimesis as a fraught endeavor. "Mimesis," says Elin Diamond, "is impossibly double, simultaneously the stake and the shifting sands: order and potential disorder, reason and madness. As a concept mimesis is indeterminate, (representation, imitation . . . neither separately captures it) and, by its own operations, loses its conceptual footing."[44]

My focus is on the stakes and the shifting sands because I have come to see that these authors write with limited ideas about where and how their lists would land. There is *drama* in the attempt to contain something while also feeling some anxiety about the adequacy of the container to do its work. Thus, my own imaginative labor is invested in staging the struggles for power and meaning that animated the production of the texts at hand.

As in theater, my aim is to conjure an immersive experience that is also interruptive. Theater calls attention to itself—actors enter and depart a stage, a seatmate coughs, lights fade, a curtain drops. The script, with its reiterative block letters, is visually interruptive. To bring the logic of "scripting" and "staging" to the poetics of writing history requires giving careful attention to the limits of the texts themselves, that is, to appreciate their edges, seams, and crossouts. The historian is instructed to perform mastery, but we depend upon texts that terminate suddenly, fail to list everything, and leave stories unfinished. Instead of adopting a synoptic view, I let the curtain drop when an actor puts a signature at the end of a page, or when he simply stops writing with no explanation whatsoever. The shift to new scenes is marked by juxtaposing texts without "papering over" the intervals between.[45]

I am attentive to these gaps because they lend an important rhythm to my own performative writing. In Diamond's words, this syncopation is "the visceral and cognitive sense of temporal otherness, [that] becomes methodological, a praxis of seeing/knowing and performing/writing in which the object belongs not to me but to a historical force field which is never fully knowable." In writing/performing/acknowledging the gaps, "linear functional time gives way to spatial intensities."[46] I take a conceptual approach that is somewhat technical.[47] The limits, the endpoints of manuscripts are to be acknowledged and evaluated: Is this an ending? Or a pause? Or maybe a cliff? The gaps are absences that "play" in the same way that provocative pauses in experimental music force us to listen to silence, to wonder what might be coming next, to experience the decay of the last sound.[48] Here attention to incompleteness and decay is key to a historiographic method that privileges manuscripts as partial and fragile objects that yet undeniably resonate according to the rhythms of now absent actors.

Reading for embodied spatial intensities is no simple task precisely because the authors of these inventories both pull us in and push us away. Their own performative practices take place within (and often paper over) the syncopated nature of space-time not only because, as Diamond says, nothing sits still for scrutiny,[49] but also because this is a history of people on the move whose tasks of observation are taken up at intervals. My attention to the pauses and gaps is a nod to the historiographical actors' anxieties *about not knowing* while in the very midst of crafting the knowledge that might anchor them, however temporarily. Especially in Acts II and III, I am tracing the syncopated time of migrant unmooring. Their writings attempt to "bear witness," but because these writers are in motion, they continually adjust their own textual framings to accommodate a shifting present.[50]

Theirs is epistemology in motion. And in the mode of a trail follower, I take note of the variety of concepts and objects, selves and others that emerge from their embodied experiences.[51] I note the spatiotemporal struggles that are written into the texts as frictions and dissonances produced by these eighteenth-century mobile writers as they traverse time-space-place.[52] Thus, what I track here are not so much "persons" as much as traces of variable tempos of knowing/valuing. In minding the gaps, instead of mending them, I do bring some moments "to life." But I also pay careful attention to what Caroline Walker Bynum speaks of as "the space between trace and departure."[53] Schneider states the problem similarly: "It is not presence that appears in performance but precisely the missed encounter—the reverberations of the overlooked, the missed, the repressed, the seemingly forgotten."[54] In performing the gaps, I explore history as "missed encounter" that, in these texts that so clearly spell out ruination, become the space of *no longer*. The archives I draw upon are performative, as is my own writing. In thinking with theater, I lean into the "doing" of historical representation but in a form that *dramatizes* how the writers of my archive experience the loss of conceptual footing, all the while still making "the thing done,"[55] that is, the inventories under study here.

LIGHTING: INITIAL GUIDELINES

Syncopation is unsettling. I invite the reader to inhabit that locational anxiety, anchored by "acts," "scenes" and "monologues" instead of chapter divisions. As Tennessee Williams indicates in his opening to The Glass Menagerie, this is a "memory play" in which "the time" is both "Now" and "the Past." I have deployed the "we," perhaps intrusively, to signal that what you have in front of you is an invitation to participate in something artificial and temporary. Williams is again instructive here: "The lighting in the play is not realistic. In keeping with the atmosphere of memory, the stage is dim. Shafts of light are focused on selected areas or actors, sometimes in contradistinction to what is the apparent center." Accordingly, I take artistic liberties with my lantern, shining it on features to which I insist we pay special attention, and to introduce "offstage" people and things that bring the stakes of my staging front and center.

No one puts on a show alone. To write a study that is both immersive and distancing I have depended not only on my three starring texts and the cast of supporting texts that you will meet, but also upon some "leading lights," that is, various philosophers and theorists whose writings function like an incredible lighting crew.

In Act I, Pierre Bourdieu and Bruno Latour are paired up. Yes, I know that neither likes to share the stage with the other, but only together can they shed light on the way that colonial power in a Catholic context runs through a networked habitus of actants, a circuitry of exchange that follows a sacramental logic. William Hanks builds upon Bourdieu to shine light on the colonial field as a space of positions and position-taking in which the latter actions are embodied and spatial but also linguistic and textual. Working with the notion that space and texts are lived, Hanks thinking sheds light on genres as generative, and how genre impacts, and is in fact intertwined with spatiality shaped by human mobility.[56]

Accordingly, Latour's mantra "no group, only group formation" drives the action that retraces "the many worlds actors are elaborating for one another." Objects and things are entry points into a network because they "authorize, allow, afford, encourage, permit, suggest, influence, block, render possible, forbid, and so on," but intermittently, and so this latter inconsistency animates what I am calling locational anxieties.[57]

Act II would not be possible without the genius choreography provided by Baruch Spinoza. His concept of conatus drives the physical drama in the second act, showing how bodies in motion move, sometimes dissonantly and sometimes in unison, thereby eroding any sense of "self" as contained. One's sense of cohesion is worn down, even destroyed, by an encounter with another. As choreographed with Spinoza, a transatlantic conversion experience transforms self into a locational problem.[58]

In Act III, Laurent Olivier's study of archaeological remains provides the shadowy lighting that complicates our sense of "having" the past. Instead, he sets up the material present as the ephemeral and disintegrating ground from which we remember the past. With Olivier we see a relationship to time that is simultaneously a melancholic, even anxiety-filled experience of having and losing. Indeed, we participate in the loss. His work is critical for conceptualizing how, in our efforts to "materialize history," we achieve the opposite. This kind of lighting is particularly important for understanding the shifting sands of Sebastián's memorialization project (Act III) who seems to abide by Olivier's words: "For this reliquary to retain its identity, I have to transform it, deform it, and in the end destroy it."[59] Latour returns to show how Jesuit "group formation" breaks down in the face of the Crown's active dismantling of its mediators. Latour also illuminates the moment when Sebastián puts down his pen and walks off the stage: "If you stop making and unmaking groups, you stop having the group."[60]

More technical instructions will be given in each act where appropriate.

Final note: Merleau-Ponty objects to "lighting" altogether. "We do not decide in advance what to see, but plunge into the world."[61]

What will be found?

Act I   Arrest

In 1767, a secret missive from the Spanish Crown informed its viceroys in the Spanish Americas that members of the Society of Jesus, the Jesuits, were to be arrested and expelled from its continental holdings. Following careful and secretive planning, the surprise announcement came in the form of a knock on the doors of Jesuit houses, colleges, and missions at dawn on June 25, 1767. Sleeping porters across the Americas were dismayed, it is fair to surmise, to open the door to the appointed commissioners and notaries who were backed by local militias, all representatives of the Crown, poised to usurp Jesuit power and wealth. Jesuits were called from their rooms and required to remain in the common areas while transportation was arranged and, importantly, their personal and collective holdings assessed. Within a few days, crowds had gathered on roadsides to watch Jesuits trek toward the port town of Veracruz, but the New Spaniards could say little. The Crown had imposed a gag order on its subjects, and to comment was a state crime.

This was a commanding demonstration of state power to quash what had been a powerhouse order of religious men. Jesuits are best known in the popular imagination for their remote mission stations, most paradigmatically in Paraguay but also in the remote regions of northern Mexico. But most *novohispanos* would have known the Jesuits for their urban colleges.[1] More than just teaching institutions, the colleges operated as hubs in a global Jesuit missionary system. Almost every aspect of the Society's tight corporate hierarchy ran through these crucial nodal points. Basically, the network of colleges functioned as a communication structure in which the superior general in Rome corresponded with the leaders of each province (the provincials), each of whom in turn oversaw operations that were directed by the rectors and procurators of the various colleges.[2] As we shall see, missionaries, money, commodities, luxury items, books, and devotional practices all moved through smaller, local networks in which the Jesuit colleges, churches and chapels, and affiliated confraternities anchored Jesuits within deeply personal communal networks. Accordingly, as made clear in the inventory of items at the Colegio Espíritu Santo, the Jesuit college in Puebla de los Angeles under study here, the colleges functioned much like sacred architecture in the sense that religious activities and experiences "swirled" around this space.[3] And the reverberations of that activity spilled out beyond the college itself, percolating into the businesses the Jesuits ran in rural countryside haciendas. Jesuits adapted a wide variety of structures to religious ends and as will become clear, seemingly "secular" edifices—colleges and haciendas—were in fact important centers of Jesuit devotional labor.[4]

Since their arrival in New Spain in 1572, the Society of Jesus had been among the colonial powerholders who cooperated and competed with both church and state authorities. In this Act, I trail after notarial actors who move from college to hacienda. But note that all staging takes place around the altar because colonial power—not merely religious authority—requires laying some claim upon the mystical corporeality of Christ's body.[5] Spanish colonialism enacts Catholic sacramentality when all people, as individuated souls and racialized bodies, are commanded to congregate around Christ's body every Sunday. This is the totalizing aim of an "ekklesial" colonialism, that is, one that has "been forged from an ill-defined yet powerful churchstateness composed of the interpenetrating and mutually constitutive forces of religion, law, and politics" in which "the body of Christ and the body politic together work to constitute the people."[6] But in this contested terrain, such totalizing aims never quite succeed because incarnation is opportunity and threat. In other words, this network of sacramental power bears within it a particular instability in that every sinner has the potential to lay hold or grasp a piece of Christ's leaky and multiplying body. We are in an environment of competing sovereignties in which "the State" recognizes that "the Church" has a monopoly over the altar and, within that field, the Jesuits "served" as key mediators of divinity. But a god that can be had, grabbed, eaten, absconded, revered, imitated, and, importantly, confer its power to things is a source of instability.

The Jesuits were no renegades; they had long worked in tandem with the colonial church and viceregal powers in New Spain. They were, however, so adept at navigating the divide between papacy and Crown that the Society of Jesus was accused of being a sovereign power. There is truth to that accusation, best seen in the network of commodity production that linked colleges such as Puebla's Colegio de Espíritu Santo to its haciendas, *fincas*, and sites for animal processing and sale, but also in the way Jesuit colleges functioned as banks, offering investments that paid interest or making loans.[7] These proceeds (untaxed) went to further the Province's missionary work in the cities and in northern New Spain and enabled the Society of Jesus to accrue spiritual capital via its missions, its charitable work, its sponsorship of religious sodalities, and its educational ministry. The colleges served to put young Jesuits through their paces as both scholars and teachers, but they folded in a wider group of laity in their sponsorship of lay confraternities, as well as in the way they loaned books in the vast collections that comprised the college libraries. All of this furthered the "soft" power of the tight affiliations born of Jesuit education.

In New Spain, the Jesuits established colleges to teach both young Spanish American men and, in segregated colleges, the sons of elite indigenous leaders. The Jesuits developed a following among Spanish and Indian alike, as well as among the newly arrived African enslaved persons—some of whom they purchased and compelled to work on their haciendas. Indeed, an enslaved family was sold to fund the foundation of Espíritu Santo, the Jesuit college where the central drama unfolds in this Act. By the eighteenth century, the Jesuits also had followers from among urban slaves and freed Black communities who participated in the social and devotional world structured by confraternities affiliated with Colegio Espíritu Santo.[8] Crucially, haciendas were more than sites of commodity production. The hacienda complex operated in the devotional orbit of the Jesuit college and was a key nodal point in a regional Jesuit sacramental network connected by personal—if very asymmetrical—religious relationships of paternal dominance, in which the Jesuit administrator of the hacienda demanded spiritual and bodily obeisance.

Put differently, much ordering and shaping of colonial subjects had taken place in and around the Jesuit colleges that served as hubs in the high-stakes and never-ending game of individuating, segregating, and assembling "the people" of New Spain as the body of a colonial church.[9] The Crown's anxiety about Jesuit power is apparent in its aims to make their absence complete. In the inventory from the Colegio Espíritu Santo under study here, the lists of items related to Jesuit haciendas and colleges did not merely mark valuable "prizes" that the Crown wished to own. Rather, in the wake of the arrest, the things that moved in and beyond the walls of Jesuit institutions were perceived as sources of power that the Crown was keen to coopt or redistribute, or whose circulation would be foreclosed altogether.

The Spanish Crown makes its initial appearance in a confident top-down display of bureaucratic action backed by force. In the initial twenty-four hours leading up to the arrest of Jesuits who lived at the Colegio Espíritu Santo in the city of Puebla de los Angeles, our vantage point is provided by a notary. On the very morning of the arrest a scribe named Manuel del Castillo, armed with pen and paper, stands alongside the militia, tasked with memorializing the event and documenting Jesuit holdings.[10] A notary recorded actions and transactions in formulaic language. As Kathryn Burns has summarized the scribe's role: "They made legible countless transactions people might eventually want the state itself to see, judge, adjudicate, or that the state might want to see."[11] She calls notaries "truth's alchemists," by which she means that they transformed singular events into formulaic language "in accordance with prescribed recipes to produce the written, duly witnessed, and certified truth. Their truth was recognizable not by its singularity, but by its very regularity. It was truth by template—*la verdad hecha de molde*."[12]

In the Newberry Library inventory, notarial description captures in a dry, factual voice the dramatic tension of the unfolding of the day's events. In "papering" the scene in front of him, the notary not only represents the sovereign's commanding power. His inventorying itself is key to the legal process that worked to immobilize a rival sovereignty, the Society of Jesus. To distinguish this high-stakes arrest from any notarial labor our scribe may have undertaken in the past, the Crown published a set of detailed instructions on how to put ordinary notarial skills to the extraordinary labor of processing an order of religious men.[13] Akin to a probate process, all Spanish American Jesuit holdings are categorized, valued, and slotted for future redistribution. Yet the Jesuits have not died. Rather, they have awoken to a new reality: Their way of life is being dismantled and sorted right before their eyes. After the Jesuits are conducted via military escort to Veracruz, we stay behind with Castillo as his inventory of items does the work of "arresting" any remaining Jesuit influence in absentia.[14]

Among the most interesting aspects of the sorting process in those initial hours following the arrest is that the state's first move was to dust away the layer of items that *did not* belong to the Jesuits. As the notary navigates the space of the college, we see that the Jesuits had cultivated a wealth of deeply personal entanglements, evidenced by the fact that the college had served as a place of safekeeping for items important to individuals in the community. As each Jesuit names money, clothing, books, instruments, and other things in his room that belong to the townspeople outside the college walls, what emerges is a fine-grained view of how Jesuits are deeply embedded in local community. The Crown may indeed have its eyes on diverting or draining the larger arteries of Jesuit "treasure," but the arrest and expulsion cauterized the very local, capillary connections that extended beyond the corporate body of the Society into *poblano* society itself. In stemming the channels of interpersonal connection large and small, the Crown dismantles what are often highly charged remnants of the hierarchical affective spiritual relationships that had been foundational to the way Jesuits had competed for sovereignty in this colonial setting.[15]

The notary is tasked with noting, marking, sorting. Yet in making sense of the great variety of items listed, historians of religion are faced with a "sorting" problem of our own. Clearly, this litany of items offers clues to how the Jesuit college, a crucial nodal point in a multiscaled long-distance missionary network, is made possible by its densely rooted local networks. But the inventory itemizes objects that, upon closer examination, are not easily categorized as sacred or profane, religious, or political. Accordingly, I resist categorizing the items individually, instead suggesting that we gain a new appreciation of how devotional practice is intertwined with colonial power if these things are understood collectively as accumulation, a kind of dust, that is, the differentiated but sum total of the many individual relationships between Jesuits and local *poblanos*.

Staged this way, the scene explores the notion of a God incarnate whose oscillating absence/presence is central to the accrual of small items in college inventories. The God-man will be introduced when he makes his appearance in an inventory of silver altarware. But I will say in advance that to read inventories for the presence of mystical body of Christ requires making scene adjustments. To trace the contours of a sacramental field in New Spain, I have taken cues from theopolitical anthropology because it attends to the way that human power relations take the divine into account in a way that mobilizes matter, sacred and mundane. As Carlota McAllister and Valentina Napolitano argue, theopolitics are forged in a space and time that is best described ethnographically to attend to the "material thickness of the political stories in which we are enmeshed." In this early modern setting, the "substance" of politics defies categorization along a "church-state" divide.[16] "Theology" is a systematic intellectual description of the nature of the divine, while political theology names an approach to secularism that depends upon a genealogical understanding of how secular power has and continues to find its grounding in theological conceptions. As an amplification of political theology that also demands attention to fine-grained detail, theopolitical anthropology depends upon ethnographic methods to trace how the flow of power in the Catholic body politic takes shape as lived experience.

Thus, theopolitical questions about *which* things might mediate the divine come into view when the Crown effectively shut down Jesuit networks of exchange and influence not only by arresting and exiling men, but also by immobilizing books and objects. These things had to be evaluated to mitigate any possibility that they would continue to mediate Jesuit power. Note that to characterize Jesuit sovereignty, I am evading terms such as "religious" or "moral authority" because Jesuit authority and influence in this colonial setting was not simply devotional or moral—words that signal personal ethics in today's terminology. Rather, as I have already suggested, colonial power is materially structured by incarnational theology. The expectation is that in the priest's hands bread can be transubstantiated to become the material body of Christ. The Eucharist is among those "sublime substances that forge the bonds of community."[17] In fact, as Charly Coleman writes, in eighteenth-century economic theology, Christ's body was "a unit of exchange . . . because his body and blood served as the measure of all value."[18] Incarnational theology structures potentialities for position-taking around the altar because this potency accrues to the things and people near the altar. In other words, to borrow Durkheimian language, *mana* moves through a traceable material network that reveals how the Jesuits obtained and maintained their key role in this colonial scene as mediators of the potentially transformative power of the incarnate God. The concept of sacramental logics that I began to outline in the introduction will become important in what follows, because tracing a sacramental network not only offers a view of the power structure from which the Jesuits are uprooted, but also choreographs a novel scene in which Catholic theopolitical power comprises a materially entangled web of people and things that circulated around the body of Christ. Staged this way, my argument about ruination becomes more precise: The Society of Jesus never reclaims its dominance as *mana* workers within this Mexican sacramental network. Looking forward in time, we see a weakened body of Christ that loses much of its theopolitical capacity to hold a people together. Simply put, one would be hard pressed to characterize material networks of political power in contemporary Mexico as *sacramental*.

But during the colonial period, the Jesuit college is a unique setting in the colonial sacramental network. While an early modern Catholic parish church demands its parishioners attend weekly Mass and to fulfill the annual precept to confess and take the Eucharist once a year, participation in activities sponsored by Jesuit colleges were voluntary. Jesuits were known for their advocacy of frequent confession and communion. This means that those drawn to the Jesuits were choosing frequency, both in the examination of self and in the consumption of the body of Christ. Through these person-to-person relationships, Jesuits mediated access to the divine by shaping the theological practices and the salvational expectations of their followers. The desire to know oneself and understand God's will more intimately through the sacrament of penance was driven by a hope to be worthy to sustain a frequent relationship with Christ's body incarnate. The Jesuits are mediators of divinity, and sacramental logics put in motion a range of people and things that moved in and through their devotional orbit. The Society's power was embedded within this swarm of activity that moved around a site of urban holiness, the Jesuit college.

As I have mentioned, my thoughts about colonial power are informed by recent scholarship that posits sovereignties in the plural that, within a single state, are in competition with one another and supported by aesthetic scaffolding.[19] This approach to church/state politics, in my view, requires the methodological approach outlined in Bruno Latour's work, in which he insists that scholars trail after actors/actants to discern the threads vivified by matters of concern. We see "sovereignty" as a matter of concern and a source of controversy lodged in material networks that themselves assemble, agonistically, multiple competing actors.[20]

In the next scenes, as we follow a notary who audits the Jesuits, we will catch a glimpse of how colonial power in the Spanish Americas is complex, not a given, reassembled daily and, more than occasionally, at risk.[21]

Scene I: Notarial Observation at the Colegio Espíritu Santo

Late at night on June 24, 1767, Francis Xavier Machado, a captain in the infantry and the commissioner charged with overseeing the arrest of the Jesuits in the city of Puebla de los Angeles in New Spain, as well as the occupation and confiscation of all their holdings, made some initial statements about his preparations. Machado is running on a tight schedule; he had been selected by the viceroy to oversee the arrest in Puebla, but he had been allowed to read the instructions only two days prior to June 25 arrest date. Machado had in his hands detailed instructions, written by the Conde de Aranda, the president of the Council of Castile and a very close advisor to the king. These "providential instructions" had been printed in Madrid and distributed to commissioners like Machado by the viceroy of New Spain, the Marquis de Croix, and were to be observed "to the letter." Puebla had five locations where arrests were staged—two Jesuit seminaries and three Jesuit colleges—and these arrests, designed to take sleeping men by surprise, were undertaken simultaneously not only across the city, but across the Americas. Aranda's instructions pertained to all the Crown's holdings—Spain, the Americas, and the Philippines, with directives written specifically to the unique situation of its overseas holdings. While Machado did not concern himself with mission stations (there were none in the vicinity of Puebla), his notes from that evening make clear that he was most concerned with Crown instructions pertaining to the speed and secrecy necessary to ensure the smooth unfolding of events.[22] His reference to *la estrechez del tiempo*—the tight window in which this would all have to take place—is very much on Machado's mind. He is also following the Crown's stipulation. "To the Scribe that you will appoint to assist you in these proceedings, you will communicate nothing until a little while before implementing them; and even then, taking care not to separate him from your side, once he has learned of this."[23]

Machado hired notaries and the man chosen to be at his own side is Manuel de Castillo. The selected notaries had been informed the night before the planned arrest. After revealing the viceregal order and the Crown's formal instructions to the notaries, all five notaries are "enclosed in a separate room under lock and key until 1:30 in the morning."[24] The commissioner, Machado, sequesters himself as well. Secrecy is imperative.

Machado's entries are not marked by the day, but by the hour: "I am now in my *posada* (inn) at approximately midnight. Present with me in a closed room are only Don Joseph Rubio, Don Juan Sevillano, and Don Matias Graihusen. I asked for a formal oath upon their honor and faith to guard this most religious secret I will reveal to them. No one will leave my sight until the order is expressly given."[25]

Francis Xavier Machado had been named after one of the founders of the Society of Jesus, yet we have no indication of his opinions. His concern is to maintain the total secrecy intended to forestall unrest. (Even the soldiers will not know the reason why they are moving into formation on the Puebla streets until the very moment that the rector of the college is roused from sleep and the arrest announced.) Two hours later, Machado writes once again, indicating that all the commissioners have moved to the house of Don Esteban Bravo de Rivero, colonel of the royal army and governor of the city of Puebla. They are, he notes, "alone in one room," and he extracted from them yet another pledge to guard *el más religioso secreto*.[26]

These several pages of quick description record Machado's compliance with Crown protocols. Then the voice in the record shifts. Enter the scribe. Manuel del Castillo, who speaks in first person, notes that Machado and the soldiers have moved into formation at approximately 4:30 a.m. "His Mercy gave the command to go down the street known as La Compañía." There is no little irony in the fact that the Jesuits—*la Compañía de Jesús*—occupy buildings on a street that happens to bear their name. The weight of this task to arrest and uproot these men no doubt prompted the commissioner's plea for help from on high: The notary observed that as Machado was about to bang on the door of the Colegio Espíritu Santo to wake up the porter, he paused and said, "Ave María Santíssima" to which in loud voices the other commissioners responded: *Por siempre sea bendita*, May she be forever blessed. And then the group moved upon the door.[27] The theatricality and the banality of these gestures are part and parcel of "the procedures, practices, discursive registers, buildings, uniforms, lawlike rules, sounds, and ways of seeing" that forge "churchstated" sovereignty.[28]

According to the *Instrucción* the college should not to be ransacked, rather, the Jesuits are to be treated well, that is, with "the greatest decency, attention, humanity, and assistance."[29] Now it has been revealed to the soldiers why they have been mobilized, and they are given further instructions to lock and guard the doors of the Jesuit churches, and to place a sentinel to guard the bell towers to ensure that no alarm will be raised and that no crowds will gather.

Castillo's notations shift briefly to an explicitly legal register, using language crafted to signal that Machado is indeed following the Crown's printed instructions. He cites and then replicates much of the Sixth Article of the *Instruccíon*: "The referred Señor Don Francisco Xavier Machado Fiesco, put into practice the *diligencias* of the legal occupation of the Archives, Papers of all kinds, the Common library, books and desks of the Rooms, conforming to that prescribed by the Sixth Article of the printed *Instrucción* and signed by the most excellent Señor Conde de Aranda in Madrid on the first day of March of this year."[30]

As the commissioner takes legal possession of Jesuit holdings in the name of the Crown, our notary is keenly attuned to space. We gain a sense of the rooms and their layout as he walks through the first floor. There are five rooms, plus two mezzanines. He notes the direction in which he walks—"entering the room adjacent, to the right." He notes all the furniture, objects, paper, and is attentive to their placement. What ensues is a form of place-marking that counters a history of Jesuit place-making. The things that had been circulated and exchanged as tokens of Jesuit power, the state now moves to mark and contain.

Castillo takes note of the cash and to whom it properly belongs, as in this example of items in the common area:

> A large cedar box with only one lock. The Fathers agreed that what is inside belongs to Don Evarde Bonilla, a neighbor of this City, who has given these for safekeeping, and that the aforementioned [Bonilla] has the key.[31]

What becomes clear at this point in Castillo's methodical notetaking is how much of the *outside* is present *inside* the college walls. Individually and collectively, the Jesuits keep things for their neighbors, a seemingly informal practice of safe guarding either money or goods for members of *poblano* society:

> In the room adjacent, entering to the right, [is] another box with *cantoneras de hierro* on its corners and a lock. The Fathers said its contents belong to Miguel Santevas, who is also a neighbor in this City, and accordingly the owner has the key and put it in this College to keep for its better safety. In the same room, another small box with a lock that the same Fathers said is destined to keep money pertaining to the pious work of marrying orphans which is funded by *licenciado* Catarroxa. And in the same room there were two large armoires with several kinds of notebooks (*cartilla*), and chalk (*de la Tierra*), and a decorated jewel box on the wall (*alhajera embutida*) with three divisions, each with its own door and lock, and each door locked.[32]

Castillo's notes mark how his entourage has moved, first toward the left side of the room, to examine several chests. These are files of paperwork "related to the College" and also to the Jesuit haciendas. He finds cupboards that hold some silver, wax, and other adornments for the church, as well as another box of funds (again with two locks) that holds the College's own contribution to the dowries for orphaned girls.[33] The fathers maintain the income of the Congregación del Pópulo (Congregation of the People) and the key should be found in the room of the padre prefect, Castillo notes, while the other two keys would be in the room belonging to the procurator. It is no surprise to find our notary marking the existence of an engraved picture (*una lámina*) of Ignatius of Loyola. More odd are "three flags said to have pertained to the eminent Religious [orders], those they said had belonged to the old Battalion of Militias of this City that had been given to [the Jesuits] to keep when the new [flags] were made." He notes that keys to one box are in the possession of the rector and can be found in his *aposento*, while the other, he notes, should be held by "Padre . . ." The spot appears to have been left vacant, and he filled in the blank later with the correct name: "Muñoz."[34]

There are more things to catalogue: A large box, locked, contained the silver jewels belonging to the estate of the Echevarria family, due to the "hundred differences that occurred between the Heirs, it is there in deposit and its key held in the same Procuraduria." In the same room there is another large box full of cinnamon (*Canela zinamomo*) from Ceylon. No specific owner is stated. And there are several bundles of "clothing from Europe" that belong to the rector, José Castillo, and the procurator, Ignacio Mozarabe. The other bundle of clothing belonged to Don Cosme Damian de Ugarte and, as we can now expect, is being held for safekeeping. As we reach the end of the description of the main rooms, our scribe notes: "All of this was seen by the Lord Commissioner and Witnesses, and by me, the rooms were closed and the keys handed over to His Merced."[35]

Next the group moved to audit the library. Without exaggeration, the library was a principal space at every Jesuit college however remote. When the Jesuits arrived in New Spain in 1572, they brought books with them, but almost immediately Jesuit leadership articulated a need for a more systematic procurement of books, considered crucial not only to support the Jesuit education ministry, the writing of sermons, and missionary labor, but also because reading was considered an important spiritual practice, and, of course, one could read for enjoyment and practical learning. Thus, by 1767 the Society had been accumulating books for almost two hundred years, its libraries, printshops, and bookstores a central component in the broad exchange of reading materials among a thriving translocal network of "lettered" society that connected libraries, printshops, and bookstore.[36]

But the task of documenting this library's holdings would wait for another day—another many years, in fact, as it took seven to fifteen years to process the Jesuit libraries, depending upon the college.[37] During this twenty-four-hour period, Castillo makes the initial foray rather swiftly. He notes the shape of the room, with wraparound shelving stretching up the high walls. "With the same subjects mentioned above, and with me in attendance, we immediately went up to the library or the school library of common books, all of which were in one room on surrounding [shelves]. Everyone agreed, upon seeing a portion of books, that the number and titles [correspond] to the works that compose the library." The padres had asserted (and the notary had ascertained) that there were exactly two copies of the general index. Accordingly, Castillo's quick work to gather the bare outlines of the library's holdings signaled the closing of a crucial nodal point of Jesuit influence and connection to lettered society. Books that had once circulated are now under lock and key.

With the indexes in hand, the commissioner closes the room, and, of course, collects the key, before moving on to the Casa de Ejercicios, another very important space that connected the Jesuits to local community.

> From the library, accompanied by his Mercy, with the stated Father Rector and Father Procurator and the aforementioned Don Fernando de Lavanda and Don Carlos Espinoza as Witnesses, we went to what they call the *Casa de Ejercicios*, where there is a Chapel and a Sacristy. We noted several Ornaments, Chalices, and others silver adornments; upon closing the doors, the keys were collected by his Mercy, the same subjects moved to the interior high chapel, in which, in the same manner, it was acknowledged to contain that concerning the Divine worship, and where the Blessed Lord is deposited, and exists therein.[38]

This "house" with a chapel had been established in 1725 as a place where the laity could make the Ignatian Spiritual Exercises. Visitors would reside on site for periods of eight to ten days to undertake the meditative retreat under the guidance of a Jesuit retreat leader. The notary's description—"what they call the Casa de Ejercicios"—offers no indication of how central were the Ignatian Spiritual Exercises not only to every Jesuit's vocation (it was how young men discerned whether they had a vocation to be a Jesuit) and their continuing spiritual life (they made the retreat annually), but also how this meditative program of self-reform was a primary and very popular means by which Jesuits around the world connected to lay Catholics. The meditations in the Exercises fostered not only the Jesuits' relationships with their innermost selves, but also with a variety of others whom they called to participate in an activist Christianity.[39]

In surveying the chapel in the Casa de Ejercicios, the notary refers briefly to space with silver adornments wherein the blessed Lord is "deposited" and "exists." At this moment the chapel is quiet, but we have to imagine the quiet bustling of monthly retreats that drew people from all walks of life, including women and Indians.[40] This was an important means by which locals became connected to Jesuit devotional practices, made them familiar with the space of this particular college, and facilitated relationships with Jesuits who gave sermons, heard their confessions, and who sponsored their confraternities. Thus, when the door is closed to "what they call the *Casa de Ejercicios*" and the keys were "placed in the power of the same Commissioner," this was very "diligent labor."

The Exercises had been foundational to many relationships of trust and authority that underwrote the material networks that will soon become even more evident in this inventory.[41]

Scene II: The Action of Subtraction

We have walked through the front door, perused the open areas of the first floor, and briskly assessed the library. We have seen Castillo's summary notations about the main arteries of cash and goods that flow to and from the haciendas. Now Castillo pivots to the processing of individual Jesuits and their belongings. The Jesuits had been pulled from their beds, presumably hours ago, and have not been allowed to return to their rooms. At that moment, the *padre ministro* is engaged in interviews with each Jesuit about his capacity to travel because, the notary comments, the *padre rector* is indisposed. The men, first gathered in a main hall, have now been called by an officer and escorted to the Casa de Ejercicios, where "his Merced has resolved to lodge them under the custody of another Official and the corresponding sentinels." Castillo notes that Machado's decision to use the Casa for detainment is due to its strategic position: It is separated from the main parts of the college, and "communication" between the two buildings is limited to a single doorway that has iron gates.[42] Now the keeper of the keys, the commissioner reopens the Casa de Ejercicios. The place that fostered vocations built upon visions of global Catholicism has become a holding pen.

The commissioner's aim in this initial survey of the Jesuits' individual *aposentos* (rooms or apartments) is to understand what belonged to the order, what belonged to the individual Jesuit, and what belonged to neither. His first step is to ask each Jesuit to point out anything in the room that is not his. The findings, given at length later in this Act, continue to offer a sense of both the formality of Castillo's notetaking and the cadence of that singular day. His language is dry but nonetheless sets an affective scene that is simultaneously a bureaucratic undertaking and a ritual display of the Crown's power, as well as a decisive end to a way of life that Jesuits meet with shock and disbelief. The German Jesuit Joseph Och wrote an account of the arrest in Mexico City that addresses the variety of emotional responses: "What manner of emotional manifestations now occurred can be more easily imagined than described. Some stood there quite dumbfounded and immobile; tears streamed from the eyes of others. Some lifted their hands and eyes passively to heaven while others sobbed. One became insane on the spot and another had a fit of apoplexy. Most stood there with well-controlled feelings and expressions."[43]

Our notary does not document the Jesuits' emotional state. Yet we have a glimpse of distress when we hear that the reason why Padre Ministro Silva accompanies the small group is "due to the Padre Rector having been indisposed."[44] We know these details because Castillo and the commissioner present their actions as hewing closely to the Crown's instructions, which state explicitly that the rector should do the job. His inability to do so is the kind of discrepancy that must be noted.

From the Casa de Ejercicios through the iron gates, each Jesuit is individually escorted to his now former room by an armed guard and required to assist in the audit. Article Fifteen of the Crown's printed *Instrucción* gives strict rules as to what each Jesuit is allowed to take with him. "Likewise, it was ordered that each Religious assist with the identification of his respective Chamber, so that in the same act he may declare if there is something in the room in which he is going to take or deposit, as well as to have his bed, clothes, breviaries, diaries, devotional booklets, tobacco of both species, and chocolate."[45] In each entry, Castillo notes the name of the Jesuit and the room number and indicates that the room's occupant did indeed "assist" in the inquiry, that at the end the Jesuit collected only the allowed personal belongings, and, finally, that the keys were put into the power of the commissioner.

In this ritualized closing down of each Jesuit's room, the social-devotional view becomes even more plain: *Poblanos* conceived of the space of the Jesuit college as a kind of bank vault wherein one could leave treasured items for safekeeping. Only a few of the items are marked in *depósito*, which indicated an item (like the Echevarría family jewelry) that is held as collateral for a loan.[46] The relationships that come into view in Castillo's notetaking were forged individually, since not every Jesuit took part in this informal economy of local exchange and safekeeping. Some men simply note that they have nothing "alien" or "foreign" in their rooms—the stock notarial phrase being "*no tener cosa alguna ajena.*" This is always followed by the all-important notation about the status of the keys. In the first *aposento* audited, Castillo notes Padre Ignacio Mozarabe's explanations about the money inside the two baskets in the cupboard: The funds belong to people whose names are written on little tickets, which are also inside the baskets, but those persons do not have documents in their power to ask for the funds. He points out a bowl, a platter, and two saucers, all made of silver, that belong to his nephew, Don Lucas de Morales. "And having taken, said *Religioso*, that which was permitted him, the door to said Aposento was locked. The Commissioner took the keys and in the appropriate manner we passed to the next." The next room belonged to Padre José Ignacio Calderón, who says that the English-language book on his desk was the property of the surgeon in the city, Don Juan Mantagas, and that they would also find among his papers a papal marriage dispensation conferred on Don Manuel Francisco Trujillo Labrador, which had been given to Calderón for safekeeping. He takes what was permitted, and then hands over the keys. Padre Manuel Dominguez has nothing to declare, so "what was allowed was given him, and the key was taken by the Señor Commissioner, who on his own terms, passed to the next."[47] This ritual notation of the key transfer continues with each Jesuit, Castillo only changing the words he uses to describe Machado's movement to the next *aposento*.

Father Pedro Gallardo declares that two large books about birds, bound in cardstock (*en pasta*), belonged to the common library of the College. The *aposento* of Juan de Arriola cannot be opened, since he is away at the Hacienda de San Pablo and must have the key with him. Padre Torrija points out the three volumes written in Italian by Padre Josef Gravina, two volumes by Padre Gecio, as well as "seis de la Racolta," that is, six that Torrija referred to simply as "the collections," although the use of the Italian word signals that, whatever the genre of writing collected therein, presumably they are also Italian works, all of which had had been loaned to him by *licenciado* Torija, a priest from Acajete.[48] Padre Eugenio Ramírez points out that the two kimonos and a piece of lace belonged to Doña Maria Ana Castro and are held in *depósito*, indicating that she had borrowed money.[49] Padre Alberto Zarzosa has a book about "the heavenly sphere" that belongs to a silversmith (*platero*) named Ortíz. Padre Ignacio Ronderos has a large bottle with a silver spout (*con boquilla de plata*) that belongs to his brother, Señor Doctor Don Vicente Ronderos, who was a canon of a church in Puebla. Ten pesos belong to a man who made the altarpiece for Nuestra Señora de la Luz, but he cannot recall his name. There is also a little bag (*taleguilla*) with money that belongs to *las Francos*, women (sisters?) who gave it to him for safekeeping. Padre Martín Vallarta has nothing to declare, collects his things, and hands over the keys.[50]

The next two rooms belonged to Padre José Castillo, the rector, who has nothing to claim. The notary remarks once again on the rector's ill health. Little wonder: He had already passed over keys to the common rooms, the library, and the Casa de Ejercicios. Now he puts in Machado's hands the keys to his private rooms. Padre José Mañan has nothing to declare; neither did Padre Mañuel Sotelo. Similarly, Maximiliano Gil and José Calderon said all things in the room were theirs (and from here forward, I will note those Jesuits who held "*nada ajena*" in the notes). Padre Bernardino Ortiz held in safekeeping a small coin box with 188 pesos belonging to Manuela de Salazar. Antonio Cid, prefect of the Congregación de los Negros, was absent, "as had already been noted" and Cid held the keys; thus, his room could not be examined. Padre Joaquín Trujillo declares a desk that belonged to Don Juán Camacho, also a book referred to as "Calancha" that belonged to Don Francisco Ronderos. He indicates that some sermons should be given to *licenciado* Benites, while a rhetoric manuscript belongs to the brother of Mariano Franquis, with some other books he had borrowed. Padre Diego de Vargas, described as a paralytic, declares five volumes of arithmetic belonged to Don Franciso Olmedo, and six volumes of Livy belong to *licenciado* Don Francisco, a notary. Padre Francisco Xavier Bonilla declares that he is holding a monstrance (*custodia*) and a silver chalice with gold plate that belong to Don Miguel Serrano, a neighbor from Cholula, who gave them to him for safekeeping. Padre Juan Francisco López occupies two rooms and noted that a key on the table opens the tabernacle (*sagrario*) of the chapel of the Casa de Ejercicios, and finally he points to some untitled books were those of *bachiller* Don Juan de Velasco. In the rooms of Padre Pedro Ganuza, there are books and various papers belonging to *licenciado* Don Manuel del Toro—again, no titles are indicated—but for a book called *Fieras de Navarra* that belong to Don Josef Mendizaval. Padre Pedro Jose Cesati points out that *Obras de Ludovico Blosio* belonged to *licenciado* Don Manuel Campurano, who is the chaplain of Santa Rosa. Padre Francisco de Aramburu is absent, and, our notary writes, "his key was not collected."[51]

Padre Josef Vicente de Silva has been occupied with the commissioner and the notary much of the day, filling in for the indisposed rector. As *ministro* he had been the keeper of the college keys until that day, when, the notary remarks, now all copies have been handed over "without exception" to the commissioner early in the morning. Now it is his turn to point to the things that do not belong to him in his two-room *aposento*. He declares that the large self-winding clock (*relox de repetición*) on the table in the first room of this *aposento* belongs to the clock man (*reloxero*) who takes care of the tower of the college. Certain books on the stand behind the door in the second of these rooms belong to Josef Paez, who is able to show his claim. The reason, he explains, that he holds so many books and ledgers pertaining to domestic business is due to his ministerial duties, which also explains why he has kept many of the books and papers of the Jesuits who had died in the time of his ministry. In addition, his apartments house a spinet (*monacordio*) that belongs to the organist, Manuel Armijo, who, it is noted, also has a key (whether to his room or to the choir Castillo does not indicate). There is a bundle of *ropa blanca* from the *aposento* of the colleague named as *ropera*; among the books he notes that the *Ohudri misterios de Cristo* belongs to *licenciado* Don Manuel del Toro, while another, titled *Le grand Filosofo*, belongs to *licenciado* Don Mariano Franquis. Finally, there is a tome of skeptical philosophy by Martín Martínez that was loaned to him by Padre Juan de Dios Cuneros from the Colegio de San Ildefonso. In an unusual ending to a room audit, the notary writes: "and said Padre declared that having made these declarations, he has discharged his conscience (*y añadió dicho Padre que ha hecho estas declaraciones en descargo de su conciencia.*)[52]

Padre Miguel de Benfumea, the prefect of the Congregation of Nuestra Señora del Pópulo, holds the congregation's *libros de govierno*, as well as scriptures and papers belonging to the congregation. He has some jewels and six bunches of silk flowers (*ramilletes de seda*) that belong to Doña Isabel del Baca, who lives on la Compañía (the street), and these must be returned to her. Juan Josef Muñoz's apartment cannot be opened, since he had actually moved to Mexico City and is now housed in the Colegio de S. Pedro and S. Pablo. (He is the "Muñoz" mentioned earlier, whose name would be added in later.) How ironic that Hermano Josef Aguirre points to a little book on his desk bearing the title *Crisis de la Compañía* (Crisis of the Society of Jesus), which belongs to Don Juan Miguel Saem. Hermano Francisco Coos had many instruments, including a spinet, a *vihuela*, and a violin, all which had been given to him for safekeeping by

Don Miguel Ruíz. P. Josef Alegria notes a sealed sheet of paper that he described as "a case of conscience," and he implores them not to read it.[53]

Padre Eligio Fernández is indignant, insisting that the works he points out be returned to their proper owners, the only Jesuit to note the volume size (one in quarto, the other octavo) of the works by Padre Miguel Angel Pasqual y Castrejon which belong to *licenciado* Don Manuel Loaiza. Another, *Speculum amoris et doloris*, belongs to Don Gregorio Quintana.[54] Padre Josef Ortega does not have "*cosa alguna ajena.*" The location of Hermano Basilio Blanco's *aposento* is noted—it is next to the sacristy—but he has nothing to declare.

In closing down the day, the commissioner returned to the starting point, the *porteria*. This was the lodging station from whence the porter had been torn from his sleep earlier that morning. With this, the notary declared that all Jesuits and their rooms had gone through the initial audit, with the exception of the four men who counted among the mentally ill.[55] The goal of the Crown has been relatively straightforward: move the Jesuits out and immobilize the swirl of activity that daily orbited in and around the Jesuit college.

"All of the keys reside with said Commissioner, His Merced . . ."

The document is signed by both Machado and Castillo.

The day is finished.

Monologue: The Sacramental Logics of Jesuit Material Remains

Attentive to ritual (the keys), ready for any legal battles (the notary and his documentation), and prepared to put down a rebellion (the militia), the Crown wields its might. The capital (spiritual, cultural, and economic) that the Jesuits had accrued over approximately two hundred years is marked for disassembly, a process of cataloguing is underway, all while the men themselves prepare for long-distance travel. In leaning over Castillo's shoulder, we have caught sight of the ritual display of sovereign power, as the Crown brought the full weight of the law to bear upon each individual Jesuit, moving person by person, item by item, to freeze and contain the moveable parts of what had been, just the day prior, the Mexican Province of the Society of Jesus.

Now, at the Jesuit college in Puebla at the close of the day on June 25, 1767, we are confronted with a list of items whose variety requires some exploration. Rooted in the Catholic sacraments of penance and the Eucharist, laity and Jesuits developed relationships of trust and authority that explain the presence of the miscellaneous items in individual Jesuits' apartments. But these small vectors of exchange between Jesuits and their neighbors are so interesting in part because they are difficult to characterize. How to sort the books about birds, the silk flowers, the silver-plated water jug, the musical instruments, the kimonos, the divorce decree, the lace, the self-winding desk clock, the silver jewelry held for the family in dispute? Clearly, these objects are what historian Leora Auslander calls "aesthetically invested objects."[56] Collectively they comprise a "scaffolding of sovereignty" that is mutable, competing, entangled, aesthetic, dramatic, staged, negotiated, and—crucially—not delimited by the "statist priority" that has dominated discussions of sovereignty for at least a century.[57] This finely grained theopolitics comes into view as an assemblage of things that locals had deemed important enough to require placement with spiritual leaders, precious items, many of which are linked to embodied existence. These are items that delight the eye (images of birds), slide across the body (kimonos), signal status (kimonos and silver-plated goblets), provide visual and sensual pleasure (silk flowers), that are linked to consumption of food (the decorative serving ware) as well as to the passing of time (the clocks). In other words, many items are connected to human sensorial experience. Even the books, which signal all manner of intellectual exchange, also mark out a space of care for precious pages protected in lambkin. Like silver altarware, a vitality resides in their preciousness, marked by material limitations. Akin to the silver that is variously touched, kissed, or polished, these are items deemed worthy of care and protection.[58]

Notably, these are relational objects. The objects denote very tiny conduits of connection, traces of movement from a Jesuit's room to the street outside, to locations across the city of Puebla, and out to neighboring locations like Cholula or Acajete, and back inside the college doors again. The placement of particular objects in specific rooms bear witness to intimate relationships that are no doubt as varied and unique as the items listed, but all of which gesture, through the priest, toward the altar. While drawing from a different devotional context, James Gentry's discussion of "power objects" sheds light on the theopolitical networks constructed here: "Owing in part to their tangibility and transactional potential, tensions surrounding the use of such objects extend well beyond the ritual sphere, bringing far-reaching implications for the nature of religious sensibilities and communal formation."[59] Many of these communal relationships with Jesuits were founded upon preparing that specific layperson through the sacrament of confession to know herself well enough to approach the altar to consume Christ's body. Whether built upon deference, fear, or friendship, sacramental logics underwrite the hierarchical relationships that authorized the Jesuits as caretakers of precious objects in a worldly Catholicism fostered by Ignatian devotional practices that found "God in all things."

Catholicism fosters material connections, we know this. From monumental churches to roadside chapels, these are the ritual centers from which flow a variety of material forms—candles, images, rosaries—which lay people often tuck into their own pockets, take home, place on shelves, or on home altars. Yet we have seen a different array of items that were not taken *from* a sacred site. Instead, they have condensed around an odd site: a Jesuit college.[60] Proximity to divinity does not make kimonos and bird books "religious" in and of themselves, the Jesuit bedrooms are not themselves sacred spaces but mundane sites proximate to the sacred. Clearly these are—also—luxury items owned by elites, precious and relatively rare. Similarly, the simple silk flowers could be the property of a wide range of *novohispanos* and do not, on their own, materialize "religion."

We find these items listed in this inventory because they have condensed around relationships with specific Jesuits. "Semiotic processes are in constant motion," Webb Keane reminds us, thus we cannot expect them to move in a single direction. In other words, we must be agile enough to follow not only the "material religion" that flows "out" from sacred spaces. Rather, we must also see the disparate items in Castillo's inventory as traces, remnants, or tokens of theologically inspired affective relationships. If, as McAllister and Napolitano suggest, the core of theopolitics is affective relationships, then these items move in and through a triangular core shaped by self/altar/priest to arrive in Jesuit rooms, like so much dust, swirling around multiple possibilities. The predominant affordance, I have argued thus far, was a Jesuit-styled understanding of salvation as grounded in the frequent reception of the Eucharist and the concomitant frequency of the sacrament of penance. Notably, the corners formed by the self-altar-priest relation do not hold things permanently. As

Michael Marder writes in his meditations on the power of dust as a metaphor: "There is nothing in this togetherness that is guaranteed to last from one moment to the next: its meanings, scales, and particles can always discombobulate and disperse."[61] This inventory has shown us "things," once circulating, that were stilled, themselves soon to accumulate dust. But we also have a glimpse of how a variety of objects once *moved like dust* to accrete around sites of sacramental power. Jesuit sacramental possibilities are vanishing, not only because the priests are prisoners soon to depart but also because the Crown has "arrested" the mobility of Jesuit objects. This first day inventory captures in freezeframe what had been a dynamic swarm, a lively salvational ecology in which the Society of Jesus had been thoroughly rooted. The Crown aims to disrupt the flow of power that might remain as material trace. The captain and the notaries are working to shut down all possibilities for Jesuit mobility that do not entail a carriage ride to the port town of Veracruz.

Scene III: Departures and Returns, Replications and Excisions

We have followed Machado and Castillo through a sleep-deprived night and one long day as they worked to guarantee that the arrest, detainment, and mobilization of the Jesuits unfolded as smoothly as possible. Castillo probably passed another long night, checking over his work, dotting "i's" and crossing "t's" to produce the documentation that ensured that all had proceeded according to Crown instructions or, as we have seen, to note when and why there were any deviations. His manuscript covers the next few days closely, as preparations are made for the Jesuits' journey to the port of Veracruz. The Crown had specified that Jesuits must be removed from the colleges within twenty-four hours, if not sooner. Yet Machado's efforts for the next two days revolved around finding sufficient carriages for the journey, a task that took longer than the wishful thinking expressed in the Crown's *Instrucción*.[62]

There is another tense morning on June 27, 1767. This is the day of departure. Once again Castillo's notes begin before dawn (at 3:30 a.m.), and he concludes with a remark that there was no disquiet among the numerous people who gathered near the sentry station, the *garita de Amazoque*, the assigned convergence point where Jesuits from the five different

Table 1: Road Trip List

Thirteen fine tablecloths of European thread (*género de hilo de Europa*), about four or five varas in length. They belong to this College.

Five of the above, in ordinary cotton from this land, of the same length; from this College.

Seventy-seven napkins, in cotton from this land; idem.

Five rags/hand towels (*paños de manos*) of the same and very long; idem.

Ninety-three complete sets of cutlery with their respective knives: sixty-three from this College and the rest from San Ildefonso.

Three serving dishes of pewter; of said San Ildefonso.

Nine smaller dishes of the same (pewter) of said College.

A crate (*frasquera*) with eighteen large bottles, sixteen full of wine, and the other two of *aguardiente el casco y caldo* of this Colegio del Espíritu Santo.

Two large copper *fonteras* (?). Idem.

Two more, smaller, of the same. Idem.

An egg frying pan, of the above [copper]. Idem.

Two spoons of the same. Idem.

Two spatulas of the same. Idem.

One straw/tube (*una bombilla*) of the same. Idem.

A slotted spoon of the same. Idem.

A machete to pick teeth (*un machete para picar canine*), also of this College.

A set of earthenware plates (*platos de barro*); candle holders of the same. Idem.

The same of *faras calderas* (?)

Two large baskets/containers of chocolate of idem.

A pitcher of oil. Idem.

A suitcase/trunk (*una petaca*) for all the "*ropa de Mesa*" and eight wooden crates (*huacales*) in which went the rest, also from this College.

Ayer 1128:35–36

colleges are gathered to begin the trek to Veracruz.[63] Meanwhile, Castillo continued to inventory items. Next he lists the things that will be sent with the *padres* to make sure they are comfortable on the way to Jalapa, their stop on the way to Veracruz.

There is no silver altarware let alone silver tableware in this inventory, no trunks full of books, nothing to conduct the liturgy. While everyone knows who they are and there are huge crowds that gather in the streets to watch the spectacle of their departure,[64] nothing in this list indicates that these travelers are Jesuit priests. This is the packing list of civilians.

But not all Jesuits leave Puebla immediately. Notably, the procurators are held back for two months to assist with documenting the Jesuit holdings.[65] These procurators had performed a crucial role in the running of the Jesuit college complex. From the purchase of wax and religious icons to books and textiles, even arranging for the movement of missionaries themselves, the Jesuit who held the position of procurator would have had his fingers on the pulse of the missionary machinery, including the procurement of goods and services for the Jesuit haciendas.[66] The Crown has singled out the procurators as key players in its attempt to make a precise accounting of the Society's holdings. They are not allowed to remain at the Jesuit college; rather, they are housed separately with local mendicant orders. The Crown is keen to prevent the Jesuit procurators from communicating with each other; thus they are transported to and from the monasteries under armed guard.[67]

The matter of the care of *los dementes* is also settled. Initially, a servant is hired to assist the mentally ill, who were temporarily housed in their own rooms at the college. Eventually, space is found at the hospital of San Roque for the *locos furiosos*, that is, the seriously ill, and a spot at a local convent for those who were only "touched" with this malady.[68] Eventually they will all be moved back to Colegio Espíritu Santo, to be housed together with others from New Spain who were too ill or infirm to travel. We will dig deeper into stories about the men who struggled with mental illness in Act III.

A few Jesuits straggle in from other places. On June 28, 1767, the day after the Jesuits depart from Puebla, Castillo reports receipt of a letter stating that two Jesuits are stranded approximately four leagues away from Puebla. The letter, written by Antonio Pablo Cid, conveys that he and Juan de Arriola were at the Hacienda San Pablo at the time of the arrest, where they had been convalescing. Cid described himself as damaged by his many accidents and Arriola as completely disabled. Castillo notes that soldiers were sent immediately to collect them and place them on the road to Veracruz. Stragglers from more distant locales included a Jesuit named Matias Souza, who had been at the *ingenio* (sugarcane mill) in Tiripito, Valladolid, at the time of the arrest. Castillo's notes give the impression that, upon hearing the news of the arrest, the men left the *ingenio* to join their brethren. The sugar mill they left behind belonged to the Jesuit college of San Andres in Mexico City, yet, along with Bernardino Sarmiento, another Jesuit at the *ingenio*, he traveled to Puebla, likely because the town is en route to Veracruz, but Puebla was also Souza's place of birth.[69] Did he imagine that he might be afforded an opportunity to see family before departing? Perhaps, but this was expressly against the Crown's *Instrucción*, which had stipulated that the departing Jesuits would not be allowed to communicate with families or the local community.[70] These stragglers, too, were shuttled to local monasteries and then put on the path to Veracruz.

Incidentally, by June 30, 1767, the room of the absent Muñoz had not been opened. It was one key that the Crown had not yet managed to collect.[71]

Stage Setting: Sacramental Theopolitics

If the Society's source of power resides in mediating access to the God-present and we conceive of this material network as crucial to how the Jesuits kept their fingers on the pulse of a salvational sacramental economy, then this is what the Crown moves decisively to dismantle. In the late colonial period, the accusation against the Society of Jesus is framed as *problematic mediation* of the divine. The Jesuits are not worthy agents of salvation. Deemed unfit, they are sidelined with the accusation that they propagate ideas and practices that are "morally lax."

The question—what does it take to be saved?—is far from settled business among Catholics in the eighteenth century. This means that uncertainty animates disputes about Jesuit sacramental practices. The body of Christ, in Latour's phrasing, is "matter of concern" and the altar a site of fierce contention. In the face of Luther's sixteenth-century provocation that salvation was anchored in "faith alone," the Catholic Church had countered by doubling down on the sacraments. Christ incarnate in the bread and wine was firmly established as central to salvific practices, while Peter's firm grasp on the keys meant that God's forgiveness (the sacrament of penance) and thus access to the body of Christ would be mediated by an ordained priest (ordination itself a sacrament). The Jesuits are dubbed a Counterreformation religious order because they were sent to Protestant borderlands, but they are also agents of Catholic renewal because their missionary ideology was fueled by the twinned desire to bring to Catholic laity and new converts everywhere a renewed devotional life centered on the eucharistic ritual that itself depended upon preparatory penitential practices. They gave their own spin to these practices, a fact that had always garnered some critique.

But long-standing Jesuit ideas pertaining to the who and how of salvation had come under serious scrutiny in the eighteenth century. The debates that raged about the Jesuits in the eighteenth century bore an uncanny resemblance to those that were central to the Reformation but were now fought out among Catholics. Both sides agreed that God is present in the bread and wine. But *how much* could sinners participate in their salvation, or better put, how often could this sacred flesh be ingested? The Jesuit answer was grounded in an Ignatian spirituality that held the relatively optimistic view that humans had free will that was inherently guided by what the sixteenth-century Jesuit theologian Luís Molina dubbed "sufficient grace." In contrast, "rigorist" Catholics in the eighteenth century adopted an attitude implied by the name: Salvation is difficult, and the theologies and devotional practices espoused by the Jesuits had cheapened salvation. Jansenism represented a newer (or renewed) strand of Catholic thinking that argued for the fundamentally fallen nature of human will. They found the Jesuit emphasis on frequent confession and communion particularly appalling. For the Jansenists, the Eucharist was to be *set apart*. Wouldn't it be nice, these critics complained, if Christians *could* commune frequently with Christ? Who would not desire such a thing? But are humans actually *worthy* of frequent communion? Rather, Catholics should cultivate an aspirational distance in their Eucharistic devotion. In the Jansenist view, shoddy Jesuit confessions had deluded fallen sinners into thinking that they could approach the altar more frequently. In making salvation "easy" and "available" to a wide variety of people, the Jesuits were accused, at best, of diluting Christian tenets and, at worst, of heresy. When Jansenism first emerged in the seventeenth century, the Jesuits successfully went on the offensive, dubbing Jansenist sensibilities a "reboiled Calvinism." But the tides had shifted by the late eighteenth century. Rigorist Jansenist theologians abhorred Jesuit "adaptable" and "flexible" methods that promoted moral laxity and cheapened Christianity.[72]

To be clear, the reformers' theopolitics had a new inflection. For example, they placed high value upon reading Christ's teachings in the Bible, and they depended upon ancient church founders for interpretations that were "closer" to the original church. The primary aim was "to free the illuminated interior conscience from restraints to its development, and to free the church herself from the centuries' corrupting accretions."[73] The Eucharist remained central, but the "table" should be set more modestly, and, really, must Christ be exposed so frequently? Pamela Voekel has dubbed this a "sacramental stinginess" that valued anguished compunction about sinfulness over the easy accessibility proffered in Jesuit advocacy of frequent communion. And the sensuality of adoration of the saints presented a greater problem for reformers who advocated a narrower focus on Christ alone. Good works would remain an important set of tools in the Catholic repertoire and the Eucharist remained paramount to achieving salvation. But Catholics—and the commoner, especially—should stand back from Christ and anxiously ponder what might be done to make oneself *more* worthy to see, touch, and consume his body.[74] Thus, their theopolitical concerns stipulated that more guardrails be put up to foment a deeper probing of conscience. The altar remained central but, for the sake of the interior life, should be free from distracting clutter.[75]

And in Castillo's inventory, we see clear evidence of these sacramental politics on one Jesuit's desk.

Scene IV: Aramburu's Desk

Padre Francisco Aramburu straggled back to Puebla de Los Angeles in the first days of July.[76] He had been among the handful of Jesuits who were absent from the college when Machado and Castillo knocked at dawn on that Thursday morning. He was attending to business at the Jesuit hacienda of San Gerónimo, the main site in a complex of smaller haciendas and farms whose agricultural production financed the educational, devotional, and evangelical undertakings of the Jesuits at the Colegio Espíritu Santo.[77] Aramburu returned to the college where, just as his fellow Jesuits had a few days prior, he was escorted to his locked *aposento* where he collected his own belongings and pointed out items that were not his.[78] When Aramburu pointed to the Bible on his desk, the notary scribbled down a partial title: *Pueblo de Dios*. This shorthand notation refers to a

Spanish translation of *Histoire du peuple de Dieu*, a French-language Bible, the very controversial work that had been written by the Jesuit Isaac Berruyer (1681–1758).[79]

Aramburu told Castillo that the Bible belonged to the Holy Tribunal of the Inquisition. Castillo describes Arramburu as having been tasked with "correcting" the Bible, which could indicate that as a prohibited book he may have had to cut out or black out parts of the book to be licensed to read it.[80] But Arramburu was not the only Jesuit with a copy of the French Jesuit's Bible on his desk. His fellow Jesuit Joseph Vicente de Silva had all twelve volumes in quarto on his desk, and he is named as the owner.[81] Had Silva or Aramburu been able to pack the books in their sparse luggage, they would not have been able to hold on to them for very long. As the Jesuits left New Spain and entered Havana, more copies of this Bible were found among the Jesuits' things. The Havana officials, strict in their interpretation of what constituted "devotional literature," confiscated these copies of Berruyer's "morally lax" Bible.[82] The Spanish Crown had singled out Berruyer's Bible to be removed from circulation. In fact, as Dale Van Kley notes, this Bible is among the books that "figured in the cases of all the states from which the Society was expelled."[83]

What was controversial about this Bible? Its author, Isaac Berruyer, had caused theological controversy because, when grappling with the effect of Christ's birth as divinity breaking into historical time, he emphasized Christ's humanity over his divinity. The work was also notorious for the fictionalized elements included within it. Berruyer drew upon contemporary literary trends to depict the inner thoughts and desires of biblical figures. The modernized language coupled with a heightened sense of drama aimed to make the scriptures approachable, entertaining, and accessible to a broader Catholic readership. As a young Jesuit, Berruyer had been recognized as a talented poet. He brought his literary sensibilities to bear in writing what he defended as a "paraphrase" of the Bible. Daniel Watkins's scholarship describes the controversial Bible as a hybrid of eighteenth-century literary and historical trends. Watkins traces how Berruyer took cues from the newly popular *roman*, or romance novel, to depict characters engaged in recognizable human struggles. Berruyer forsook what he considered the stilted language of an imagined biblical past, replacing it with contemporary vernacular French. His success is verified in the response of a contemporary critic who deplored the fact that Berruyer's John the Baptist spoke just like a fishmonger at the Place Maubert! He also included historical explanations, including visuals like maps and charts. In addition, he incorporated his own biblical commentaries seamlessly into the text. His Bible can be distinguished from those of eighteenth-century philologists who, aiming to write more authoritative translations, demonstrated a keen understanding of the original languages and subsequent translations.[84] In contrast, Berruyer accepted the approved Catholic Reformation Bible, the Clementine vulgate. His innovation, however, is a smooth narration of events peopled by vivid characters. He hoped his short, imaginative narratives would speak directly to eighteenth-century Catholics.

Berruyer's aim to be "accessible" was not novel for members of the Society of Jesus, who had long depended upon the evocative powers of the imagination from the moment that Ignatius of Loyola made "contemplation of place" a central component of his Spiritual Exercises. Ignatius instructed practitioners of the Exercises to foster a personalized vantage point on the scenes from Christ's life, imagining the most detailed aspects of the setting of the Gospel stories to bring to life, for example, the affective experience of Mary when she joyfully experiences the news of the risen Christ. Or, more humbly, one might envision oneself occupying the vantage point of a maidservant present at Christ's birth.[85] The fact that no maidservant was referenced in the gospels was momentarily controversial for the first Jesuits, but they eventually dropped the debate. Accessible imaginative experience would underwrite the Jesuit evangelical project.[86] Thus, contemplating the emotions experienced by biblical characters had been key to Jesuit meditative practices for two centuries.

Whether considering Christ's passion, or Job's despair, Berruyer's Bible offered affective engagement as a valuable reading practice. For example, more than a century before Kierkegaard's famous commentary on Genesis 22, Berruyer asked his readers to place themselves at the scene of Abraham's journey to Mount Moriah. Here he takes a literary approach when describing an Abraham weighted down by the knowledge that he would murder his own son. Berruyer's Abraham struggles to command his own visage on the long road to Mount Moriah so as to not give Isaac any notion that dutiful Abraham was following God's horrific command.[87] The reader is guided to consider what it must have been for a father to ponder killing his son. Berruyer's commentary describes how fatherly pain is overcome by a commendable stoicism:

> Everything would contribute, it seems, to justify Abraham's resistance in such circumstances. The sacrifice of human blood, ordained by a God who is always offended by such barbarities: to take the life of a child, by the hand of his own father, and by mandate of a God, who confesses to be the Father of all men. . . . It was a long road, and the journey lasted three days, in which Abraham's reflections would have been very bitter. Notwithstanding, he did not regret anything. His soul was penetrated by the most vivid pain, but he mastered himself always, never allowing what he perceived in his heart to be visible.[88]

These rhetorical aims, touching the hearts of the reader, were aligned with Jesuit modes of accommodation that had been practiced locally and globally. That is, Jesuits had long practiced meeting people where they are and translating Christianity into comprehensible terms, of course with the aim of converting them. Scholars often study accommodation in the context of remote mission stations where the Jesuits comprised a tiny minority. Most famous are Matteo Ricci in China and Roberto di Nobili in India, both of whom adopted the clothing and cultural practices of their potential converts.[89] But Berruyer's paraphrase is yet another mode of Jesuit accommodation, here "clothing" the Christian scriptures in provocative contemporary literary methods. Rigorist Jansenist theologians abhorred Berruyer's Bible, citing it as another example of "adaptable" and "flexible" Jesuit practices that promoted moral laxity and cheapened Christianity.[90] Down with the Jesuits, irresponsible mediators of the divine! Just look at their latest Marian devotion.

Scene V: Madre Santísima de la Luz, Owner of the Means of Her Own Reproduction

Indeed, the Berruyer Bible is not the only controversial item on Aramburu's desk. Some of the *cosas ajenas* that this late-arriving Jesuit points out have a very interesting owner: "And that to the image of María Santissima de la Luz, whom they venerate in the Church of this College, belong the following items." He lists a woman's dress, some emerald earrings, a Chinese mat (*petate de China formado de cotone*), two new paintings, a belt of fabric and another of silk, two altar covers and a little curtain, a Cross of Jerusalem, a heart made of silver, forty little paper notebooks, two plates for making prints, and another cord of silk.

The Jesuits promoted devotion to the Madre Santísima de la Luz (the Most Holy Mother of the Light) beginning in the 1720s, when an Italian Jesuit priest commissioned a painting for his itinerant missions in the countryside of Sicily. He asked a woman known for her visions of Mary to consult with the Virgin about how she wished to be portrayed. Mary appeared to the unnamed woman and conveyed her wishes in detail. But a disappointed Mary returned, this time to complain that the artist's first attempt had been poorly executed. Mary doggedly pestered the woman to travel to Palermo to confront the artist, but the woman voiced reluctance: "Why me? I am just a vile worm." Having performed the proper self-abasement that authorized an early modern woman's decisive action, she traveled to Palermo on Mary's behalf to speak to the artist herself. At this point, Mary appeared once again to give the woman precise instructions that the artist should be certain to follow on his second attempt. With Mary guiding the artist's brush, the second painting proved satisfactory.

The miracle of Mary's self-portrait was described by the Italian Jesuit Giuseppi Maria Genovese in 1733, and the devotion moved promptly along Jesuit networks. A Spanish translation by Luis Rincón, SJ, was published in Mexico four years later.[91] The legend referred to a painted image, but literature promoting the devotion reminded readers that even the engraved images contained within the pages of this very devotional guide "could inflame a love in our heart for this Lady under the glorious title Mother of the Light."[92] In this invocation of Mary, Christ is referred to not as the "Word" made flesh but as a sacred light that has become human with Mary as the mother of the Light. As Madre de la Luz, she is dedicated "to the eternal Light made Human, so to win eternal health of souls, redeemed by his divine Blood."[93] Emphasis on salvific *light* was intended as a spiritual counterpoint to the *luces* propagated by the new philosophy.[94]

Multitasking, Mary holds the Christ child in one arm, and with her other arm she reaches out to grab a sinner before he falls into a monstrous hellmouth. The gist of the image is how devotion to Mary can prevent one from being consumed by the flames of hell. In the standard image, she is crowned by angels, while another angel holds up a basket of flaming hearts that the Christ child reaches down to grab, usually

FIGURE 3. *Madre Santísima de la Luz*, eighteenth-century painting by Miguel Cabrera, oil on canvas. Author's photo, courtesy of Museo Galería Mariana, Guanajuato, Mexico.

absentmindedly. In some depictions, the person saved from falling to damnation is an Indian man. In others, saints are plugged in variously, kneeling in the foreground.[95]

As described by her promoters, her clothing is intended to be sumptuous and radiantly beautiful. "Her virgin body is covered by an ankle-length garment, more splendid than the Sun, and whiter than Snow, gracefully girdling her waist [is] an enameled belt made of the most precious jewels of the Empire. She wore a blue robe that lay beautifully on her shoulders, and a crown of angels in splendid vestments attended as the retinue of the Queen."[96] The devotional art dedicated to her in New Spain took shape as paintings and engravings, as well as in medals and in sculptures, both relief and three-dimensional.[97] Although the paintings often had three-dimensional ornaments such as crowns or necklaces that could be attached to the finished canvases, the items on Aramburu's desk seem more appropriate to adorn a sculpture, either relief or in the round, that could be dressed, belted, and adorned with jewels. Aramburu maintained this closet full of sumptuous accoutrements, likely because he served as rector of the Congregación del Pópulo. Its members would have been the privileged devotees of this Jesuit-sponsored devotion who would have had the honor to dress and decorate her, place the emerald earrings on her ears, the belts and cords of various kinds around her waist, before carrying her to be shown off in diverse locations, bringing along the necessary items—Chinese mats, altar covers, and curtains—to appropriately stage her appearance.

But all of these, Castillo notes, "belonged" not to the college, the Church, or the confraternity but to the image of María de la Luz herself. One might point to an ambiguity in the language Castillo deploys to indicate ownership. He uses the verb *pertenecer*, which can mean both "to belong" and "to pertain," and it is possible that Castillo merely means that the items "pertained" to the devotion to la Santíssima. But his words differ from the language deployed in other inventories. For example, in the inventory from the Jesuit college of Veracruz, an unnamed notary deploys the verb "correspond" to mark books that "corresponded" to the devotion of our Lady of the Light.[98] Notably, in the Puebla inventory, Castillo deploys the same language to describe items that "belong" to neighbors near and far.[99]

Most interestingly, he notes that the Madre Santísima de la Luz owns not only her sumptuous accoutrements but also the means of her own reproduction. The corresponding paintings, the forty little paper notebooks, but most notably, the two copper plates for making prints—presumably of her own image—all offer a means of mobilizing devotion to la Luz, as if an extension of the founding story in which Mary fastidiously monitors the production of her image. From her resting place at the Jesuit college, by means of the plates, she extends herself to new audiences. But printed images were still a relatively new technology in the eighteenth century.[100] Manuscript replication existed alongside print copies. The forty paper notebooks are intriguing in this regard because it is quite possible that they, too, are dedicated to her replication. She not only directed the paintbrush of the painter, but she may well have been central to a small factory of Jesuit students who copied or pasted her words and images into paper notebooks. Jesuit colleges put notetaking and commonplacing at the center of its education because students were not allowed to write in the printed books that belonged to the college library but were taught instead to create *libros de papel* or *libri bianchi*. Paul Nelles demonstrates how Jesuit students were expected "to invest a considerable amount of time outside of class in constructing and maintaining notebooks." The Jesuit college librarian was to supply all of the materials for notebook making—"paper, ink, pens, knives, scissor, and a stylus." Students used such booklets to study together, quizzing one another.[101] In the years leading up to the arrest and expulsion of the Jesuits from New Spain, it was rumored that the students at the Jesuit colleges in Puebla were engaged in copying pro-Jesuit literature that leaked into New Spain.[102] It is quite possible that students were assigned with copying tasks related to her devotion.

In the inventory, Our Lady of the Light is described as "owning" the tools to continue to replicate herself. Mary's agency—what she can and cannot do for sinners—is precisely what is at stake in the controversy about Jesuit promotion of devotion to Our Lady of the Light. Who can be saved? Who can do the saving? While rigorist critics conceded that devotion to la Luz had been sanctioned by the church, they complained that the Virgin's arm reaching out to save the sinner from falling into the hellmouth is potentially confusing. Peter holds the keys, not Mary. She could advocate for or assist the fallen but could not herself save the sinner. Rigorist reformers had a low opinion of the discernment skills of the average Christian who, they argued, could interpret this as Mary overstepping her bounds and reaching to *pull* the damned soul *out* of the fires of hell.[103] This was corrected in many existing paintings by blacking out the sinner who hangs precariously above the hellmouth, either replacing it with a different image or leaving the left bottom corner unambiguously blank.[104] The controversy over this artistic depiction of a path toward salvation was part and parcel of the rigorist claims that Jesuits habitually fostered "lax" penitential practices.[105] Even Jesus's mother cannot overstep sacramental boundaries, although she is notorious for hovering near the edge, ever a threat to priestly sacramental authority.

In the aftermath of the expulsion of the Jesuits from both Spain and the Americas, the efforts to uproot Jesuit devotions depended largely upon the depth of the anti-Jesuit zeal of individual bishops. The accusations of moral laxity lay behind the move of many reforming bishops to destroy books, images, and the means of making stamps and engravings, so as to prohibit the continuation of Jesuit devotions.[106] At the Fourth Mexican Council (1771) anti-Jesuit vitriol was, "from start to finish, one of its most significant characteristics."[107] Rigorist reformers took direct aim at the Madre Santísima de la Luz. Taking the lead, the archbishop of the diocese of Mexico City, Francisco Antonio de Lorenzana (1722–1804), insisted that because this devotion had been introduced by the Jesuits, it was necessary to "destroy and erase the memory of all her things."[108] Vicente Antonio de los Ríos, who represented the absent bishop from Michoacán, seemed disturbed by the vitriol. He himself may have been a devotee. He wrote in his diary that the discussion about "mi Señora de la Luz" was "full of blood." "The business of Jesuits became that of my Lady of the Light, and the matter was taken with such art, that they would have made cause for Jesuit and fanatic any who would have wanted to oppose that torrent."[109] Lorenzano's torrent included condemnation of the sumptuous jewels and clothing used to adorn the image, that is, the very items that Aramburu held in his *aposento*. He singled out the problem of "effigies" of the Virgin brought into laypersons' homes to be dressed, quite inappropriately, he thought, "with worldly adornments" like necklaces, bracelets, and other items that were "very far from any semblance of her singular modesty."[110] The clothing used to adorn religious statuary more generally, he complained, had profane necklines that were not only entirely unbecoming to the Virgin Mary and the saints but also spelled trouble for the laity. "Dangerous desire (*concupiciencia*) can enter into the sacred via the eyes upon seeing naked women and children; what they believe is tenderness and devotion is but pure sensuality."[111] Reforming bishops in the eighteenth century clearly found something worrisome in the plethora of holy objects that could be, as Caroline Bynum has noted, "dangerous in their varieties of potentialities."[112]

Bishops continued to discuss Madre Santísima de la Luz for two hours, folding in a subsidiary criticism of the five hearts of the Holy Family (Joachim, Anna, Mary, Joseph, and Jesus), which then morphed into a heated discussion about Jesuit devotion to the Sacred Heart of Jesus. One bishop pointed out that the heart of Jesus was no more sacred than his feet, while another added that the heart is just a muscle that distributes blood. One attendant dared not speak but noted in his diary that no mention was made of other heart-centered devotional practices, including devotions to Saint Augustine and Saint Gertrude and Christ's exchange of hearts with Saint Teresa.[113]

Monologue: Reiteration, Replication, and Reassembly

In closing the door on Aramburu's *aposento*, I pause to consider this Jesuit's work as a *"revisor."* Consider for a moment all the labor represented on Aramburu's desk: Why does Berruyer need to write a new Bible? Why is there a need for yet another image of the Virgin? Why does the Virgin herself intervene to say, "it will be done right" even if she had to do it herself, instructing the painter through the voice of the unnamed "pious woman"? Why do bishops demand the revision and excision of the hellmouth from her existing images? There is an urgency to the reshaping of ideas and images, a felt investment in the pressing controversies about what "our times" or "our views" demand. Aramburu's labor to save books from error enables their continued circulation, la Luz replicates herself to save more souls from hell, the bishops, in contrast, seek to quash replication and circulation in a quest to save sinners from their purported credulity and sensuality.

If the story of Aramburu's desk is analyzed in terms of investment of time, effort, and vitriol in competing views of biblical interpretation and the role of Mary and the saints, then these items provide a snapshot of the continuing and contentious reassembly of the eighteenth-century Catholic world.[114] In freeze frame, the inventory captures the replication and reorganization of touch relics, prints, paintings, and books that comprise the scaffolding of competing sovereignties. This is a dynamic system of political-devotional aesthetics—that is, a theopolitics whose stability had long depended upon these kinds of replications, checks, and countermoves. And then—quite suddenly—there is a systemic "correction" in which the Jesuits are pushed out, deemed "not too big to fail." And so the story of Jesuit ruination begins with the loss of the position they once guarded quite fiercely, that is, their privileged ability to shape the daily reiterative processes in which *novohispanos* anchored their salvific desires in a relationship to Jesus (and with his mother, a crucial conduit to both Father and Son). So just as we require a historical understanding of the realms in which notaries could act in the world, so too do we require some historically specific explanation about the capacity of the mystical body of Christ to act in the world.

Who is this Christ?

Character Study: The Mystical Body of Christ

When the priest exhibited and elevated the consecrated host, this was—as Richard Kieckhefer makes clear in his study of the mystical presence of Christ in late medieval Europe—"the manifestation of the breakthrough of eternity into time."[115] In the sixteenth century, Tridentine Catholic theological reforms had reaffirmed the doctrine of transubstantiation, the latter made highly controversial when Protestant Reformers reduced the Eucharist to mere symbol. The Catholic Church insisted that Christ's actual body and blood were corporeally present in the consecrated bread and wine. Tridentine reformers, seeking to promote eucharistic piety while also regulating miraculous action, published new liturgical missals and catechisms that were intended to ensure global orthodoxy on every Catholic altar.[116] Trent's edicts had established the correct veneration of sacramental presence, emphasizing universal orthodox practices that reinforced priestly authority. There were even new regulations controlling the production of chalices, the vessels that would hold the consecrated wine. These should be made of precious metals. Primarily, altarware in Mexico was made of silver, to which we will turn shortly.[117]

Spanish missionaries brought the body of Christ to the Americas, where church and state together enforced a habitus in which indigenous lives were restructured around the parish, thus imposing a sacramental culture whose rituals called for Christ to appear as bread and wine on elaborately decorated church altars.[118] Brian Larkin describes church interiors in New Spain as an "ornate staging grounds for the liturgy" and documents how *novohispanos* from all walks of life "poured wealth into ornamentation of sacred space."[119] Jennifer Scheper Hughes demonstrates how indigenous communities built a future-oriented vision of how autonomy might be gained via the new religion. Recognizing the altar as a powerful place, they moved to assert some control over it.[120] For example, *pueblos de indios* demanded their churches be properly attended and cared for by ecclesiastical authorities in the wake of a series of late sixteenth-century epidemics. Throughout the colonial period, investment in eucharistic devotion is evident not only in the theatrical productions that commemorated the passion and death of Christ,[121] but also in in the last wills and testaments written by a broad swath of Catholic Mexicans who bequeathed cash to local churches, with instructions that the funds be used to enhance the ornamentation of church altars. As Larkin's scholarship makes clear, "The central mystery of the Catholic faith, the eucharist, depended on the notion that symbolic human performances could invoke God into the world. . . . This real presence was physically approachable, and baroque Catholics often made contact with it in and through their bodies."[122] Most telling about the centrality of eucharistic devotion in New Spain are the testamentary gifts that included wax, candles, and oil that were bequeathed to illuminate the Eucharist.

Importantly, Christ's divinity made him a shape-shifter. Note the spatiotemporal language that Kieckhefer utilizes to describe how Christ "is not bound to the particularities of time and place as a historical person must be."[123]

> He was present in various modes: sacramentally, in the consecrated bread and wine; ecclesially, in the Church as his mystical body; vicariously, in the needy whose care or neglect was the criterion for distinguishing the sheep from the goats; morally, by grace; mystically, as the bridegroom in relationship with his brides. *He might be present in one mode but not others. He might be experienced in one mode but not others.* In any case, it was because he was divine that he was

necessarily ubiquitous and thus guaranteed present even when his presence was hidden.[124]

This created a problem for sorting items that sat on Jesuit altars. In the next scene, notaries are tasked with documenting how Christ's presence on the altar touched and transformed the silver items on and near the altar. In 1774 Aranda wrote an addendum to the directives to clarify how silver altarware should be sorted. The notaries are given precise instructions for how to inventory the shape-shifting power of the God-man and bring material made sacred by his presence under the purview and judgment of the imperial state. Adopting an action-oriented approach, I read the inventories for clues as to the way its authors organized and edited the text.[125] That is, I follow their deliberations to understand how they approached the task of inventorying the agentive power of the holy items wrought what they understood to be Christ's transformative actions, mediated by priestly power.[126] Notaries are engaged in the epistemological labor of documenting a metaphysical entity as part of a state containment action. They are to ascertain with some specificity how silver altarware serves as channels of sacramentality and which objects remained functionally "live" conduits of sacred power. In other words, notaries have been authorized to inventory the nature of God.

Scene VI: Counting the Silver

In the summer and early autumn months of 1767, Castillo works with the captive Jesuit procurators to understand the cash and commodity flows. Up to this point his job has been to determine who owes what to whom, from whom payment can be demanded, or who might demand a payout. His final act entails noting how money moved, from the cash in the little baskets to the loans made for the purchase of a local *tocinería* (pork processing shop). After filing his report, Castillo exits the stage.

Entering the stage now is a document titled "List of the Gold and Silver Adornments, divided by class, belonging to the Five Colleges occupied in this City, 1774." The inventory includes instructions copied from Aranda's updated directive for how to inventory silver altarware, as well as the resulting list of silver items. Helen Hills has described how colonialism, refinement, and salvation were inscribed into the silver that decorated early modern Catholic churches. She has suggested that silver be understood in its overlapping potentialities: profit and salvation.[127] The Crown also sees silver this way, asking what can be melted and what is untouchable. In the years following the arrest, all silver adornments are meticulously evaluated, with some silver marked as an asset to be "liquidated" while other silver items, although counted and evaluated, can remain in use on or near a church altar. This documentation of silver belonging to the Colegio Espíritu Santo and the institutions that orbit around it offer detailed descriptions of both simple and ornate altarware that belong to the colleges, individual Jesuits, Jesuit churches, Jesuit-sponsored confraternities, and the haciendas affiliated with the Puebla colleges. The inventory appears to have been compiled by different notaries in a process that took approximately seven more years to complete, its final signatures dated August 29, 1781.[128]

The process of inventorying according to the Crown's categories of "degrees" or "classes" of silver items is not straightforward. Care went into the classification process as evidenced in notes indicating deliberation over items. There are queries and corrections in the margins that illuminate some of the head-scratching that went into the process. In examining some of the issues to be ironed out, it becomes apparent that proper classification of silver altarware is a matter of concern—those involved want to get it "right."[129] One might assume that the "correct" distribution is one in which the Crown gathers the maximum amount unto itself. But this supposition is dismantled relatively quickly when the notes in the file make clear the number of items categorized as "third degree." The third-class items consist predominantly of lamps, candelabras, and chandeliers (*lámparas, blandones, y arañas*) as well as jars, vases, and silver flowers. All items in this class fall within the purview of the Crown, but the document states outright that the sum total of third-degree items is numerous, large, and unwieldly. Specifically, the chandeliers, lamps, and candlestick holders are described as simply too costly to remit to Spain.[130]

NOTES ON HOW TO LIGHT A SACRED NETWORK

The action in this next theopolitical scene will be businesslike yet subtended by low-grade anxiety. Notaries are themselves novohispanos *who harbor expectations that the incarnate Christ, mediated by the priest, would regularly appear on the altar. But they are also aware that ecclesiastical authorities harbor worries that the God-man might appear in other places or that people would* abscond with his body or with the sacramentals that adorned it. On a more mundane level, special white linen cloths called "purificators" and "corporals" were designated to wipe the lip of the chalice, and sit under the Eucharist to catch any stray sacred drips or crumbs. Theologians even addressed what might happen should a mouse consume the Eucharist, with advice given about how to address the issue, namely, "the capture and the burning of the mouse."[131] My point is that unauthorized movement of the body of Christ was a matter of concern. In following the archival grain of these post-arrest inventories, we see how notaries, working within a baroque culture that put a high premium on sacred immanence, labor to catalogue with great precision which silver ornamentation had been transformed.

The lighting should focus on each object that the notaries identify as sacramental silver. Fresnel lighting is suggested for organizing silver altarware according to its proximity to the body of Christ. The bright light at the center ring would indicate the silver touched by the body and blood of the God-man. The glowing light is circular, and fades on the edges, to give the effect of concentric circular space that is less powerful on the edges. Circles of light, softening with distance from the silver altarware, catch the edges of the growing pile of non-sacramental silver that is being stacked at edges of stage, where it falls into the brown light.

But the scene is rather dynamic; thus the lighting requires a bit of rhythmic augmentation (but not a strobe light!) to convey inventorying as an action-oriented hermeneutics that lights up some objects but not others.

Andrew Pickering usefully suggests the rhythms of a dance scene: "We act in the world, and the world acts on us, to and fro, in a dynamic process I call the 'dance of agency,' in which all the partners are unpredictably and emergently transformed.... There is nothing mysterious about this. It is just how things go in science and, indeed, everywhere else."[132]

What should be brought to light in the bureaucratic listmaking is in fact a dance of agency between scribes as state representatives who are taking turns on the floor with a more-than-human power.

An occasional wave pattern washes over the entire stage, to mark that the state is concerned with imperial distance. The Crown must "see" the arrest of the Jesuits from across the ocean to gain some certainty that the missionaries will not remain influential in absentia.

But the dance must also be seen from the vantage point of Ayer 1128, a document. Use a simple spotlight on the notary's pad of paper when he pauses to make notes to put the process of inventorying front and center. When the notary locates first- and second-degree silver objects (sacred) the circular colored lighting mentioned earlier will mark them out, but stagehands can enter the stage to move the third-degree silver altarware to one side of the stage. This growing pile of silver is half visible on stage and half in brown light.

The brown light on the edges of the stage marks "the present." On these dark edges of the stage hovers the historian who watches, occasionally tripping over the growing pile of third-degree silver in the brown light, as she moves to pick up and read the papers that the notary puts down on a desk that is, also, half in full light, half brown light. She does bring certain leading lights out from the brown light to a front corner of the stage, lit by a lighter/brighter brown light. The role of these thinkers is to explain a bit of what is going on in some of the more obscure dance scenes.

First onstage is Bruno Latour, who points out how sacred objects enable (or disable) points of connection. He explains how to study "actants" as those things that "authorize, allow, afford, encourage, permit, suggest, influence, block, render possible, forbid, and so on."[133] Another lighting expert, Leo Cabranes-Grant, takes the spotlight to discuss the way that material figurations (like silver altarware) translate theology into ongoing labor. According to Cabranes-Grant, nothing is static, rather "identities are networks re-performed through a series of relays and labors."[134]

Within this active sacramental field, what kind of mediator is silver altarware? Notaries are not always certain which way sacramentality moves. They need to remain agile; the lighting trails after them. While Latour and Cabranes-Grant are speaking, lighting technicians continue to use followspot lighting (best for tracking mobile performers) trained on the notary, tracking the notary as he makes decisions about where and how to define the space around him.

In this scene, the mystical body of Christ appears and disappears as a quality of light, a flickering "on" when the individual pieces of sacramental silver light up/fade, but the lights demonstrate how, collectively, the individual pieces forge a sacramental network.

Meanwhile, the historian draws another lighting expert, Emile Durkheim, to the spotlight, but as rewired by William Mazzarella. If a hologram is not within the budget, then two actors can play Durkheim and Mazzarella, who tag team in explaining the concept of mana and how it operates like as a force that is at once structuring and unruly, a source of order and excess.[135] The *historian will nod excitedly from her darkened portion of the stage when Mazzarella explains how mana's provocation is dual in that it provokes classification and routinization but is also a calling forth, a potential for becoming. She steps forward to quickly explain to the audience that the Body of Christ, as mana, is a source of authority and volatility, order and unruliness, thus, is a concept that requires the audience to pay attention to both taxonomy (in the present scene) but also the potential for transformation that will be shown in future scenes.*[136]

In sum, to properly light incarnational theology we need a combination of Fresnel lighting that situates the body of Christ as central but acknowledges eucharistic power waning slightly with distance from the altar; occasional use of a patterned light filter to signal when Christ is actually present (i.e., when there is ritual action taking place upon the altar); finally, followspot lighting is key to trace the movement of the various people and things that comprise a sacramental network that is in near-continuous motion.

Mobility presents a question mark: Who has sacramental power, and who can attain it? This anxiety underwrites colonial theopolitics in New Spain. So now it is ok to end with a bit of strobe light action, just to add a measure of distress.

The list of silver items belonging to the first class bears fewer corrections and notations. This makes sense: A chalice or ciborium would *always* belong to the first class, having touched the blood or body of Christ incarnate. Wherever found, its purpose is expressed in the object itself. But silver lamps and candlestick holders are situational objects. If they are on an altar, they are deemed second-class silver. An example is a set of six plain silver candle holders with roman feet (*pies romanos*) of three quarters height with lettering at the foot that says "Nuestra Señora de Loreto."[137] The implication is that these silver candlestick holders adorned a holy image or were on an altar (likely both) and thus are second degree silver. But sometimes a silver lamp on the list of second-degree items is corrected, marked as truly belonging to the first-class list, as in the following description: "An old silver lamp, five palms high, including the Cross with a Weathervane (*una veletas*) as a finishing touch, which they said at the time of forming the inventory, corresponds to the Altar of Señor San Josef and since this is the one where the Divinisimo was placed, the described lamp seems to correspond to [that] class."[138] Similarly, a silver reliquary of plain silver with the signature of San Ignacio, "topped with a

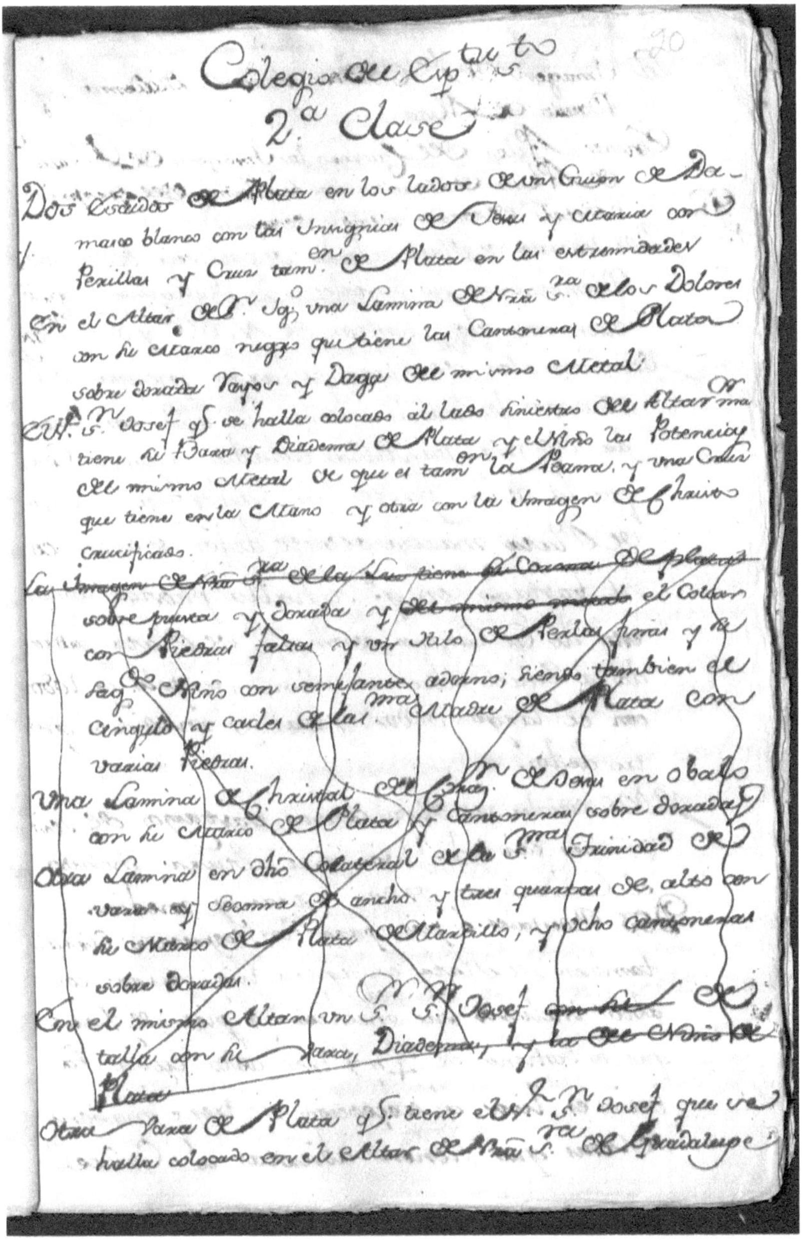

FIGURE 4. Inventory of silver altarware from the Colegio de Espíritu Santo, demonstrating how notaries marked and changed the class of altarware that had touched the body of Christ. Courtesy of Biblioteca Histórica José María Lafragua de la BUAP.

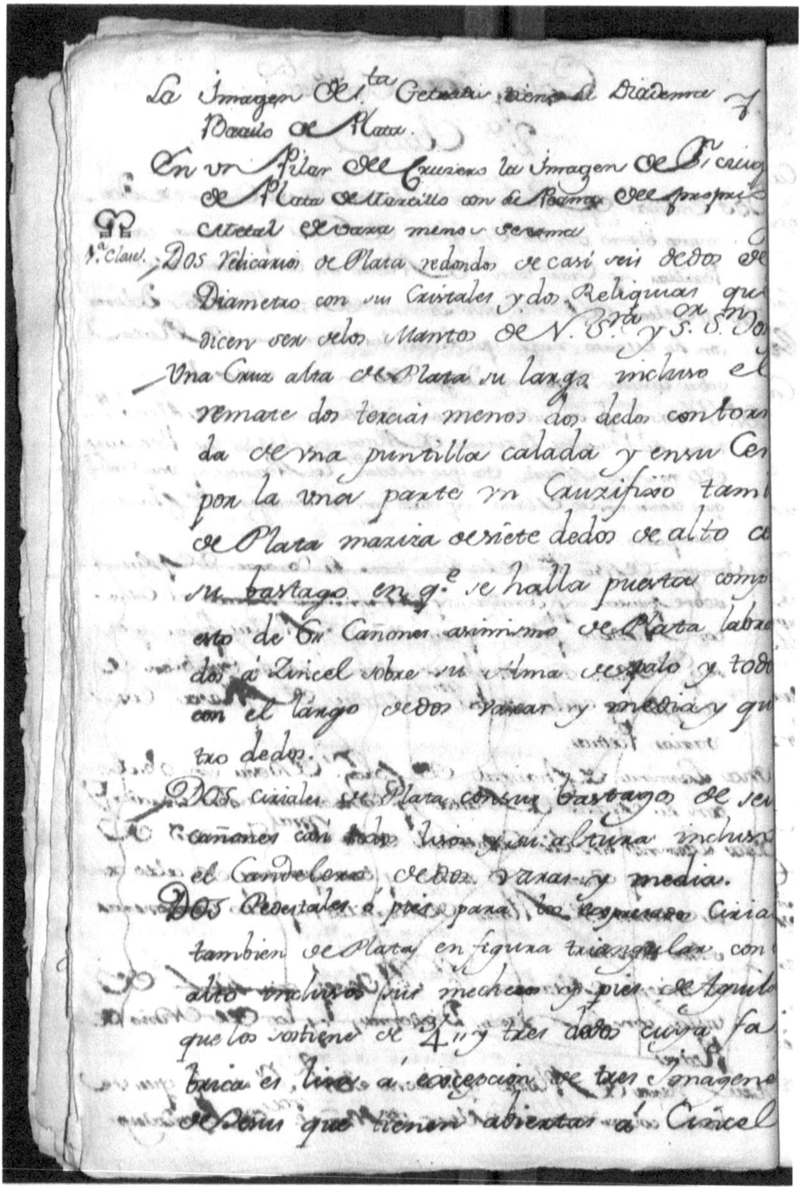

FIGURE 5. Inventory of silver altarware from the Colegio de Espíritu Santo. A marginal note signals that the reliquaries are mislabeled and should be on the inventory of silver belonging to the first class, or God-touched silver. Courtesy of Biblioteca Histórica José María Lafragua de la BUAP.

silver Jesus" is noted as belonging on the *"primera clase"* list.[139] In both cases, notaries are concerned to elevate lamps and candlestick holders to a higher status when necessary, as in this case of the signature of Ignatius. The handwritten name of the saint is considered a surrogate for his sainted body, and so the silver reliquary is accorded first-degree status.

The amount of silver does not appear to matter. The silver corners of an ebony frame, for example, are listed on the inventory of second-class silver. The gilt corners adorn an image of the Holy Family, implying that the image of the Holy Family holds sacred qualities. It is simply a matter of these small corners of silver being proximate to the object adorned. Sometimes the adorned object is unknown, as is prevalent with jewelry. While there are a few pearl chokers and bracelets that are described as adornments for the arms and neck of the Christ child,[140] most of these items have no place-markers. Prominent among these are the belts, necklaces, chokers, bracelets, pendants, and earrings, some with emeralds or garnets, many more made of pearl. But the notary's assumption is that they were made to decorate holy images and statues, thus they are all considered second-class.

Sometimes a few silver items stand apart, as if surrogates for the holy image or sculpture itself. Among these are "las potencias de Nuestro Señor Crucificado" (the "powers" of Christ) represented by hammered silver decorative "rays" that are attached to the head of Christ in some sculptures and paintings. But in this instance Christ's powers stand apart from his human representation, and Christ's *potencias* are displayed together with items that function similarly as surrogates for his holy and suffering mother. That is, Christ's *potencias* are displayed in a niche alongside the silver rays of a halo that would usually be seen glowing behind the tear-stained face of Nuestra Señora de Dolores. In the same niche is a little silver dagger, referring to her own pierced heart. The niche housing the three sets of silver items decorate a side altar for Saint Joseph and together comprise a distinctive representation of the Holy Family. Similarly, a display of sacred hearts belonging to Mary and Jesus stand side by side in another niche.[141] The inventory lists yet another set of *potencias* and describes them as corresponding to a Niño Jesus, but unlike the *potencias* displayed in the niche, their location is not marked and appears to be located outside of any specific network of sacramental power. Yet in the process of sorting, the notaries return them to their proper status

FIGURE 6. *Our Lady of Sorrows*, or la Dolorosa. Author's photo from Templo de la Compañía, courtesy of Museo Galería Mariana, Guanajuato, Mexico.

within the inventory. Thus, these moments of puzzling over proper location confirm a sacramental network that makes sense of the silver objects according to a logic that is organized according to where they took up their "positions" around the altar.

Monologue: Weighty Matter

The Eucharist appeared during the liturgy and disappeared when consumed by both priest and laity. The iterative quality to Christ's presence posed a problem of *duration* that was implied but not directly addressed in the resulting notarial documentation. Silver, by contrast, remained visible even when Christ was not making an appearance. The silver objects had been permanently transformed—ostensibly made eternally sacred. And that made those mobile sacramental objects powerful. The transformation of silver altarware is part of a *longue durée* history of Christian materiality that, as Caroline Walker Bynum states so elegantly: "Miraculous matter was simultaneously—hence paradoxically—the changeable stuff of not-God and the locus of a God revealed."[142] That flickering quality—God/not-God—underwrote the Crown's directives, as notaries were tasked with making explicit what had been an operational yet unstated doxa about the organizational power of *mana*. Local Catholic notaries toiled to account for the ways in which transubstantiation touched and transformed some silver into sacred altarware, while marking others as playing a largely aesthetic supporting role. The marginal notes and the cross-outs offer evidence of bureaucrats in a deliberative mode. They paid careful attention to the emplacement of silver objects. Notaries likely based their judgment upon prior existential experience of sacred settings. That is, their knowledge of the status or importance of each silver object and its likely proximity or distance from the body of Christ is situational knowledge, knotted into their repeated phenomenological experiences of shining silver on many altars in a variety of Eucharistic settings across their lifetimes.

These notarial investigations produce results that bring me to the following conclusion: Clearly not all Catholic "things" are always "religious." But note that I have said little about "religion." It is a flabby term. Instead, I have tried to be specific about the nature of *mana* in a sacramental field, using the word "sacramental" to bring some specificity to how we conceptualize *when* Catholic materials could wield power in colonial Spanish America. So I have been asking, do objects have or convey sacramental power? Or are some more decorative? Commercial, even?

To riff on Latour's words, silver altarware is *matter* of concern. Yet nothing is "religious" in its essence.[143] Space and place determine when some silver objects emerge as entangled with Christ's body and are thus "untouchable," while other objects can be transported far distances from the altar or even melted down. This is not a matter of metaphysics. These are ethnographic and historical questions about the location of power. If we are to reframe the social, cultural, and political history of Catholicism around the concept of "sacramentality," then a clear-eyed attunement to spatiotemporal emplacement is key to interrogating changing patterns in the ways people and things move in relation to the altar. Giving adequate attention to where and how objects occupy space as people pick them up (or are restrained from doing so) is a way of determining if and when materials are Catholic "power objects" and to discern what makes them so. What should be clear by now is that neither economics nor aesthetics give an adequate account of the importance of silver altarware.

What these inventories allow us to see is that within this highly competitive theopolitical landscape, the scaffolding of sovereignty consists in part of *sacramental* objects.[144] In fact, silver performs a previously unrecognized function because if, as McAlister and Napolitano contend, there is a gap when the God-present retreats, then God-touched silver functions as a *stopgap*. Silver of the first degree is material that reverberates with the presence of a momentarily absent God, a glow that fills the space between an experience had and, perhaps more alluring, its promised reiteration.[145] And the fact that the Crown was not only compelled to bend its knee to the body of Christ but also had to stand back from the stopgap silver makes concrete how the theology of incarnation has material weight.

What we move to explore next is how incarnational theology weighed upon social relations. The scene changes so we can follow silver altarware past the outskirts of town to where precious metal adorned an altar at a Jesuit hacienda. In existing historiography, haciendas appear as economic institutions at the margins of the dense cosmopolitan centers. So why is sacramental silver held on Jesuit haciendas? In tracing the contours of a sacramental network, hacienda and college are folded into a single

Table 2: Silver on the Hacienda de San Gerónimo

Alhajas de plata (Precious Items of Silver)

1	*custodia* (monstrance)
1	*baldoquín* (pillared canopy, over tabernacle or altar)
1	*Evangelio con cantoneras de plata* (Gospels with decorative silver corners)
1	*copon*—ciborium/covered cup/chalice
3	*calices con sus patenas* (chalices with their patens)
2	*cruces con sus christos* ("crosses with their Christs" or crucifixes)
1	*Sacras con su pie* ("Sacreds" on a stand—an engraved bookholder?)*
2	*Candeleros* (candle holders)
1	*Incensario* (incense burner)
1	*Naveta* (incense boat)
1	*Lampara* (lamp, lit when Christ "present" on the altar)
1	*concha para Baptisar* ("shell" for baptism)
3	*chrismeras* (holy oil jars)
1	*báculo con su calabacito* (staff with its little decorative head)
1	*Tiara* (crown)
5	*Coronas* (crowns)
2	*corazones* (hearts)
1	*plato para vinageras* (plate for the vinegar holder)
6	*ceras de Agmuil? dhos de Madera y Latón en formal de custidas de madera negra gunorendas de latón*
2	*Evangelio y Lavavo de cristal y latón* (Gospels and Bowl of crystal and brass)

Ropa de color

12	*carellas aviados* [?]
3	*capas*
3	*muzettas*
1	*palio* (canopy)
2	*estolas* (stoles)
8	*Singulos*
15	*hijuelas* (sashes)
1	*Almaisal*
2	*Vestidos de Santa Rosalia completos*[146]
1a	*capa de San Geronimo* (cape)
8	*Frontales*
15	*Palias*
2	*guarda polvos de altar* (altar cloths)

(Continued)

Table 2: (Continued)

Ropa blanca	
10	albas (white vestment)
9	manteles (tablecloths)
18	corporales (square white linen cloth to collect any crumbs of Eucharist)
24	purificadores (small cloth to wipe lip of the chalice)
3	connaltares
Utensilios	
1	Brevario (breviary)
6	Misales (missal)
4	Bonetes (bonnet)
1	Manual (manual)
3	llaves de sagrario (keys to the sacristy)
8	faroles de vidrio (glass lamps)
8	cortinas (curtains)
4	alfombras (cushions)
6	opas de misionarseloo?
1	paño de tumba (funerary cloth)
2	Companillas de metal de mano (small hand bells)
1	organ pequeño (small organ)
2	ciriales con sus pedestarles todo de madera dorada (wooden candlesticks, gold plated)
1	cruz con su pedestal de lo mismo (cross with its own pedestal)
10	candeleros de metal y cobre (metal and copper candlesticks)
12	dhos de palo plateados (the same, with silver plated wood)
4	atriles de idem (music stands, silver plated wood)
14	Ramilletes (vases of flowers, usually metal/silver)
1	Niño Dios en su urna de cristal (the Child God in his crystal case)
12	estampas de humo
[margin note says Yglesia y Sacristia]	
1	christo de madera
1	lienzos de varios tamaños
35	estampas
3	campanas de maior a meno en la torre (three bells, major to minor, in the tower)
6	colaterales con varias Imagenes de b.to y pincel
2	confesionarios de madera (confessionals, wooden)
2	Escarios
2	Bancas

FAJML, Legajo 139:66–67v

devotional field. What becomes clear is how the hacienda is, like other Jesuit institutions, configured to host wide-ranging devotional opportunities rooted in eucharistic practices. The critical distinction is that Catholic laborers (both free and enslaved) are *compelled* to put the sacraments of baptism, marriage, last rites, but especially penance and the Eucharist at the center of their highly monitored lives. Indeed, devotional life at the Jesuit-run hacienda is a command performance. Engaging in evening prayers and attending Mass around silver-adorned body of Christ is not a choice but an aspect of how "devotional productivity" shaped labor practices. These overlapping spheres were geared toward this-worldly *and* otherworldly profits. Accordingly, everyday practices of Catholic racialization bore a distinctively Jesuit stamp.

Scene VII: Care for the Sacramental Silver on the Jesuit Hacienda

Recall how Castillo had worked quickly on the day of the arrest, pausing in his studied perambulation around the college to briefly examine documents pertaining to haciendas. He had quickly delegated teams to take up the future work of auditing those locales more distant from the city center. This is the paper trail that will lead us away from the city of Puebla to the Jesuit-run sites of commodity production in the countryside. An inventory of silver altarware held by the haciendas and ranches owned by the Colegio Espíritu Santo provides a vantage point on how sacramental silver was deployed in a racializing labor system. To see this, I juxtapose the notary's list of altarware with a manual written to guide the Jesuit who does not live in community in a college, but rather lives among laity in his mission to run a hacienda. The silver inventory recedes to the background as the guide quickly brings into view how labor administration on the Jesuit hacienda was organized around the altar.

Thus enters the scene a text titled "Instructions That the Brothers Administrators of the Haciendas Must Observe." The guide to hacienda administration, hereafter referred to as the directive,[147] is held in the Archivo General de la Nación in Mexico City. The manuscript was written for an administrator who had little to no experience running a hacienda.[148] The silver inventory, as we know well by now, exists because the Crown is documenting Jesuit holdings. But the Jesuit administrator is a master at inventorying as well. The process of keeping inventories of the actions he takes is key to his role as a virtuous leader of what is cast here as a devotional community. The anxiety that subtends this guide is a concern with how mobility affects the lives of the hacienda inhabitants, both the Jesuit and his workers. Notably, the Jesuit's charting, marking, and inventorying is key to this containment of self and of others. Thus, this scene is performed in the even tone of an instructional guide, yet palpable is its undercurrent of worry about the moral management of racialized laborers.

The *hermanos* in the title refers to the special grade of Jesuit called *temporal coadjutor*. These members of the Society of Jesus did not take the final or fourth vow and were usually not ordained priests. Jesuit brothers primarily ranked among those most often tasked with the occupations of cook, nurse, or doorman. In New Spain, *hermanos* were frequently hacienda administrators. This guide covers all aspects of hacienda life, beginning with how the Jesuit ought to manage himself, the altar, and the lives of servants and slaves so they would develop habits conducive to virtuous living. Adopting a paternalistic role, the Jesuit administrator structures his own everyday life to, as the Jesuits often say, find God in all things. His inventorying process marks practices of "care" as a form of containment: Care/containment of self, care/containment of others, and care/containment of the silver altarware are intertwined management processes dependent upon charting, noting, and inventorying.

For the Jesuit administrator, this involves managing a potentially destabilizing sacramental power, as becomes apparent in his care of silver altarware. These efforts to gather hacienda residents around the adorned and illuminated Eucharist is central to how he organizes the daily movement of bodies and souls. Although the document does not address emancipation directly, the directive nonetheless reveals ways in which sacramentality held within it transformative potential that could be harnessed to practices of freedom, as evidenced in what amounts to a throwaway line for the author: "slaves, where there are any." This casual turn of phrase is tacit acknowledgement that slavery is disappearing in New Spain, in large part due to the active pursuit of emancipation undertaken by enslaved persons and their kin.[149]

Well before the administrator is advised about managing the fields or the livestock, he is given a list of what must be done to care for "all that touches upon the divine cult and the things of the chapel."[150] The directive offers detailed advice to the Jesuit administrator about how to maintain the devotional objects that are so central to the sacramental rituals around which the hacienda community congregates. The Jesuit cares for the chapel "so God will care for the fields and multiply their fruits." In keeping the ornaments in good order, the Jesuit assures that the chapel remains a worthy space for God to visit. The administrator is to prepare and to "ask what the Church asks of God on the day of Corpus [Christi]: *Sic nos tu visita sicut te colimus*. Visit us, you [*tú*], Señor, as we have gone to great lengths in your cult and service." Like a good host, the Jesuit lays the silver to invite Christ incarnate to come to the hacienda, and as we shall see shortly, he also commands that hacienda workers and slaves be in attendance.

First, to comply with his obligations as a host, he is to see that the chapel and sacristy are kept neat and clean. The administrator must keep a written inventory of the precious items (*alhajas*), but he can elicit the assistance of a lay person whom he can name as sacristan. Given his proximity to the altar and as custodian of all things related to the liturgy, the sacristan's "emblems of office were the keys he held—to the church, to the sacristy, and to the cabinets were the linen, chalices, and other equipment for the mass were kept."[151] The keys, once again, enact authority.

The sacristan has unique access and special responsibility to attend to silver altarware, holy water, holy oil, and the cloth that has covered the altar. His tasks include the care and prevention of damage to the various ornaments, but he is also to assist the chaplain with the Mass. Twice a week, he should sweep the chapel and sacristy. He should ring the bells at noon, but also to mark prayers for departed souls or ring for prayers if a storm threatens. The sacristan's own access to sacramental power can be shared when he delegates the ringing of bells on feast days either to "two Indians or *muchachos*." He is to ascertain on Saturday afternoons whether the Padre Capellán has sufficient wine and hosts for the following week, and he must keep track of the appropriately colored liturgical ornaments. He is to make certain that water, soap, and a hand towel are in the sacristy for the priest's hands. There should be a sink of clean water in the sacristy and a little plate of ground salt on Sunday mornings "so to bless the priest."

Water that has already been blessed can be placed at the doors of the church, the sacristy, and can be carried to the bedrooms in the house.

Thus, remnants of eucharistic sacrifice seep into the sleeping quarters, connecting the domestic sphere firmly to the chapel. Note the care that goes into disposing of the remainders of Christ's appearance on the altar. The sacristan should wash the *ropa blanca* of the sacristy whenever necessary. The *purificadores y corporales* are cloths specifically set aside for cleaning the chalice. When items that have touched the body of Christ require washing, the sacristan can carry them in a basket for the Father Chaplain to wash. Only an ordained priest can launder Christ's dirty linens. The water in which they are washed can be carried and poured into the drain that is in the sacristy for this purpose, but if there is not one, it should be poured into a tomb (*sepultura*). These instructions demonstrate the limits placed on how God-touched matter could circulate, as well as who can come close to the altar outside of liturgical time. While sacramentality may have seeped out from the chapel, not many on the hacienda would have had such complete access to the generative space of the altar as the chaplain. To make certain, the sacristan must "lock the chapel and sacristy with a key and not leave it open during the day, unless there are penitents who will confess, in which case, consult with the Chaplain." The author "omits" additional instruction, allowing that in other matters, he can follow "the practice and style of each hacienda."[152]

The level of detail in the instructions indicate that these tasks are critical to maintaining the sanctity of the hacienda chapel and its altar as one among many important nodal points in this Jesuit network of sacramental power. The care of the chapel and its sacristy, with the attention paid to ornamenting the chapel with precious metal, is necessary precisely to signal that this small community is linked to those who congregate around the Eucharist in the bustling cities: "The Mass that is celebrated on the haciendas in the countryside, and the Holy Sacrament that is consecrated there, is the same that is consecrated in the most populous cities and deposited in the tabernacles of those churches. Accordingly haciendas should not be inferior in decency and in the adornment of sacred things if they lack a flourishing gathering (*por falta de concurso florido*), for this is not done by men, but by God."[153] In other words, it does not matter that hacienda communities are small in number. This imagined Catholic community envisions inhabitants of both city and countryside united in the sacraments.

Scene VIII: Charting Virtue, Enforcing Devotionalism

The silver monstrance and chalices signal a God-present on the altar around which the hacienda community congregates. In the directive we see how the Jesuit administrator oversees this command performance. Enforced devotionalism is clearly a containment practice, but servants and slaves are not the only targets of this mode of subjectivation. The Jesuit administrator's labor to manage "the help" is devotional labor undertaken to *manage and maintain himself* as a virtuous subject. In fact, he depends on this cast of actors to support his own spiritual self-fashioning as an authority of a particular type: the father figure. To harvest souls and worldly fruits, Jesuits are advised to care for servants as if "fathers" in a family.[154] Indeed, many laborers were born and raised on the hacienda, were baptized, with godparents, so the semantics of fictive kinship has some play.[155] The language in the directive slips back and forth between "servants" and "Indians," implying that most hacienda workers were indigenous. Notably, the term *mestizo* is absent in this text.[156] I have already noted that the directive gives its advice about slaves with the caveat that on many haciendas there are no longer very many.

The Jesuit administrator is instructed that "just as there are seasons for sowing, so one must put great care in the cultivation of souls and the good education of the servants and their families. . . . God has promised abundant harvests of worldly fruits to those who keep the holy Law." The Jesuit administrator is admonished to manage the spiritual lives of the workers on the haciendas, just as any good father would do, reminding him that Saint Paul railed against fathers who neglected the education of their servants as "worse than infidels."[157] Meditating upon his role as a father of a family, the administrator is instructed to consult and reread every year "*plática* 36 of Padre Parra's work." He is referring to Juan Martínez de la Parra, SJ, who wrote the three-volume work titled *Luz de verdades católicas y explicación de la doctrina christiana*. The sermon that the *Instrucción* mentions is titled "On the Obligations That Masters and Slaves Must Observe." Parra begins by pointing out that the Latin root *famel* links slaves (*famulus, famuli*) with the Spanish term *família*. The father of a family ought to be a father to his slaves.[158] Parra refers his reader to "the genius" of Seneca, and in particular his Letter 17, to advise them to learn lessons from their forebears who taught that "neither should masters become hateful through the tone of their domination, nor should slaves always be face to face with their powerlessness."[159] The sermon also stipulates that slaves ought to focus on ultimate salvation in the afterlife where "souls have no color,"[160] but that here on earth they should consider the slave master's commands as an opportunity to turn tribulation and fatigue into merit and glory. "Thus consider everything you are commanded to do is the same as if God commanded it."[161] These are words upon which the Jesuit administrator is advised to meditate, but we can also imagine that these words had the visual authority of being read from a book or paper resting on the *sacra*, that is, the bookstand listed in the hacienda inventory whose silver plating adorned the authoritative words preached by religious authorities.

But it is not only preaching that takes place at the altar. A large portion of the Jesuit's paternalistic responsibilities are related to structuring and monitoring devotional life that is centered on daily activities at the hacienda chapel. Each night, following the bookkeeping, and after giving orders to the *mayordomo* about the next day's tasks, he is to ring a little bell to call to the chapel the servants and possible slaves. The residents of the hacienda should congregate to pray a "chorus" of the rosary, first together, and then they can pray on their own "from any devotional guide" (*algún librito manual*). The prayers should finish with a litany to the Virgin. The Jesuit is advised to limit evening prayers to this simple series of prayers, remarking that inhabitants can pray on their own and that communal prayer should not be an onerous aspect of the schedule of daily devotions.[162]

Sundays are for all kinds of accounting: The betterment of souls and the payment of wages and the distribution of rations go hand in hand. Everyone living on the hacienda is to attend Mass and take communion every Sunday of the year. On Sundays and feast days, the administrator is to ring the bell three times at thirty minutes before the start of Mass and once more at the start of the services. He is to make certain that everyone attends Mass weekly and on feast days, and in so doing to inculcate the value of punctuality.[163] He may call upon the hacienda chaplain (if there is one) who can be an important support to the running and regulation of devotional practices. The administrator should foster a cooperative relationship with the chaplain, who will help to make sure the servants in his charge go punctually to the chapel, and that they attend the *pláticas de doctrina cristiana* before the Mass and, importantly, that they remain until the end of the Gospel. The chaplain, here, is like an extra pair of eyes, but this also marks an area in which the Jesuit brother (*hermano*) addressed in the text has limited power: He has not taken vows as a priest so cannot himself consecrate the bread and wine. Like second-degree silver, the coadjutor plays a supporting role, but he has no power to make Christ present in the bread and wine.

Attendance is taken as they depart the Mass. "Have written on a chart [*tabla*] the names of the Indians of the hacienda along with their women and children. When the Mass is ending, [you should] leave by the door of the chapel, along with the *mayordomo, ayudante*, and *fiscal*" (the assistant to the priest/chaplain). Roll call takes the form of a prayer. "As you call out the names in a loud voice, they are to answer *Ave María Santísima*." The administrator is to note who failed to attend and commit to making inquiries the following Sunday. If no "rational excuse" is offered, the *fiscal* will be instructed to give them six to eight lashes. The same is to be practiced with slaves "on haciendas that have them." The Mass is described as "an important means [*un medio*] to attain the well-being of their souls; as is the frequent reception of the sacraments during the major fiestas of the year."[164]

A similar schedule holds for feast days, but only if Mass can be said at the hacienda. In other words, when feast days land on workdays, laborers will not be trekking into town to attend Mass. The Jesuit administrator is to keep track of the required communion days (*comuniones de regla*), and he is to pin it to his wall so that he will not forget. There is greater attention in the directive to the discipline of the hacienda Indians who miss Mass, because unlike slaves, they have more control over their own movements. The rules are listed explicitly: All of the Indians at the hacienda are required to arrive a half hour before the Mass to pray the *doctrina cristiana* "*en mexicano*," that is, in Nahuatl. "For this, find a blind Indian to teach [the prayers], and give him a donation (*limosna*) on that day for his work." If it is not possible to pray together before Mass, then they can do so after, in which case attendance would be taken after the *doctrina* instead of immediately after the Mass. Later on Sundays afternoons, from three o'clock onward, the Indians on the hacienda should gather once again at the ringing of the bell "to pray now just a chorus of the Crown of María Santísima and at the end of their Litanies to pray again from the Doctrina Cristiana, but this time in Spanish. This should conclude with a reading from the short Catechism of Padre Castaño."[165]

For the most part, "fathering" servants entails the labor of what today is gendered parenting. The administrator is akin to a devotional "soccer mom," that is, the parent who keeps on top of the schedule, utilizing lists and charts to maintain a working devotional order. This is a management process: The Jesuit monitors the fulfillment of Christian duties and, with his numerous charts, "pins down" his family of laborers, making the Mass and the Eucharist central to the mechanics of everyday governance of servants and slaves.[166] But remember that these inventories aim not only to manage the devotional lives of laborers: This is the work the administrator must do to maintain *himself* as a Jesuit.

Next the directive turns to the issue of the "good governance of slaves, where there are any." The directive continues to advise the administrator on methods for training ethical workers whose inculcation in their duties and status as slaves includes the memorization of prayers and Christian doctrine. This is especially true for young, enslaved women who, we shall soon see, require additional attention and a period of segregation from other slaves. Unlike freed laborers, all enslaved persons are to live in segregated and locked quarters. The administrator is to be certain that the slave barracks (*el real*) is securely fenced, and always locked at night, to be reopened in the morning. The secured door is to be visible from the main house. A bell is to be hung over the door, which can be used to call the slaves to work in the morning and to pray the rosary at night and at other times of the day when they are required for different tasks.[167] Here one sees that slaves were physically restrained and kept segregated from other workers on the hacienda, with their movements visible from the house. Clearly slave mobility is a source of anxiety.

As with servants on Sundays and after working hours, the ordering of slaves' time takes a devotional shape. Young slaves undergo training, first in the prayers and Christian doctrine, and second in the modes of physical labor in which they are intended to one day participate. Both modes equate physical labor with the inculcation of moral values. The earliest forms of training take place in or near the hacienda chapel.

> Do not have laziness among the young slaves, give them some work from the time they are *niños* up to the age of eight, occupying them in

some work proportionate to their strength. To help them, designate an old female slave who can no longer work, who will bring them to the morning mass every day. But before mass, have them pray in the cemetery of the church, and seated on one side the boys, and the other the girls, where they pray the Doctrina Cristiana, the old slave who cares for them, teaching them, or a young man who knows it well; if there is Mass, they go in to hear it with devotion, keeping the above stated separation; if there is no Mass, they will sing el Alabado at the end of the Doctrina and then they go to have breakfast. After this she will bring them to the fields where they have tasks like gathering stones, cleaning roads, hoeing seedlings, sweeping away trash, and similar things, following what the *mandador* or the *mayordomo* orders, and, when the big slaves finish their work, they should return the young men with their mothers to the barracks.[168]

Containment and continence coincide in managing the lives of girls who are over twelve because "grave problems that are always experienced" when young girls are separated from one another. He calls them *doncellas* or "maidens," an honorific that is tied to the state of a young woman's virginity. The potential source of grave problems to be avoided was loss of virtue due to rape, *rapto* (kidnapping), or the experience of sexual pleasure outside of marriage. All of these would impugn the honor of the patriarch and put future marriage possibilities at risk. As administrator-father figure, he should gather all young girls who are twelve years old (and older) in a capacious room that is separated from the slave barracks. "This should serve as a school for the *doncellas*, where they will live and from which they do not leave until they marry, in order to conserve, by this road, their virtue and integrity. They should be housed with a slave, a widow of good judgment, who will be a teacher who lives with them, and takes them out to the field, and works with them, and cares for them in everything, and who gives an account to the Administrator if there is any disorder."[169] The Jesuits, then, are charged with monitoring marriage and reproduction in this makeshift *recogimiento*—a withdrawal from public view that, as Jessica Delgado has shown, is a complex mode of containment that protects the honor of men/the family while also marking a form of virtue that can confer spiritual status for the women.[170] Discourse about honor also signals systems of constraint that can serve as (very complicated) avenues toward attaining a modicum of control over one's social status in this transactional society. Recall the example in the story about the woman who travels across Sicily to promote the Madre Santísima de la Luz. Her claims to "vileness" and virtue underwrite her ability to take action. In most cases, however, modesty, chastity, and obedience are enforced via segregation, and this enables the author to paint an idealized portrait in which the imagined young slave woman earns the honorific "doncella" for living an enslaved life, *muy recogida*.

The inventory notes a silver "shell" used to pour holy water over a baby's head. The use of objects made of precious metals on the hacienda marked the seriousness of the sacraments. The Jesuit administrator, too, was tasked with celebrating the sacraments of marriage and baptism. And he should document that he has done so, making yet another chart that notes what has been distributed to the enslaved couple upon marriage, when a child is born, and when the child is baptized. His inventories were to include gifts made at Easter and Christmas. "Keep this list on the wall of your room and refer to this always when these occasions present themselves, so that the slaves do not take it upon themselves to introduce new imposiciones, especially when a new Administrator enters, but that all conforms to the *arancel* that has been checked prior with the Procurator and approved by the Superior."[171] In another section the administrator is admonished to be sure that slaves do not sell the church clothes that they are given each year. This hints at the reality of hacienda life in the central valley of Mexico wherein its inhabitants had much tighter material and spiritual connections to other non-hacienda wage laborers, markets, the parish system, as well as connections to the devotional options and market cultures of not-so-distant urban centers.[172]

"Be sure," he writes, "to foment devotion among them, the frequent reception of the sacraments, and the *pláticas* (spiritual talks) and examples from the novenas of the Virgin, at night where there is a Chaplain, more when there is not one to make up for this with reading, on these nights, some examples from the *Año Virgíneo*, or another book that treats devotion to the Virgin." He is to read to them on Sundays, after the Mass, "from the Catechism of Padre Belarmino or the Roman Catechism of Padre Eusebio [Nieremberg], and during Lent give some spiritual talks from Padre Parra, who treats the topics of confession and communion, and in the case of the *Doctrina Cristiana*, they will pray it before the Mass." These were very popular Jesuit writers—Bellarmine, Nieremberg, and the *criollo* Parra—a sign that slaves and servants were groomed spiritually in a Jesuit style. "Finally, remember to do well for the souls of the slaves who have died; for each one who dies, everyone is charged with praying the Rosary for eight days, and the Mass on the first Sunday following, and command that Masses be said in the Parish, giving an offering of one peso (whether there is or is not a Chaplain); take out an announcement of the dead (*una bula de difuntos*) and apply in writing the [slave's] name, and give this to the living whenever there is new publication of bulls, distributed to all who are twelve years old and up. All this can be obtained by the Administrators as they wish. Make good Christians of the slaves, and they will be good servants, and God will cast upon all his blessing."[173]

Monologue: Hacienda Subjectivities

Clearly Jesuit labor relations pivot around the altar. David Sweet noted this years ago but contended that the Jesuits had been driven by economic goals, leaving "spiritual" concerns to trail in profit's wake. "The Jesuit priestly commitment to spiritual welfare of individuals was allowed to take second place to their institutional commitment to the material welfare of a socio-economic system."[174] He intends this as critique: The Jesuits are not living up to their Christian mission. But I contend that Jesuit discourses and practices of "care" are not screens intended to distract from an extractive racializing system. Rather, we have had a glimpse of how racializing disciplinary labor practices grew out of an intimate encounter with the Jesuit, who figures himself as the stern but caring father who is mediating an encounter with Jesus. The Jesuits project an image of the idealized "family" bond that develops in relation to the body of Christ, even when the fictive kinship is purchased and some members of the "family" live in bondage. The Christian notion of the sacrificed body as *profitable* is the proposed horizon, a salvific narrative presented to both free and enslaved workers on the Jesuit hacienda. In his closing comments on slave management, the administrator is asked to look closely at himself, to evaluate the care he is giving to the slaves, especially because they "have no other superior to care for them."[175]

The guide makes clear and urgent that the salvation of the Jesuit administrator himself depends upon making labor management the center of his own devotional life. As the father of a family, "the Administrator must give a tight account to God, of the harm he does out of carelessness, and of the good he has omitted to do." Much of this ordering is embodied—he is to master his passions and adopt the patriarchal norms of fatherhood modeled in classical literature.

But the littered room of the Jesuit administrator indicates that inventorying is key: How many charts, tables, lists is he required to keep or pin to his wall? Such administrative practices run parallel to his spiritual self-management. He has been trained, via the Spiritual Exercises, to make marks in a notebook that break up the day into manageable segments in order evaluate what he needs to do/change/think after morning prayers, then before noon and again before the evening meal. The notetaking accounts for his spiritual progress as well as his habitual weaknesses. The Jesuit is well trained to mark up the page in management exercises.[176] On the hacienda, the management of others offers yet another avenue to produce an "inventory" of self, here as the virtuous father tasked with constructing an ideal devotional world among the hacienda's servants and slaves. Profit accrues in the "fruits" of souls as well as in the commodities produced. And so if the maintenance of one's spiritual life can depend upon the patriarchal management of servants and slaves, then surely the Jesuit adage has a brutal edge: God can be found in *all* things.

If this ideal Jesuit administrator presented in the guide had reread Parra's "On the Obligations of Masters and Slaves" every year, as instructed, what would he think of the advice to the slave to take the command of his master as a command from God? Perhaps this resonates for him: Especially as a coadjutor, he is obedient to his own superior, instructed to be as if a cane in the superior's hand, a mere tool. This was especially so for the "brothers," that is, the lower-status Jesuit coadjutors to whom the manuscript is addressed. Does the Jesuit administrator read the directive and imagine himself running an idealized familial-monastic world, wherein the wise Seneca authorizes the humble coadjutor to take on an expanded role as patriarch among the largely Indian familial units that circle the hacienda? The directive emphasizes how his spiritual training at the Jesuit college is replicated here, with the quasi-monastic inner core of single men. There are echoes of the closed utopian Christian world aimed at in the Jesuit missions of Paraguay. Later among exiled Mexican Jesuits in Italy, hacienda scenes are reimagined as a kind of model for Christian living.

In sum, this future-oriented Christian life on the Jesuit hacienda holds out salvation as the ultimate profit, while quotidian labors on a Jesuit hacienda are envisioned as the pathway to both thisworldly returns and otherworldly rewards. The economic and the spiritual profits are in no way separated on the hacienda when both take place within the orbit of the silver clad body of Christ. This finer-grained understanding of how a Jesuit-run hacienda was centered on the transforming and transformational body of the Catholic God-man indicates that Jesuit disciplinary devotionalism is implicated in the ways that racialization and emancipation played out in colonial Mexico. Sacramental power flows through the haciendas—sites of commodity production built upon hierarchical and oppressive labor systems—because they are also structured as devotional spaces. This simple insight about *compulsory congregation* underwrites Ingie Hovland's attention to what she calls local Christian theories, that is, "how specific Christian communities use and think about their places."[177] The hacienda is a space where segregation functions within a system that privileges *congregation*. In fact, "segregation" reads like an imported descriptor. *Segmentation* within a system that privileges *congregation* better explains both racialization *and* the possibilities for position-taking within the hacienda-college complex, and in colonial society more broadly.

Jesuit hacienda administration is theopolitical in its efforts to congregate and segment a mobile colonial workforce around the altar and according to sacramental logics. Theorizing a sacramental field expands the scene such that we see the hacienda, long considered to be an "economic" institution, within a larger colonial power complex in which position-taking around the altar shapes space, conduct, and language.[178] But it also matters that these hacienda regimes are empowered by *mana*. In that vein, I have come to appreciate how the starring role—the exemplary Jesuit administrator—necessarily issues a casting call in which supporting roles are played by the devotional community.

And yet there is room within these assigned roles for improvisation and interruption. Mareike Winchell insists that scholars ought not reproduce and reify settler fantasies of total racialized dominance.[179] We should also pay attention to discourses and practices that point toward the "what else" in the history of colonialism. One trace of this in the directive is the very disruptive little phrase "slaves, where there are any." The directive does not give us access to the lives of enslaved persons nor to the freed peoples of African descent who began to outnumber those enslaved by the end of the eighteenth century. But we can get a glimpse beyond the idealized vision of Jesuit patriarchal dominance if we turn back to the inventories of silver to see how silver altarware—power objects—were wielded by Afro-Mexican congregations in Puebla. In the next few scenes, we see more clearly how colonial hierarchies are shaped according to positionality around the altar. Formerly enslaved people were also *mana* workers.

Scene IX: Silver, Salvation, and Racialization

Silver is a crucial thread to trace because it can change form, flow, harden, be molded to different shapes, from the medallions to the mouth of a crystal pitcher, or the cup that holds sacramental wine, and the crown that adorns the Santísima Madre de la Luz. And so can social positions and identities morph and change in the Spanish Americas.[180] Jesuit reproduction of Catholic society's asymmetries of power carried within it the possibility that Christ's transformation might become one's own. A Jesuit-styled devotional life contributed to this transactional colonial hegemony wherein the spiritual subjugation of self could potentially be exchanged for a taste of sacramental power.[181] We have seen how Jesuits sorted people but now we move to catch a glimpse of how Jesuit followers sorted themselves to be proximate to the sacraments. In all of this, we follow the notaries documentation of items made of precious metals to see how silver once indexed the ways in which colonial ethno-social positions could form, flow, change shape, and harden, only to change again, all in relation to the altar.

Returning to the documentary work taking place at the Colegio Espíritu Santo in the years following the expulsion of the Jesuits, we see racialization and silver linked in the notary's move to mark out the silver items found on the desks of Jesuits.[182] In these last scenes, I continue to trace how sacramental power moves in and through Jesuit institutions and, notably, how sacramental power shapes racializing colonial hierarchies, but here flipping the script so we can see how the body of Christ allowed subaltern peoples to "*mana* work" their way into a higher social status. Take note of the silver altarware in the room of the Padre Rector Joseph Castillo, where there "can be found two chalices and their patens that were not inventoried in this *aposento*, because engraved around the bottom it says they belong to the Congregation of the Morenos." The formal title of this religious organization is Congregación de la Escalvitud de Nuestra Señora la Virgen Santísima de la Anunciata, or Slavery to Our Lady, the Holy Virgin of the Annunciation. The reference to *"esclavitud"* refers to the spiritual subjugation of its members who modeled themselves upon the devotional slavery of Joseph, Anna, and Joachim to Mary. This Jesuit-sponsored confraternity was originally established in Rome in the seventeenth century, its "slavery" indicative of the spiritual profit in assuming an abject devotional attitude. Many of the Annunciata congregations in New Spain are similarly formed, but in 1685 the Annunciata sponsored by the Colegio Espíritu Santo in Puebla established this subdivision of the Annunciata as a confraternity for freed blacks called la Congregación de la Santísima Virgen de Morenos y Pardos.[183] In the documents pertaining to the arrest and exile of the Jesuits, references to this congregation take different names: Notaries variously jot down *"congregación de negros," "de pardos," "de morenos,"* and *"de mulatos."* Differences in nomination may reflect of attitudes accorded by each individual notary.[184] Pablo Silva describes *morenos* and *pardos* as labels that, denoting freedom, were key terms through which freed persons demanded a greater social respect. For this community, congregation membership was central to claiming honor in this status driven society.[185]

Thus, it is not surprising that the ethno-spiritual status of black confraternities in the existing documentation is marked in terms that signal contention: The variability in how one names "blackness" marks the way in which status was *fought out* in socioreligious terms. And such disputes are indexed in the inventories of silver adornments. When the notary moves next to list items belonging to Jesuit-sponsored confraternities, he inventories these Eucharistic objects as belonging to the Congregation of Nuestra Señora, *"que llaman de los Morenos."*[186]

Status and silver go together. These members marked their ownership of a silver chalice by engraving the name of the confraternity on its base.[187] Belonging to this organization made them owners and custodians of silver of the first degree, a marker of a form of respectability. The chalice not only *represents* status but is also a power object that *confers* status.[188] The chalice with the group name engraved on its base empowers the Congregation members to enter theopolitical transactions that, in turn, reassemble their social world.

In addition to the chalices and patens, the inventory shows that the Congregación del los Morenos also owns an image of the Annunciata that, like Our Lady of Sorrows, has her own "*rayos de plata*"—silver crowning rays. They own the stand upon which her image is displayed, which is also made of silver. The congregation owns a gold reliquary decorated with two emeralds and two garnets; a cross with five stones, one of which appears to be emerald; and a belt with a pearl decoration in the middle, ostensibly a decoration for the Virgin Mary.[189] The confraternity's "third degree" items include a silver lamp described as two yards (*dos varas*) in height with the chains by which the lamp would have been hung "very well treated." The other item owned by the confraternity also makes a powerful but more clear statement: The confraternity members own a silver pen and ink set (*tintero y salvadero de plata*), indicative of how the power of literacy when coupled with the pen confers status in this religio-legal society. In sum, the Jesuits mediated access to "the Divine worship," a place where the Crown's power was limited, but where slaves or freedmen could take hold of sacramental power to amplify their own. This small silver story hints at how sacramental logics made for different modes of enslavement and emancipation than the model of Mexico's northern neighbor too often considered the paradigmatic story of enslavement and emancipation.

In New Spain, the ethnopolitics of religious respectability extended into and strengthened Afro-Mexican kinship networks. Members of freed Black communities congregated in urban centers and, often together with *indios* and mestizo kin, they worked to bring individuals out of the condition of enslavement.[190] Freed persons of African descent often "married up," but as Silva clarifies, not "out" of social networks. What this means is that, as Silva establishes in his study of Black-Indigenous relations in Puebla, the strength of these socioreligious and commercial—and, I would add, *sacramental* relationships—is that they assisted one in forging networks that supported and financed a slave's self-purchase.[191] Racialization is contested materially not only with cash, but also in the devotional practices and symbolics that denote and facilitate position-taking around the altar. Clearly, silver objects were relays that rendered some social/cultural asymmetries more enduring (a nod toward the durability of habitus). We have seen that the "swarm" of activity around the altar moved in a far more regimented way on the hacienda, where sacramental logics shaped everyday racial-religious disciplinary practices. Most clear is how the mutability of racialized identities in the Spanish Americas cannot be explained by appeals to models of racial segregation. Rather, in this colonial society, *the* primary demand is *congregation* around the body of Christ. It is a demand that shaped social relations and power structures because sacramentality also afforded a means to accumulate and wield *mana*.

Theopolitical place-making includes the ways Afro-Mexicans resituate themselves in relation to where the God-man most reliably appears, opening possibilities for claiming status, greater liberties, and emancipation.[192] In sum, the notion of a God-present in the sacraments simultaneously justified asymmetrical power relations while also providing what Larissa Brewer-Garcia has called Catholicism's "gestures of inclusion."[193] These "gestures" were a partial credit—a small amount of sacramental power—that Indians, slaves, and freedmen transacted in devotional and legal forums to forge freedoms for themselves or for their families. This extension of credit may sound abstract, but when wielded like a concrete tool it becomes key to understanding the line that marks "slave" as a disappearing category in New Spain—"slaves, where there are any." With silver altarware, *mana* is *held*. God may sit at the center of a patriarchal master-slave relationship, and the God-man is called upon to support the Jesuits' insistence upon subservience. Yet sacramental power is a kind of material credit that confounds the master's total dominance when the silver clad body of Christ can be positioned like a wedge that cracks open a few exit doors.

Monologue: Mutability

Silver indexes potentiality. Silver changes shape, objects made of silver can be mobilized, and, moreover, their changing position within the sacramental network matters. Bureaucratic notaries *and* Afro-Mexican confraternity members had an innate understanding of the stakes of being proximate to the silver altarware that carried and adorned the body of Christ. Eucharistic ritual *enlivened* the material world in this colonial setting. Crucially, while these silver relays of sacramental power can be held by some, *mana* is not fully containable, neither by priest nor king.

In this setting, theopolitical maneuvering is at once an effort at elite levels to manage the flow of sacramental power, thus the debates among

Catholic rigorist bishops about Jesuit devotion to La Luz were anchored in a material reality. But theopolitics also encompass the claims that lower-status individuals make in the sacramental field, thus marriages, proper burials, memberships in confraternities are sacramental status markers. Thus, the altar can be the space for a power grab, where jurisdiction and sovereignty are contested, and where smaller players can "catch power" by taking hold of sacramental objects.[194] So too is the *deliberating* about the categorization of a silver candlestick holder on a government inventory a theopolitical consideration. And who can hold that power? What does it mean when Jesuit devotional practices encourage frequent communion at silver adorned altars? Among the many critiques launched at this order of religious men was that their devotional practices were sufficiently "adaptable" and "flexible" to meet people at their various states of life. Critics at the time accused the Jesuits of promoting a moral laxity that had cheapened Christianity, a dangerous accusation.[195] This is a promise of mutability and one that had informed the Crown's worries that Jesuit-mediated sacramentality had seeped into everyday life, putting lower-status members of society within reach of these potentially empowering objects.[196] In fact, as we have begun to see with evidence from the silver items held on haciendas as well as the pieces owned by Afro-Mexican confraternities, *people* are sorted—and they sort themselves—around the altar.

A Concluding Monologue: Ruination Is a Spatiotemporal Argument

To study how power operated sacramentally is to foreground questions of the duration and decay of a *mana*-driven network of people-thing cohesion. How do people and things connect through a desire to touch God; how do those relays disintegrate? As I have been insisting, this is a reiterative system that is best mapped with an ethnographic eye attentive to the knots of relations among very mobile people and things. In the case of Jesuits operating out of the Colegio Espíritu Santo in Puebla de Los Angeles, the inventories of the items left behind after their departure demonstrate a lively sacramental field animated by moments of people-thing coherence that, in turn, also show us how both the Jesuit college and the Jesuit hacienda were once configured within this emergent and recursive sacramental system. Importantly, to understand Jesuit positionality within this sacramental power structure is to acknowledge that Jesuit sovereignty did not "wane" over time. They were arrested and exiled at the height of their popularity. Jesuit ruination began with well-considered state action, a consideration that signaled the Crown's keen awareness of how sacramental power moved along spatiotemporal relays. In other words, what the inventories make clear is how agents of the Crown theorized materiality according to these sacramental logics with the intent to strip the Society of Jesus away from the circuits of power that hummed around the altar.

The bureaucrats hired to do this work demonstrated a conviction, shared with other *novohispanos*, that God appeared in a tangible form. The Catholic divinity was sometimes experienced as absent or hidden, but this is not because the *divinismo* was ethereal. In the colonial Mexican culture of baroque immanence, the sacred was tangible because their God was reliably present on the altar, the priest as *mana* worker having sacramentally transformed the substances of bread and wine into the body and blood of Christ. Thus, *novohispanos* actively decorated the space where he most often appeared, adored his body, and illuminated his presence with their testamentary gifts of wax and oil to ensure that his silver adornments would blaze with appropriate glory. There was also general agreement that Christ's appearances changed the nature of things. Paying careful attention to how silver objects had been organized spatially, these state agents took precise notes on how God's power could extend into human-made objects. Some objects were deemed sacred due to their use as containers of divinity; others drew their specialness from their emplacement near those divine containers.

While attempts to both utilize and restrain power objects has long been part of Catholicism's approach to the miraculous,[197] it is crucial to emphasize that what we have seen here is the management of Christ's body but not by Church agents. The priests are offstage. Now the notaries are the ritual specialists, serving as masters of the ceremony on behalf of the imperial state. Their inventories produce—for both local government and the more distant Crown—what a state might see, judge, and adjudicate. And what they account for is how the mystical extends into the concrete. As they map the sacrality of silver according to sacramental logics, we see precious metal valued neither for its economic value nor or its aesthetic beauty. Rather, notaries organized their inventories of silver to specify the spatiotemporal logics through which sacred power had enlivened Jesuit altars and the things on or near them.

Scholars have linked bureaucratic documentation and colonial domination.[198] In this Act, we have seen this relation between writing and power. Notaries, pens in hand, were present during the initial moments of the arrest of the Jesuits not only to document but to represent state authority with their ceremonial labor of observing and pausing to take notes. Ann Stoler has long asked historians of colonialism to pay attention to "what constitutes the archive" and to attend not only to "the archive-as-subject," but to the work of archiving as a process. Scholars of colonialism must understand that "what form it takes, and that what systems of classification signal at specific times are the very substance of colonial politics."[199] So what does it mean when an archive is constituted by records that trace a link between *sovereignty* and *sacramentality?* Clearly, God-centered epistemological practices are key to understanding the "very substance" of colonial politics in New Spain.

The body of Christ was, indeed, a very complicated substance. His flickering presence injected some anxiety into colonial governance. Uncertainty resides in the semantics of "possibility" that inform the theology of the mystical body of Christ. Recall Kieckhefer's description: Christ *might be* present here, but not there; he *might be* experienced in this mode, but not that. The inherent *ambiguity* in human capacity to perceive the Catholic God ought to prod scholars to reconsider approaches to church-state politics because the gods are, indeed, complicated dance partners. Accordingly, sacramental logics are inherently unstable because the shape-shifting body of Christ enables *and* disrupts flows of power. If Christ's body is the substance of colonial politics captured in notarial documentation, then these same inventories offer some clues about the Crown's inability to assert total control when the divinity has *substance.* Indeed, the Crown formally acknowledged the limits to its own power in relation to the silver objects that had been enlivened by the real yet flickering presence of Christ's body on the altar. Although able to enact the termination of a powerful and popular order of religious men, while also commanding the public's silence on the topic, this same sovereign was *unable* to touch sacramental silver, let alone weigh it, melt it, or ship it to Spain. This ought to reframe our appreciation of the unruly terrain of colonial sovereignty when the God-present in the Eucharist put limits on the Crown's power to fully impose its will.

Further, the ordered labor of inventorying sacramental silver should alert us to a new terrain being charted, or better, some new moves in the church-state dance that are being tested in this eighteenth-century Mexican moment. To put it in colloquial terms, government employees are working to disambiguate a sacramental network. What are the implications when *state agents* make explicit which silver objects belonged to this material system of sacramental power? Perhaps most uncontroversially, the notaries labor to establish in a state-certified language what baroque Catholics already understood quite well: Christ appeared on the regular, and he could alter their world, spiritually and materially. This is surely the most basic takeaway.

With the benefit of hindsight, I contend that this dance of agency among the Crown and Christ contributed—as Pickering suggests these dances often do—to emergent transformations in the realm of state power.[200] We have seen a complex mechanism of capture in action. The inventories not only mark how limits were placed on the state, but the inventories also sought to *define* and *delimit* where Christ might be expected to be present, thus pointing toward a not-so-distant secularizing future in which increasing constraints determined where and how the God-man could appear in the world. We see a hint of the shape of the dance to come in the nineteenth century, when the liberalizing Mexican state has the upper hand and how its bid to consolidate state power includes demarcating and regulating sacramental power.[201] In theopolitical terms, the altar no longer holds primacy of place. But a weakened body of Christ is not a story about the disappearance of "religion" in the face of "secularism." Rather, it is in the fragmentation of *sacramentality* that we can historicize the emergence of Catholicism in Mexico as a "religion," one among an increasingly diversified field of competitors for sovereignty. The emergence of "secularism" in Latin America then, marks a contrast, not to "religion," but rather denotes a breakdown in the prior hegemony of sacramental logics and an end to an era when the body of Christ served as the primary congregating force.

Thus, Act I has provided a "before" narrative: Jesuits cultivated and retained power in a colonial landscape because they were savvy mediators of the mercurial God. To establish this, I have foregrounded a spatiotemporal understanding of power as densely material and sacramental. The Jesuits are decisively extracted from this sacramental network and thus begins the story of their demise. But my aim in telling their story this way is not only to narrate their demise, but also to argue for a spatiotemporal account of religious power in colonial Mexico. Simply put, people-thing assemblages are finite. Thus, we need to look for density, mark the duration, and note when and how the relays are strengthened, or indeed, weakened, that is, where connections endure, and where there is decay in the system. *Mana* does not flow without these material relays.

The scenes that follow focus closely on the transient Jesuits. In the last years of the eighteenth century, their spatiotemporal situation changes and subsequently their material networks weaken. We will see how Jesuit relays no longer "fire" as they once had. The missionaries no longer occupy a central role in the dense materiality of people and things that had once swarmed around their altars in Mexico and there is no authoritative place for the Jesuits at the altars in Italy.

And yet the Jesuits struggle to persist despite the dispersal and fragmentation. In the case we will examine next, they even experience moments of profound hope.

Change of Scene

Floor opens through which Jesuits make abrupt exit. Grunting, confusion, only a few screams.

Floor closes.

CURTAIN DROPS

LIGHTS: Sacramentality continues demonstrated by a quick replay of the sacramental lighting sequences on the closed curtains.

SOUND: Clattering & crashing of silver being hauled off stage, then silence, followed by sound of footsteps.

ACTION: Swedish man, young, walks out in front of the closed curtain; he is engrossed in Voltaire's *Candide*.

CURTAIN RISES

A large ship is center stage. Black-robed Jesuits are on deck; they are praying the rosary. The Swede steps on to the boat and it lurches, moving in a see-saw fashion. In the struggle to stabilize himself, he throws the book into the sea as he grabs and holds tight to a Jesuit. The Jesuits turn into a chorus line, singing about their triumph, not noticing as waves pick them off, several men falling overboard, one by one.

Act II   Possibility?

The world is full of possibility for a young Lutheran Swedish merchant named Lars Birger Thjülen who, in 1768, departs from the Spanish port of Cádiz on a boat destined for the French island of Corsica. Here we meet this young man as he finds himself among two hundred Jesuits who, recently expelled from Mexico, were en route to their exile in Bologna, Italy. In close confines with these recently expelled and soon-to-be ex-Jesuits for the duration of his five-week journey, Thjülen chooses to convert to Catholicism and, shortly after arriving in Italy, he decides to take vows as a Jesuit. As Thjülen tells it, the transformation took place gradually; his quest for true religion—a religion in accord with "Reason"—had begun with his love of French literature, particularly the writings of Voltaire. This and his mother's death left him with a brooding sense that he ought to seek answers in the world. He took up life as a merchant, and in September 1767 he set sail for Spain, where he worked for the Swedish consulate and later joined the crew of the *Stockholm*, a merchant ship bound for Corsica. Conversion and his decision to take vows as a Jesuit removed him permanently from family and friends in Sweden; he described this as profoundly painful. We might think him an odd bird, this Swedish Lutheran convert to Catholicism, yet he found birds of a feather aboard that ship and in Italy, an exile among exiles in Bologna, where he lived a long and productive intellectual life.[1]

This is a story of hope for the Jesuits who are literally and figuratively "at sea." Thjülen's conversion is their success story. The Lutheran's choice shines a spotlight on the continuity of the Jesuit mission under conditions of great duress. For a narrative undergirded by an Enlightenment-themed quest for authenticity and truth found in the world through reasoned disputation, the narrative seems, oddly enough, deeply invested in Catholic Reformation polemics. In reaching for a well-worn script that generates a particularly Catholic feeling of confidence, the Jesuits cast Thjülen's conversion as a decisive victory of the Society of Jesus over Luther's minions. Note that these men from the Americas have never met a Lutheran. Nonetheless, the Mexican Jesuits have a good sense that the tale should be elaborated in the time-honored tropes of Marian triumph over a Lutheran devil. Yet in the following scenes, hope meets an inadequate inventory. While unfolding as a series of optimistic attachments, the "mission accomplished" overtones do not completely distract the reader from seeing what must have become painfully obvious to Thjülen by the end of the story he is writing: Thjülen trails after "a cluster of promises" that shape a uniquely mobile story of cruel optimism.[2]

We think about conversion narratives as marking the formation of new selves. He is stepping away from the familiar ground of home and confessional affiliation. Yet Thjülen describes conversion as *loss*, or alternatively, as *anxiety* about the tentativeness of *finding*. This is because his bounded, rational, Enlightenment self is disintegrating rapidly within an affective encounter with these Catholic others. Crucially, Thjülen is struggling because these shifting intersubjective relationships make it difficult to locate *himself*. His sense of "self" has become vexingly elusive because his horizons of possibility are anchored in Manuel Iturriaga, the Mexican theologian whom he calls the father of his soul.[3] He struggles to contort himself into the shape of an aggravating desire that has him chasing Jesuits in his attempt to shore up his sense of self. This task is all the more arduous because the Jesuits are unsettled, always on the move.

In the aftermath, the young Swede composes an inventory of self. That is, he writes to unravel, evaluate, name, sort, and *stabilize* the entangled threads that converged in his life-altering experiences. What aspects of self are to be kept, what can be discarded? Thjülen categorizes these moments of instability variously, some as thrilling, others irritating, a few horrifying. Thjülen becomes entangled in complicated relationships among books that anger him, devotional objects that irritate him, and a caring Jesuit priest who does not solve any of his problems yet somehow makes him *feel* better. The knots of relations in Thjülen's narrative comprise palpably affective threads, even if Thjülen's stated purpose has been to construct a self that aligns with Enlightenment concerns about "Truth" and "Reason." In framing this as an affective inventory, I am drawing attention to the way his conversion narrative unfolds as a series of material and emotional stumbling blocks. The abundance of turning points make the tale believable—he is a confused human. But he also erodes the required plotline of conversion-as-transformation: Will the genre ever capture this convert? This may explain why Thjülen will find occasions later in his life to "edit" his first conversion story.[4] I have studied his subsequent "reseekings" of self, but here I pay most attention to the first two narratives—which are quite similar—both written in the first eight years of his life in Bologna. In these years, the Swede accounts for himself as thoroughly anchored in the unmoored men of the Mexican Province.

NOTES FOR "AFFECTIVE" LIGHTING

The lighting should make apparent how affect functions in Thjülen's narrative. Two of the terms I am using, namely, "affect" and "affective" are not simply shorthand for emotion. Affect theory draws attention to a prepersonal and intersubjective intensity.

Working to discern affective experience enables a mode of historical practice that is mindful of textuality even as one works with and through *religious language. Thereby, one can avoid remaining trapped in the discourse (or even the single body) of the speaker who struggles to name and contain the felt experience that comes to be named "religious" or "spiritual," or labeled as "conversion."*

One of the founding (and most original) theorists of affectivity was Baruch Spinoza. He devoted two books of his Ethics *to explaining the transmission of affect as an embodied experience and he did this by theorizing bodies not as substance, but as motion. He used the term* conatus *to describe the endeavor to persist that is an essential quality of all bodies, human and nonhuman. Importantly, this ratio of motion-to-rest persists with and against other bodies as forces. Accordingly, bodies—as motion and activity can affect as well as be affected. As Lauren Berlant says so well, "Its [affect theory's] strength as a site of potential elucidation comes from the ways it registers the conditions of life that move across persons and worlds, play out in lived time, and energize attachments."[5] The conative encounter is one in which bodies are strengthened or impeded by one another.*

My analysis is attuned to what that shared intensity produces. So to illuminate this, use lighting that moves across and unites subjects and/or objects. Given that they are in motion, and are to remain so, conatus can be captured by coloration that shows temporary people-things groupings.

Gels offer different hues that can be deployed to signal shared affective coloration.

But more creative approaches to lighting are required to demonstrate how bodies can be strengthened or impeded through other bodies. "When a body 'encounters' another body or an idea another idea, it happens that the two relations sometimes combine to form a more powerful whole, and sometimes one decomposes the other, destroying the cohesion of its parts."[6] *Composition/decomposition captures nicely the affective connection between Thjülen and Iturriaga, since theirs was not simply an emotionally sustaining relationship; rather, "emotional sustenance" is itself an embodied mode of persistence, that is, it is the very endeavor of two bodies to remain in sync, to move as one. Thjülen's conversion experience is about striving to persist in an alignment of ratios of motion-to-rest, a task made difficult by transregional mobility that makes the father of his soul an elusive figure. Here we need a sense of texture to set a geological mood that captures this Deleuzean restatement of Spinoza's thought.*

Scene I: The First Book

Relationships are key to Thjülen's narrative, from start to finish. The account begins at the story's end with the declaration that he is writing for the greater glory of God and, importantly, in obedience to his superior. In other words, he writes in a relation of subordination, embracing his new situation as a good Jesuit novice. But he has an interested audience in the general of the Society of Jesus, Lorenzo Ricci. Word of Thjülen's conversion has reached Ricci, who has written to the Swede, congratulating him on his courage, and indicating that this story is quite welcome at a time of crisis for "the sons of Ignatius."[7]

After acknowledging his new relationship of obedience to his superior, Thjülen begins to sort through the events that brought him to the Jesuits. He introduces his Swedish father, Lars Birger, with some brief but intriguing lines about a mercantile life involving two trips to China. His father's last voyage, fraught with difficulty, cost Lars Birger his health, and he died within a few years of his return from Asia. Thjülen's mother, Petronilla Pattemborg, takes up more space on the page. Her family's wealth, he wrote, imbued her with "a grandeur made all the more glorious in the eyes of man by her piety." His characterization of his mother as a spiritual model bears resemblance to Monica, Augustine of Hippo's mother, but Petronilla offered a far more problematic model since, unlike Augustine, Thjülen has converted *away* from his own mother's religion. Yet he is keen to present her as the woman who made his conversion possible, explaining that the seeds of his quest for truth were to be found in his mother's modification of "a little Lutheran prayer." The words of the original prayer, he explains, asked God to grant a *firm* faith while, in contrast, his mother prayed for "the True faith." Given that he writes from the other side of his conversion, he is concerned about the salvation of his Lutheran loved ones, and these worries condense around the figure of his mother. He cannot say for certain whether true faith animated his mother's heart—indeed, he now questions whether "true piety can take shelter in the heart of a Lutheran"—but he gives her the final word on this matter: "Son," she announced on her deathbed, "I am going to heaven." She admonished him to never take leave of praying to God: "of this do not let up, never drive him from your heart."[8]

And yet he did just that, he concedes, in large part through reading Enlightenment *philosophes*. The year of his mother's death was 1765, and he admits having both great freedom and equally great inquietude during this period. He had fallen in love with French literature but in hindsight blames "the grand reputation" of Voltaire for his uneasiness, since the *philosophe*'s impiety had entered Thjülen's own soul. "Little by little almost every idea of God was worn away and Religion became a fable, which was fine for vulgar persons, but not [sufficient] to sustain the beliefs of a Gentleman. . . . A true religion had to be in the world, and I had to find it."[9] Through his stepfather's commercial connections, he takes up life as a merchant and sets sail for the Iberian Peninsula in September 1767.

After contrary winds, storms, and the continuous danger of shipwreck, Thjülen arrives in Lisbon in late January 1768, where he remains for approximately four months. Both Lisbon and Catholic religious life fascinate the Swede. He occupies himself with making observations about the city, taking notes on the architecture, the churches, and the ruins of the 1755 earthquake. "Quite often I attended *funzioni sacre*, principally the Mass, whose ceremonies seemed the strangest to me; of every detail I took note in my diary with no other intention than to be able to recount them when I returned to my Country." Thjülen lives at a time when the notion that religions could be compared dispassionately and rationally is gaining widespread acceptance, perhaps best signaled by Picart and Bernard's comparative evaluation of religious rituals in the multivolume *Religious Ceremonies of the World*. From the safety of Holland, these Huguenot exiles had undertaken a survey of the religious ceremonies of the world with the express interest of furthering religious tolerance. Inspired in part by ethnography, in part by the burgeoning field of journalism, but primarily by "the new philosophy," they presented information about cross-cultural religious life, largely concerned to describe the rituals that marked important moments common to the human condition, such as birth, marriage, and death. "Readers were expected to draw their own conclusions from this material. . . . [The series was] an invitation to readers to make up their own minds."[10] There is no indication that Thjülen had studied Picart and Bernard's volumes, but he was clearly interested in comparative cultural practice, as indicated by his keen interest to document the strange sacred ritual called the Catholic Mass.[11]

Thjülen declared his love of Voltaire in the context of a statement about French literature. Until nearly the date of Thjülen's conversion Voltaire would have been best known as a literary star: He published his famous *Candide* in 1759 and became a *philosophe* known for his defense of tolerance only in the years after 1760.[12] Would it be safe to wager that Thjülen had read *Candide*? And if so, was he aware that his own expedition mirrored (and distorted) that taken by the fictional figure after departing Westphalia? Like Candide, Thjülen braved "near shipwreck" (Candide and Pangloss suffer a wreck off the coast of Portugal) and arrived in Lisbon to note the damage of the earthquake (perhaps taking special note of the ruins of the earthquake because Voltaire had written so passionately about this in his *Poème sur le désastre de Lisbonne*) before journeying to Cádiz (as does Candide). There the fictional character boards a ship that traverses the Atlantic to encounter Paraguayan Jesuits. Thjülen's encounter with the American Jesuits put him upon a different path, but by his own description Thjülen was faithful to the spirit of the age as expressed by Voltaire's Candide: "To know the world one must travel."[13]

Scene II: Shipboard Disputation

In June 1768 Thjülen embarks for Corsica. He describes the ten ships in the convoy as "weighted down" with Jesuits. Observations of the transport reached England in the *London Magazine* (a magazine subtitled "Gentleman's Monthly Intelligencer") which reported the transport of twelve hundred Jesuits.[14] Thjülen observes on his ship alone "at least 190 Fathers, and it is possible that it was up to 210 because after a number of days the vessel from Ragusa broke down and we had to distribute these Jesuits." Black robes and the Spanish language dominated the ships' decks and, as Thjülen's notetaking in Lisbon makes clear, he was primed to study religion. This encounter with the Jesuits provided ample opportunity to gather information about the curiosities of Catholicism. Three or four of the Jesuits know French, so he engages in polite conversation, touching upon religion, but they speak about this delicate topic "superficially, without imposition."

This changes during one very vexing conversation and, notably, this moment of extreme irritation marks the beginning of his turn to Catholicism.

> One evening one of these [Jesuits] asked me, "What is your impression of the Jesuits?"
>
> "To me, quite good, I responded. They are good people, and peaceful, and I love them [the Jesuits]."
>
> The Father replied, "And of the Catholic Religion, which we profess, what do you think?"
>
> "Oh this is another matter," I said.

The unnamed Jesuit insists that Thjülen's position is illogical, in that it was not possible to have good people who were guided by a bad religion. "So if you love the Jesuits, why do you not love their Religion?" To this Thjülen replies that it is quite possible to love people and abhor their defects. The unnamed interlocutor takes the opportunity to press him to reveal his own affiliation. Thjülen is boldly evasive: "I am Christian." Urged to name his sect, he replies: "None, I was not born in this world to be either Lutheran or Calvinist, but I had to search for the Truth, and the Religion to follow is that which seems to best conform with the Sacred Scripture and with Reason; this seems to me to have been found in the Church that is called Lutheran."

Homing in on Thjülen's sentiments about reason, the unnamed Jesuit issues a challenge. If Thjülen can be persuaded that Catholicism is the "one and true" religion, the "source of truth and health," would he be content to embrace the Catholic religion? Thjülen replies that he would not only be content, but that this would be the correct choice and for this he would be eternally grateful. But he adds his own fighting words, "I believe that your work will be received in vain. Your Religion seems to me far too Mohommetan and irrational." The conversation becomes heated as they debate the Catholic position on reading scripture in vernacular languages. Thjülen contends that this point of Catholic doctrine rests upon "insufferable arrogance" that deprives "vulgar persons of the power to examine the fundamentals of their faith."

To this the unnamed Jesuit basically shrugs his shoulders. "*Ma ché?*" So what? And then more angrily: "We are the church that is founded by Jesus Christ, and we are meant to believe the follies of the malevolent Luther, who is worshiping the Devil in Hell?" To the shock of a young Jesuit coadjutor, Thjülen replies that he would be very content to be found with Luther in his hell. "*Gran peccato!*," cries the young Jesuit, concerned that a youth with such an angelic exterior "had the deformed and horrible soul of a devil."

Emotions were already running high and, as Thjülen puts it (in an idiom that marks his historical context) these last words "fell like many sparks of fire near the powder of a Harquebus." At this explosive moment, a different figure appears on the scene: "Stepping forward with some uncertainty was Father Emmanuele Iturriaga, native of Puebla de Los Angeles, or as others say, the City of Angels. This dignified Father, who had to be by Divine Intention (as I express myself) my own Ananias, he had conceived an ardent desire for and a living faith in my conversion."

Father Iturriaga, recognizing how distressed the Swede was by these words, assures Thjülen that the other Jesuit's statements had been far too "spirited" and inappropriate. Thjülen describes Iturriaga as having "a manner and words so sweet, [that this] was enough to placate me."[15]

When Thjülen met him, Manuel Iturriaga was forty years old. He had been born in the city of Puebla de los Angeles in the viceroyalty of New Spain, had entered the Society of Jesus at age sixteen, and spent most of his career there.[16] He had two brothers, Pedro and Juan Mariano, who were also Jesuits. At the time of the arrest, Iturriaga was a professor of moral theology at the Colegio del San Ildefonso in Puebla. But perhaps more important than any biographical details is Thjülen's characterization of Iturriaga as "il mio Anania." My Ananias. Appropriate to the genre of conversion narrative, this is a reference to the paradigmatic story of Saul's conversion on the road to Damascus. Ananias had been commanded by God to attend to Saul who, having heard the words of Jesus, had been blinded. "So, Ananias departed and entered the house, and after laying his hands on him said, 'Brother Saul, the Lord Jesus, who appeared to you on the road by which you were coming, has sent me so that you may regain your sight and be filled with the Holy Spirit.' And immediately there fell from his eyes something like scales, and he regained his sight, and he got up and was baptized; and he took food and was strengthened" (Acts 9:17–19).

Our early modern Ananias relies upon Mexican chocolate to strengthen his budding friendship with Thjülen: "From this moment forward, [Iturriaga] continued to cultivate me, treating me with an extreme affability, he often invited me to join in their Chocolate break, and gave me, from time to time, little gifts. For these tokens of affection, I bore him great affection. Nor did I have difficulty with him in discussions about Religion. I always disagreed and defended myself as best I knew without ever ceding, unless obliged to do so by reasonable evidence."

The parallel between friendship and spiritual life is that both must be cultivated. Iturriaga set a certain mood, bringing with him a spirit of conviviality that kept the two men together and communicating, even when they disagreed on particulars. The "little gifts" are an offering from a friend. But Jesuits often carried medallions or prints, and other religious tokens, and were advised to have such things on offer. Thus, inextricably intertwined, is a budding spiritual and intellectual friendship that becomes the hinge upon which Thjülen pivots toward Catholicism. And if I insist upon the affective contours of the spiritual friendship between Iturriaga and Thjülen, I do so in large part due to the details Thjülen subsequently reveals. Two things, he writes, make their "conferences" difficult.

> The first was the defect in language with which to express ourselves and to understand each other well because Father Iturriaga did not speak any other language other than Spanish and Latin, and I only had begun to stammer some Spanish words, and the Latin that I had was in great part forgotten; also, as spoken in the mouth of a Mexican, the pronunciation [of the Latin] made it seem an altogether new language; [Yet] where science fails, one supplies industry, and we came to be able to communicate with each other some concepts.

"Reason" remains the name of the game, thus their "industry"—their common work to relate to one another—but this labor builds an affective intensity that supersedes the deficits in shared spoken language. Equally important in this case is the manner in which Iturriaga's stronger *presence* dissipates, softens, reshapes the tone and mood of Thjülen's various moments of vexation, aggravation, distress and it is this "meeting of the moods" that serves as his passage, with and through Iturriaga, to Catholicism and eventually to the Jesuits. Understood in a Spinozist frame, Thjülen moves toward and with the stronger body, his transition results from the effort to remain in sync with the empowering *conatus* of Iturriaga.

But this took some time, for Thjülen's inventory marks moments in which he is confounded and impeded by the moods, motions, and activities of others. For next we learn that the captain of the ship is his other source of difficulty. The captain, a Lutheran, attempts to dissuade Thjülen from fraternizing with these Catholic men, cautioning him that "the Jesuits would have me hooked and fastened with their sophism." To Thjülen, this is all "solemn nonsense," and he continues to do as he pleases until "the sad man continued to pursue me, emphatically goading [me] at every hour with his bitterness, and making me disgusted as never before, such that I was exhausted by the end, determined to avoid (at least in his presence) the conversation with the Fathers."

Yet the passions of the captain ultimately deliver Thjülen to the Jesuits, or as Thjülen described it: "The Lord desired my great liberty, demonstrating on this occasion, that He knows how to use the passions of Man to promote His own designs." The captain had a large store of delectable items in his control—wine, *aquevite*, pastries—and these he wishes to sell to the Jesuits.[17] Despite his prohibition about conversing with the Jesuits, he occasionally uses Thjülen as a middleman in this exchange. Thjülen's language here is interesting: "There were some Swedes on the ship, but I remained only with the Padres and took on the color of their language and since I had recourse, he asked me to give a hand to his illicit trade. I willingly accepted the job." What took place during those conversations with the Jesuits? Thjülen never offers any details.

Scene III: Off the Page, or Things Thjülen Is Too Self-Absorbed to See

Thjülen is entangled. But the young Swede's conversion narrative is necessarily *self*-absorbed. In accounting for the turning points in his conversion, Thjülen mentions only the fact of the expulsion, offering no details about the journey that the Mexican Jesuits had undertaken. Remember that these missionaries were not "returning" to a homeland. Approximately 500 among the 678 from the Mexican Province had been born and raised in New Spain and thus are far from home. Thjülen mentions neither the shock of their arrest, nor the existential crises of homelessness. He said nothing of their long stay in the disease-stricken port town of Veracruz, nor the next period of limbo in the port of Cádiz, Spain, nor of the fresh discoveries that his new Jesuit friends had made upon arrival in Europe.

He must have heard the stories: At each new landing place in the exhausting journey—from Veracruz to Havana, from Havana to Cádiz, from Cádiz to Corsica, from Corsica to Bologna—as Jesuits encountered one another anew, the men told and retold stories about the first days of the expulsion and about the last legs of the journey.[18] We have seen the first moments in this drama, how the Jesuits were swiftly kicked out of the colleges, houses, haciendas, and mission stations in the Americas and hurried toward the Gulf coast under military escort. Approximately thirty overland expeditions were made by Mexican Jesuits in groups ranging in size from five to eighty-six persons. In the port town of Veracruz, what had been relatively well-oiled machinery broke down, and the exodus stalled. There was not sufficient housing, the heat was ponderous, as was the wait for seaworthy ships to carry them on the first leg of the trip to Havana.[19] In overcrowded lodgings and depleted by the tropical heat of the Caribbean town, one Jesuit wrote that "souls were well purged of their faults, and bodies of their ill humors, for day and night one would continuously suffer and sweat, due to the excessive heat and the crowding of persons who were enclosed in said Monastery."[20] Many Jesuits sickened and died of *vómito prieto*, the dark vomit that signaled yellow fever. There were eventually twenty embarkations from Havana for Cádiz between 1767 and 1768, followed by another four months of limbo in the port of Cádiz, Spain. Many near-catastrophes accompanied their transatlantic journeys. Everywhere the theme was much the same: cramped conditions, worse for those who were accommodated at the hospice, better for those housed in local monasteries. One Jesuit wrote in gratitude for the fathers of San Francisco who cared for them, "not with the strictness of their rigid poverty, but with the Caja Real wide open. . . . We were to be assisted in everything, serving us personally, gifting us and consoling us in our hardship."[21] These are topics to which we will return in Act III. But none of this information is accounted for in Thjülen's inventory of self.

We obtain a different point of view of life on the *Stockholm* from another *poblano*, the Jesuit Antonio López de Priego (1730–1802).[22] In 1785, López de Priego wrote an account of the expulsion with details about his adaptation to life in Italy that he sent to his sister, María Josefina de la Santíssima Trinidad y Priego, a nun in Puebla. He included a catalogue of names and dates that another Mexican Jesuit, Rafael Zelís, lists the birth and death dates of each exiled member from the Mexican Province. "Do not forget them," López de Priego wrote, aware that the list and "his little sketch" would have to serve in place of a fully painted portrait to keep the absent and dissolved Society of Jesus present to mind for those back home who might read his account. López de Priego wrote that he wanted to satisfy her curiosity about life in Italy, but it is also important to him that his sister pray for him, and he hopes that she will keep the memories of his Jesuit brethren impressed upon her heart. "Receive this book, print it in your heart, and pray for me to our Lord, as I pray for you always."[23] Most poignant is López de Priego's description of taking leave of his native Mexico: "*Adiós*, shouted the sailors, *y un buen viaje*; we repeated, goodbye Indies, goodbye Mexico, goodbye parents and relatives, goodbye brothers and friends, goodbye happy land, you gave us life, yet we did not have the solace of your cover after death. Between these tears and sobs sounded the shot of the Captain, with which he signaled [the departure of] the convoy."

How to explain sea travel to his sister living in a convent in Puebla? Sailing is awful, he wrote. "Why do men sail?" God wants men to have commerce with one another, he mused, and this explains the discovery of the New World. But he turns to the quest for self-discovery that, on board a ship, had taken on a new meaning for López de Priego. Upon his departure from Veracruz, the captain of his ship offered some basic counsel: "Know thyself." This advice was neither spiritual nor philosophical. Rather, once the ship was in motion, either one knew how to keep his food down, or not, and this was nothing "even Galen could cure." And when the storms began, so ensued the stock-taking—*los balances*—because sailors fear God, he comments, or at least they do during such storms.[24] But he also refers to maintaining one's balance quite literally. He reminds his sister about shared moment of chaos when the earth's shaking had turned the brother and sister upside down and it seemed as if their house would collapse; he tells her to imagine such an earthquake and its aftershocks not as a series of terrifying moments, but as a single enduring event that lasted for the more than two months that he was crossing the Atlantic. "This is what happened to me."

These journeys were different from those that some European Jesuits would have made *from* Europe to American missions across the Atlantic (and for some then further afield, with New Spain as a stopping point while traversing the Pacific Ocean to missionary sites in Asia). First, the would-be missionaries traveled in smaller groups, maybe with ten or twenty Jesuits maximum. "From stem to stern of each carrack lay numerous occasions for preaching, teaching doctrine, caring for the sick, hearing confessions, performing humble chores, and begging for alms. . . . The essential task throughout was raising the tenor of piety on board the ship. The Jesuits contributed to it by teaching doctrine, praying and explaining the rosary, reading devotional books aloud, and instructing others how to make examinations of conscience."[25]

The shipboard experience provided an opportunity to hone their missionary skills, a situation that has been described as key to the formation of the missionaries as men who could modulate their fear. The Jesuits were also advised to pray (for their survival), care for their own health, and assist fellow passengers in body and spirit. But they were also advised to seek "diversion from the crushing tedium of the voyage"—anything to get out of the unhealthy cabins below, activities which included reading stories aloud, but also playing cards. Sonora missionary Benito Ducrue wrote that the emphasis on routine was similarly important on the long journey the expelled Jesuits made to Europe.[26] He mentions the Mass, praying novenas, reading, etc., as key to maintaining their spirits.[27]

Yet the sheer number of men on the *Stockholm* made this journey quite distinct from the outward-bound oceanic journeys described earlier. The implication is clear from Thjülen's initial characterization of the ship as weighted down with Jesuits. Now their black robes dominated the ships' decks—and new black robes at that, wrote German Jesuit Joseph Och: "Since we had arrived [in Spain] in rags, we had to be newly clothed. Because of this, for a month no store in Cádiz or the port of Santa María contained a single piece of black cloth."[28] Crowded on deck in dark soutanes, they were something of a spectacle to behold.[29]

One can imagine how happy the seasick López de Priego was to arrive in Spain on March 30, 1768. "The fruit is good," he noted, "even if not as various as what we have in the Indies." The hospice of Santa María was sufficiently capacious to handle a hundred people, he adds, but now four times as many Jesuits are packed in, but at least they can say Mass in the chapel there. The Jesuits remained in Santa María until June, when they began the leg of the journey from Cádiz to Corsica. López de Priego described leaving Spain as another sorrow, this time to "depart from our Kingdom for foreign lands, leaving buried in that port fifteen of our *compañeros*.[30] The German Och, with his wry sense of humor, took this view on the departure from Cádiz: "All other citizens and artisans were also very much dismayed and sorrowful, partly because of sympathy for us, partly because of what they would now lose. The Jesuits in the city had caused money to circulate and had kept everyone busy." Och was assigned to board the *St. Elizabeth*, a ship captained by "an exceptionally arrogant man [who] did not condescend to exchange a single word with us." He describes the other Jesuits as better off: "Billeted aboard Dutch, Swedish, and Danish ships, they received better food and more civility, affability, and humane treatment from the Protestant captains and ships' companies than we did, for all priests were immediately permitted to say Mass. These Protestant gentlemen only begged that the Spanish great admiral be not informed about the prayers, out of fear that in Corsica proper compensation as promised in Cádiz would not be paid to them. It certainly would not have been paid, for a most stringent order had been given forbidding entirely the saying of Mass."[31] This is another reminder of how the Jesuits had been stripped of their religious authority that they had as mediators of divinity, although on paper, they were clearly allowed to be in charge of the rhythms of their own prayer lives, which was left at the discretion of the Father Superior.[32]

López de Priego boarded a ship called *The Stockholm* where, as the ship's name might indicate, Lorenzo Thjülen was employed.

> I was assigned to *The Stockholm*, a ship belonging to Lutherans. Do not be alarmed, my reader, even though you have heard me say "Lutherans." Nothing terrible happened, they correspond to the name, but we were treated with attention, principally by the Captain, and all was well. The ship was free of crawling bugs (*sabandijas*), rats, and cockroaches,

which in other embarkations was just the way of life. Here, around four o'clock in the afternoon we passed the celebrated Strait of Gibraltar, with weather so serene and clear that we were able to see Ceuta without any glasses.

Do not be alarmed, he says. What did Jesuits like Iturriaga, López de López de Priego, and the multitude of unnamed Jesuits on board know of Protestants, and of Luther? An ocean separated the Mexican Catholics from the religious conflicts that had riven central Europe. The encounter with so many "pagan souls" in the Americas had been understood as compensatory for the loss of souls to the Protestant "heresies." In Spanish American discourse, Luther figured as monstrous. Both in print and on canvas, as well as in sermons, Luther was invoked as a metaphor for evil, and juxtaposed against the figure of light, the Virgin of Guadalupe.[33] The majority of the Mexican Jesuits, especially those born in the new world, had likely never encountered a Lutheran. Yet the idea of Luther, as well as his much-maligned image, was a feature of Catholic culture in New Spain. López de Priego's words of warning about the word "Lutheran" are indicative of a particularly Mexican point of view. But he countered this with a description of the Mass, which would have been quite familiar to his sister, although here made strange by its shipboard setting:

> Mass was celebrated during the days that weather allowed, but with compassion to see those people who did not understand the Mass. Really for them it was something of a comedy. Notwithstanding, God makes use of everything for the good of our souls, accordingly on this occasion, [he made use] of Don Manuel Iturriaga, who had become close with the Accountant of the ship, who was a capable young man; by the time we jumped ashore in la Bastia, God had, by means of this hook, secured the fish. Despite the fact that he was distinguished and had authority at home, he renounced his own, his kingdom, his assets, and, following the Jesuits, he reconciled with the Catholic Church in the City of Ferrara. Such great tenderness! But even greater [tenderness] will it cause you to hear, that he was called by God to Religion. He wanted to become the same as those who did him so much good. This same Father took the necessary steps so that he entered the Venetian Province. This *hermano*, Lorenzo Chulen (this was his name) passed through the Jesuit novitiate in the City of Bologna. In a manner that was edifying and apostolic, he would write letters to his home for his

mother and his family, with the aim that they convert. The prize will come in heaven for the Father who converted him, for I am told that even in the poverty in which we exist, he sold his clothes in order to maintain his godson before he could enter into the Religious life. This digression you will find very satisfying, as well as the fact that in the three hundred leagues that we traveled by sea from Spain to la Bastia, we had no particular misfortune."[34]

López de Priego says no more about Thjülen—he moves to a new topic—a trunk fell on another Jesuit's head, the blow should have killed him, but he is relieved that there were no deaths on this portion of the trip. We do not have another sighting of our Lutheran Swede in other Jesuit expulsion narratives.

Monologue: Horizons, or, Appearing to Disappear

Thjülen describes the oscillations between agitation and illumination, a roller coaster that shapes the remainder of his conversation narrative. His relationships with Jesuits are antagonizing, they provoke anger, irritation, and occasionally, disgust.[35] In the guise of an Enlightenment tale about Reason's approach to Religion, the document that Thjülen produced is, as I have been describing, an affective inventory, a retrospective accounting of the waves of turmoil that accompanied his tortured decision-making process. Even though Thjülen has his reader in the thick of the journey, it is worth restating that Thjülen is writing from the other side of his decision to convert and become a Jesuit. He memorializes some details better than others.

Moreover, this is not a solitary journey. The Swedish youth has fallen into the thick of unfolding Jesuit struggles. The Mexican Jesuits' battles against disappearance *appear* for Thjülen in the dwindling alternatives that remain available to him if he is to remain with them, while the Mexican Jesuits rely upon his successful conversion as a vital argument against the disappearance of Jesuit ways of being. This interdependence shapes how Jesuit ruination appears in the archives as an episodic narrative of one man's transformation. Iturriaga—the father of his soul—figures as an enabling object that is *also* disabling because Thjülen's ability to take hold of himself is enabled and impeded by Jesuit transregional mobility.[36] Thjülen's attachment to the mobile Iturriaga means that Jesuit demise brings

Iturriaga and Thjülen together; yet Jesuit demise marks their ongoing life together as problematic, because the Jesuits are always moving toward an unknown horizon, and Thjülen continues to choose to anchor himself in their unpredictable mobility. We are still in the "coming together" phase. But this relationship is unsteady.

Scene IV: Missing Books

We return now to the way that Thjülen records the weeks that followed the heated argument aboard the decks of *The Stockholm*. The journey proved to be the opportunity Thjülen had wanted to have deeper conversation about religion with Iturriaga and while no details about their discussions are documented in the conversion narrative, we read how the highs and lows of his spiritual awakening push him toward Catholicism. In the devotional literature of the time, his resolution must be tested. Cue the Devil.

> As such, I proceeded to question one or another article [of faith] and saw ever more clearly the light of truth. Then suddenly the Devil presumed to foment war with me. One day in the small room of Padre Iturriaga, I observed on his little desk a book with the title *Modus disputandi cum Protestantibis*. One glance staggered me and, accordingly, altered the course; I said to him that never once had I purposefully studied religion, that to him it was too easy to vanquish, given that he was armed with his book against one unarmed, one who had no other defense but his own reason. In this business of such importance, I did not have anyone in whom to put my trust, no one on my side, but for my own ability to examine the reason supporting one part or another. It was an enraged passenger that Padre Iturriaga had to endure with great hardship before he could return me to the original tranquility; but I did not go easy, that wild beast Enemy drove a machine that was something very formidable.

What irony that the Devil arrived in the shape of the Jesuit way of proceeding, that is, in their studied adaptation to other cultural modes![37] The book packs a punch, and he is staggered, but what precisely is the nature of Thjülen's utter dismay? We can only guess: Their relationship is not special, he is just another Protestant, to be "hooked" as López de Priego had put it, like a simple fish? The playing field is much less even than he had previously understood as indicated by his discourse about unfair battle. The armed Jesuit vs. the unarmed man of Reason is pitched in terms of David versus Goliath. Or perhaps this is about authenticity: Authentic Reason stood the lone player against the heavy artillery of inauthentic "Book Learning."

The book. It is an odd piece of the story and clearly a matter of controversy among the two friends. I pause here to shine some light on the informal material networks patched together by these men on the move that made this explosive moment possible. First, do we imagine that Iturriaga had the foresight to pack this book on his departure from Puebla? This would have been difficult, for as we have seen in detail for the Jesuits at the Colegio Espíritu Santo, the Jesuits were required to leave behind all books, minus breviaries. Joseph Och's expulsion narrative offers a hint that Jesuits managed to smuggle out a book or two here or there. Och was among the 170 Jesuits who were in Mexico City at the time of the expulsion. In his wry account, Och tells how at the moment of the arrest, all students were dismissed, compelled to leave the colleges "half-clothed." Och himself was crippled with severe arthritis, so his vantage point on the dramatic events of those two days was his bed, where he lay in hope that the Indian servant who attended to him would be allowed to come to him. The latter had been detained by soldiers until he finally bolted past them, shouting, as Och remembers it, "I have a sick father to take care of!" Och took advantage of the young man's devotion to him and, in the guise of preparing the afternoon chocolate, the servant helped him burn his manuscripts. Och sketches a scene that confirms what we know from Act I: Jesuit movements were very restricted—men sat in public parts of the house for long periods of time, and even their bathroom visits were supervised. He gives us a glimpse of occasions when isolation was breached. A friend of the Jesuits managed to pose as a doctor, the disguise made more realistic when he haughtily dictated in Latin an exceedingly long prescription to the great frustration of the soldier who struggled to write it down. Soldiers forgot their posts when Och produced some pictures that he had brought with him from Augsburg twelve years earlier. The blue and red inked etchings were novel, and the soldiers fought over them. Despite a prohibition against writing, pencils were not confiscated; moreover, he was allowed to purchase "Chinese or India ink."[38]

But Och makes clear: The Jesuits lost all access to their books. "On this occasion I lost all the books I had brought with me to the Indies from Germany, Italy, and Spain, contrary to all laws and contrary to the intent of the royal decree wherein it was ordered that none be deprived of his personal property. They left us only our breviaries and the little book of Thomas à Kempis. . . . Ink, pen, and paper were in all cases removed and it was forbidden on pain of death that any be permitted to come by them. They even cut the blank end page out of the Authenticus and from the Documentary Letters of the Relics."[39] Och's ability to remain in his room is rare: Most Jesuits were well supervised and compelled to remain in the public area of the Jesuit houses and colleges for the several days that passed while the viceroy commandeered a sufficient number of carriages for the journey to Veracruz, a task made difficult because carriage owners preferred not to donate vehicles, either because the carriages would be ruined or they did not wish to play a role in the exodus of favored priests.[40]

Would they have had opportunities to pick up books along the way to the port town? In both Veracruz and in Cádiz, many of the Jesuits were housed in monasteries, that is, in locales where book acquisition may have been possible. Among the most interesting tales is that of Rafael de Zelís, a Jesuit studying at the novitiate in Tepotzotlán. Native to Veracruz, he was able to send notice to his mother who hurried to meet him in the town of Antigua Veracruz (about five leagues from the port city), bringing with her two of his sisters, and other relatives, all of whom passed a day and a half with him before the Jesuits continued the sojourn toward Veracruz proper where restrictions were more strictly observed. Yet during the several months delay, waiting for the ships to arrive to port, Zelís was housed in a Franciscan monastery where his hometown advantage continued to pay off. Although the Jesuits were forbidden to have any commerce whatsoever with lay persons, Zelís's cousin was among the soldiers assigned to monitor activity at the monastery. Zelís's mother was able to arrange a surreptitious visit underground, beneath the sacristy (where the bodies were buried, Zelís noted) but then she eventually moved into the monastery and remained a secret guest there for the duration of his stay. They met for several hours every evening. "During this time my small suitcase, which as I have said carried only a small change of clothes, had grown, becoming a trunk prepared by maternal love to sustain me for the rest of my trip."[41] If this overflowing chest of items included any reading materials, he did not say.

Yet we should not be too hopeful that he would be allowed to keep any books for very long, for Och reported that all of the Jesuits' belongings were subject to inspection in the days prior to embarkation in Veracruz in October 1767. "Many days before embarkation our baggage and the keys for it had to be sent on to the warehouse. There it was inspected, and all papers, sermons, and letters were confiscated. Even the written general confessions were collected and were not returned, despite many entreaties. Instead, a white paper was wrapped around them, sealed, and the words written thereon: *Matters of Conscience*. The Father in charge of the baggage wished to burn these in the presence of the inspectors, but this was refused."[42]

Their possessions were subject to even greater scrutiny upon arrival in Havana. The governor of Cuba, Antonio María Bucareli y Ursúa, was notoriously strict with the Jesuits. Many of the books that Jesuits had been allowed to pack in Mexico because categorized as "spiritual reading" were confiscated by Bucareli's agents in Havana. Among the books confiscated in Havana were "catechisms and bibles, parish manuals, confession manuals, sermons, Augustine's *City of God*, Bellarmine's *Doctrina Cristiana*, the Ignatian *Spiritual Exercises*, Berruyer's *Pueblo de Dios*, many works by Virgil, Cicero, Ovid, Luis de Granada, Jacob Wal, Busembaum, y Tamburini; Jesuit apologetics; lives of the saints, books about orthography, poetry, art, agriculture, Nebrija's grammar, guides to the study of Greek, dictionaries and vocabularies for the Italian, French, and German languages, and, finally, a book of rules for the Society of Jesus, catalogues of the Mexican province, and biographies of illustrious Jesuits."[43] The prohibition against having paper and writing instruments was not taken as seriously. But deliveries of food and laundry to the Casa de Depósito in Havana were searched to make certain that letters and books were not passed on to the men under guard.[44] Even servants could not come and go without being checked.[45] There are occasional remarks that lead one to assume that the Fathers surreptitiously tucked away a book here or there: "Had not some of the Fathers thoughtfully hidden away a book for meditation or spiritual reading, we would have had nothing to read."[46]

The precise title of the book about disputation with Protestants remains a mystery, as does the question about the informal networks of exchange that enabled Iturriaga to have this guide with him on the *Stockholm*. What we do know is that the encounter with the book, so offensive to Thjülen, shows us how disgust and abhorrence function as affective mobilizers that bring him closer to Iturriaga and, with him, to Catholicism.

Monologue: Separation Anxiety

Conversion experiences are elusive occasions. The conversion narrative is a kind of machinery of capture. That is, the process of writing entails a confrontation with the prior experience and whether it can be adequately located. What Thjülen's unfolding account names is the way that his growing intimacy with Iturriaga builds as each obstacle presented is countered by an experience of solace.

What is this solace?

The Jesuits had a name for it. They called it consolation. The Jesuit Jerónimo Nadal's (1507–1580) description of the consolation found in prayer and meditation formed the basis of the Jesuit mission to "console souls": "There is also in prayer another thing that is from God and He purely gives it; that is a consolation, an interior happiness, a quiet moment of understanding, a pleasure, a light, a better step forward, a better understanding of things: all of this is the particular grace of prayer and that which encourages one to go forward and offers relics to help on the way."[47] We might call this "the consolation prize," the silver lining of Augustine's life of the troubled spirit. These *reliquias*—translated both as "relics" and "heirlooms," words which imply a materiality or tangibility—provided small tokens or gifts that would ease one's path toward spiritual advancement and, like stepping stones, paved a way into the world.[48] "A better step forward" was construed figuratively and literally. Consolation could be sought not solely in retreat, penance, or quiet. For the Jesuits, consolation was moving because these moments of "light," "pleasure," and "interior happiness" were to be found in the action of bringing spiritual consolation to others, all the while living a life of obedience to God. The Jesuits wrote about finding stillness in movement, locating moments of quiet and inner peace in mobility. This was the tension that animated the way of being Jesuits described as "contemplatives in action."

Here is what a Jesuit theologian like Iturriaga would have known about discerning God's will in one's own life. The imaginative search for unknown objects—a self, a God—formed a path upon which one could be attuned to glimmers of God's presence. But vexingly, God could not be permanently had. This self, this path, was a road that rolled out behind, yet could not be fully left behind. One leaned toward transcendence while remaining bound inextricably to a self that could be only lightly held, continually formed and reformed through embodied memory arts and narrative techniques.

Notably on the ship they are not bound by the hierarchical relationship of spiritual father to spiritual son. And yet he calls Iturriaga the "Father of my soul." On one hand, this indicates that with or without vows, he had turned himself over as a novice to be mastered.[49] His path moved from self-direction (he wished for reasoned disputation with intelligent priests) to necessity (he needed to remain with Iturriaga). But it also means that with and through Iturriaga he found spiritual consolation. Their friendship here is, as Brenna Moore argues, "the constituting force in the formation of religious sensibilities." Consolation is more than an essential *aspect* of the transformation of Thjülen's religious sensibilities.[50] As will continue to be evident in Thjülen's narrative, affective intensity of friendship *is* the religious experience of consolation in which he endeavors to persist. And as I have noted, Thjülen's struggle for "self" often appears as external. But to catch up to himself, he must keep up with the mobile Iturriaga. Separation from Iturriaga is an anxious experience.

Scene V: The Virgin Mary Conquers Lutheran Heresy

What I have found so surprising is that Thjülen takes no pains to explain his transition to Catholicism after the incident with the book. He simply claims that he "was already convinced that Lutheranism seemed a truth amassed with error, contradictions, and impiety," and he offers no discussion of the errors. He is soothed by Padre Iturriaga, but is he hoping to make a leap of faith in which he can have Padre Iturriaga *and* have Enlightenment Reason? He is never entirely sure about the tenets of Catholicism—the adoration of the saints is troublesome, so too the sacramental nature of confession and communion. Yet he feels a sense of urgency: His journey is drawing to a close. Does he imagine his enabling object disappearing on a watery horizon? He appears willing to anchor into an unclear future, to accept the ambiguities of the new religious life because he does not want to part ways with Father Iturriaga, who "had spurred me to remain with him."

That Thjülen deems this change of life a real possibility, that he has begun to feel a sense of security about his chosen direction, was merely another invitation for the Devil to put him to the test.

> Here is where the Devil began to fight me. In vivid colors, he made clear to me the consequences that would follow should I change Religion, the contempt of my relatives, the exile from the homeland, that I would be reduced to a state of begging, still it seemed to me that to flee/escape and, to unite myself with the Jesuits would make me odious to the World, I would be reproached for all eternity as having been sold the fable, and I would be the curse of all of Sweden. What confidence (I said to myself) what confidence could I have in these foreign persons, who perhaps did not nurture in the soul those affections they had demonstrated with words? What if after a number of years I found that the Catholic Faith was insufficient or uncertain? I would have lost the time with which to secure Eternity for myself. Overall, my heart was cruelly torn by the tender love that I felt for my sister who remained in Stockholm, and the perpetual neglect to which I would abandon her; to me this seemed an ingratitude, an impiety, an unheard-of barbarism, but I had no words sufficient to express my extreme anguish. How for many days I was tormented!

It should come as no surprise that instead of struggle or explosive frustration, he now simply turns to Iturriaga. "I revealed this wound so profound, and so painful to the Father of my soul, who used every means to cure it." His spiritual doctor prescribes frequent yet careful consideration of "the Maxims of the Gospels, now the sweetest, next the strongest, or the most appalling." He also makes clear to Thjülen that the Jesuits live well and that he would never be reduced to the feared state of begging. More poignantly, Iturriaga offers his own family to Thjülen, suggesting that after converting, the younger man could "journey to Mexico to his own relatives where I would be well-off and well-treated." Most interesting is what amounts to Father Iturriaga's money-back guarantee: "If nothing else (said the Father) were our Religion not to satisfy you, you would always be at Liberty to leave, and I myself promise to return you once again to Sweden." This is a pragmatic leap, then, for safety nets are in place.

Now the only thing left is for God to concur. Father Iturriaga's words "had made some inroads into my Spirit, but to be submitted entirely it was necessary to find relief [*soccorso*] in a more powerful grace. This Grace I recognized as coming through the powerful intercession of the Virgin Maria." Father Iturriaga had "managed to light in my heart some small flame of Devotion toward the Divine Mother." Iturriaga had accomplished this with the help of an irritant: the rosary. Only at this point do we learn that from the time of Thjülen's earliest entanglement with the Jesuits he had been drawn into Catholic prayer, an experience that was sonic, material, and he now tells his reader, disgusting: "I was induced to recite their Rosary each day publicly with the other Fathers. I confess that I did it with many scruples and disgust; but I did it nonetheless, and the holy Rosary I wore always around the neck under my clothing."

Iturriaga had continuously prayed to the Virgin on his behalf, and now, as Thjülen described it, he had confirmation:

> By intercession of the most pious Great Virgin Mother, everything fell together [*improvisare*] in a flash, with a ray of light, I recognized [*conosceva*] that the Catholic Religion was the only true Religion, and that I would not err in embracing it. At the same point, I felt infused in my Heart, with such a force, a generosity, waves of crying out to God that I abandoned everything to his hands, that I sacrificed everything to him, that I took whatever country for my new homeland, wherever I would find the health of my soul, and that my family, my friends would now be found in the Fathers of the Company of Jesus, which whom I allied myself with so much love.

Reason may pave the way *toward* religious conversion (here the Augustinian case is paradigmatic), but, in the end, conversion narratives must describe the *relinquishing* of human reason. We could say that the nature of Thjülen's conversion was prefigured in the reference to Ananias, in that Saul did not follow reason but rather adhered to God's command. Ananias was simply the conduit of the Holy Spirit, who shook the scales from Paul's eyes. What does it mean that Iturriaga was Thjülen's conduit? He shaped the affections of this young man and, as I believe the text makes quite clear, moments of inquietude or instability dissolved into the soothing presence of Father Iturriaga who figures as a resting place, as well as a conduit to Thjülen's deeper sense of his own ratio of motion-to-rest. Toward the end of the voyage, Iturriaga turned him toward another relationship, this one with the book, the Word, that is, to scripture. Yet even here it is clear that the conversion was made firm through affective spiritual exercise: He instructed Thjülen to choose the "Maxims of the Gospels" *that made him feel*. No matter whether sweet, strong, or appalling, affect anchored the pivot point of his turning.

With his turn to the Jesuits and to the Virgin Mary, Thjülen's conversion takes a decidedly Mexican turn. As we saw on Aramburu's desk in Act I, the Jesuits had been key to the promotion of various cults of the Virgin Mary, from Our Lady of Sorrows to the Virgin of Guadalupe to Our Lady of the Light.[51] Notably, despite the restrictions on the movement of the Jesuits as they made their way to Veracruz under military escort, their petition to break in Tepeyac in order to pray at the basilica of the Virgin of Guadalupe was begrudgingly granted by the Viceroy. The Virgin of Guadalupe symbolized the purity of the Americas, and she was known as "La Patrona." Catholic sermons called for prayers to Mary to support Spain, the torch-bearer of the true faith. Under her watch, the New World was not to be defiled by "wolves, wild beasts, venomous serpents and dragons," specifically, Luther, Calvin, and their "henchmen."[52] The Society of Jesus and the Virgin of Guadalupe were linked in a global effort to quash heresy.[53] Deploying bellicose language, she was compared to Nike, the Greek goddess of war. The Virgin (her purity signaled by a white flower without spines) would annihilate the Lutheran monstrosity; her sharp sword could cut through Luther's soul.[54] She was the light against the darkness, or the beloved *Lucero* who conquered the despised *Lutero*. In other words, the Mexican Jesuits were leaving a land of metaphorical purity and their destination—Europe—was the place where heresy threatened Catholicism. Thus, Thjülen's invocation of the Virgin not only met the requirement for a sign of grace in a conversion narrative, but the story also conformed to Mexican expectations about Luther, namely, that he meet his end at the hand of the Virgin Mary.

This Reformation script is waved like a victory flag, but the mission-accomplished rhetoric cannot draw attention away from the ongoing instability that troubles the Jesuits' attempts to anchor themselves in a new place. We see how their world disintegrates further as they continue to move across the Mediterranean Sea.

Scene VI: Chasing Spiritual Union across the Mediterranean

In the remaining ten additional days on board, the men aboard the *Stockholm* become spectators to the bloody battle between French troops and "le Nazionali" of Corsica. Thjülen describes the battle as a terrible "show" that evoked compassion and disgust. But this means that Corsica, suddenly overtaken by the French, is no longer hospitable to the exiled Jesuits. The destiny of the Jesuits shifts—the pope finally agrees to accommodate them in the Papal States—and so Thjülen pivots to align his destiny with Iturriaga's.

He has told only a few of the Jesuits about his decision to convert. They raise their hands to the air and praise God, truly delighted, and assure Thjülen that they are bound to "an inviolable silence." But nothing stays secret for long in such close quarters. The Swedish captain hears, and he is scandalized. He locks the Jesuits below deck to prevent them "from deceiving people." Thjülen struggles to find ways to speak to them, but in vain, which only adds fuel to the fire of his desire to flee from the ship to remain with the Jesuits when they disembark.

The *Stockholm* eventually docks at S. Fiorenzo, and now that the Fathers have disembarked, Thjülen is consumed with the idea of joining them. He sneaks off the ship to find Iturriaga.[55] He describes Iturriaga as astonished, but the Jesuit points out that it would be impossible to hide Thjülen without exposing the entire Mexican Province, already so compromised and under the watch of various Spanish officials. Iturriaga counsels him to return to the ship, sending him off with a letter requesting assistance from his brother, Pedro Iturriaga. It was difficult to persuade Thjülen to return. "I took that letter with tears in my eyes. Full of bitterness I returned to the ship."

In the days that follow, he remains driven to find a way to reunite with the father of his soul. Packing only underwear, "country" clothing, and his diary, he jumps ship again at Ajaccio. He finds Pedro Iturriaga and spends a nervous but hopeful night, imagining the ship pulling out of the harbor without him. Yet the winds keep the *Stockholm* in port, and the captain uses the delay to put out a search for him. Thjülen is arrested. He is interrogated by a Swedish commander who serves under the French Comte de Narbonne Pelet-Fritzlar. During the interview, Thjülen does not at first admit to his plans to convert, because he fears his fellow Swede may attempt to dissuade him. But a night in a makeshift jail changes his mind. Thjülen's holding pen is an abandoned chapel furnished with what he describes as "an ancient altar table" that is to be his bed. But the altar is also full of mice—fat mice, he tells his reader, that came streaming out of the old wood at night. He spends the night awake, reading Catholic doctrine in the Spanish language. Thus, he had a diary, underwear, change of clothing, *and* a pocked-sized *doctrina Christiana*. More books! This title indicates that he is studying Spanish and Catholicism at the same time. The book is a small object but a sign that he is attaching himself to a new future.

When the Swedish officer returns to him the next day, he confesses to him that he is "changing his Religion" and wants nothing more than to follow the Jesuits. The Swede does indeed attempt to dissuade him, citing Thjülen's duties to country and family, as well as the verity of the Lutheran faith. The officer departs, but when he returns next, he announces that he has come back to liberate him. Thjülen runs to Pedro Iturriaga, and there is a joyful reunion. Pedro wants to take him to meet the vice provincial of the Mexican Province, but a Spanish commander wants to see him first. The latter simply tells him that should the Jesuits ever abandon him; he is welcome to come to Spain. *Everyone* is excited, his conversion a victory for Catholicism that both the Jesuits and their captors can share. The next day he pays a call to the General Comte de Narbonne to give thanks for his release and to obtain a passport that would allow him to travel to Bastia to rejoin "my very dear Padre Manuel Iturriaga."

But this reunion will have to wait. He is advised that the Padres have already begun the next leg of the journey to the Papal States. He obtains a new passport, this time for Genoa. Next, transport presents a problem because, as much as he loves the Jesuits, he is not a Jesuit. This is a reminder that the Jesuits have been arrested and that he is prohibited from traveling with these closely monitored refugees. He finds passage aboard a French boat. He finally arrives in Bologna and seeks out Padre Iturriaga, but his hopes (and ours) are dashed as we are not yet witness to the long-awaited reunion scene. The father of his soul is not in Bologna, but in Ferrara. On the October 5, Thjülen—finally!—is reunited with Padre Manuel Iturriaga. "I cannot say what a consolation, and I was surprised— what a joy to find myself, after so much time, with the Director and the Father of my Soul, to kiss his hand anew, and to recount the adventures that I had experienced." He has found himself.

Can he maintain this self?

Monologue: On Conversion

Thjülen aims to channel moments strange and incommunicable into the genre's recognizable pattern of a life split neatly into a before and an after. But as Christopher Wild reminds us, to convert is to turn, to rotate, to revolve, to turn around, or upside down. These spatial semantics indicate a change of position from which new realities emerge. Wild draws upon Plato's description of the turn away from the shadowy back wall of the cave toward the light to demonstrate how philosophy established "turning" as key to the quest toward wisdom, bequeathing to Christian conversion this "art of turning around." Yet given the standard conversion narrative's emphasis on finality, what is often overlooked, Wild contends, is the problem of continence—that is, maintaining oneself as turned, which, in fact means that to convert is to continue to rotate, revolve, turn, to, in sum, remain in tension in order to maintain the momentum.[56]

Yet if we take conversion to entail a "turning" we must ask, toward *what* in particular did Thjülen turn? To Catholicism? Thjülen certainly described himself as curious about Catholic ritual life, as attested by his tourism in Lisbon, where he took notes about this strange religion to share with friends upon his return. This is where it becomes clear that the conversion narrative is an attempt to *contain* the topsy-turvy movements of his soul that he had experienced in chasing after the father of his soul. He remained discomfited by Catholic ritual, as depicted in his account of praying the rosary. Later in the account, he admits that he was positively squeamish about declaring his Catholic faith before the Dominican-run Inquisition, against whom he had imbibed a hatred "along with his mother's milk." Finally, the narrative ends with his decision to take vows as a Jesuit. The request that Thjülen compose the text had clear political and ideological motivations, namely, to highlight the continued role of the Society of Jesus in defending and promoting Catholicism.[57] But one wonders whether Thjülen's telling unwittingly undercuts any hard-and-fast defense of Catholicism. In fact, his narrative never completely departs from the theme laid bare in the first conversation with the shipboard Jesuits: Though he loved the members of the Mexican Province, he remains less certain about everything else.

Accordingly, oscillation best describes the rhythm of this narrative that continues to follow the ebb and flow of vexation and consolation.

Thjülen's inquietude after his mother's death is answered by his "resolve to be in the world," in the style of Voltaire. The unnamed Jesuit acted as an irritant to Thjülen, his "fighting words" a reminder that surly Jesuit missionaries were capable of driving potential converts away—although in this case, he pushed Thjülen toward Iturriaga (or, more accurately, the unsettling scene drew the soothing Iturriaga out of the shadows). The Virgin Mary figures as his ultimate resolve, mediating Thjülen's transfer of affection from his Swedish sister and countrymen to his new family and friends, the fathers of the Society of Jesus.

Can we say that this is an account of his conversion to the Jesuits? "There were some Swedes on the ship, but I remained only with the Padres," he wrote, adding, "I took on the color of their language." "I love them," he had declared early on. *Why* was he drawn to the Jesuits? Despite his allegiance to Reason, he never offers any *reasons* why he arrived at the conclusion that Lutheranism is "a truth amassed with error, contradictions, and impiety." Perhaps he considered this unnecessary. Even if he never offered an explanation for his reader, we can see that he *did* in fact arrive at some kind of reasoned conclusion, because he fears that he may lose hold of it. "What if after a number of years I found that the Catholic Faith was insufficient or uncertain?" This indicates that he *had* anchored into some "sufficient" reason, some measure of certainty.

Scene VII: Betrayal

Thjülen remains in Ferrara with the father of his soul, where the first task is to pick up a pen to sort out matters with friends and family in Sweden. But Thjülen's sorting process does not end with the Swedish correspondence. He continues to reorganize *his self* in this new place. What now? He had considered traveling to the Americas or to India. Some of the Fathers support this idea and promise to help him with some money. But Padre Iturriaga "shone a better light," suggesting that he go back to his studies. Initially, this plan is not to his taste. He is twenty-three years old and considers the notion of returning to study Latin grammar depressing and a bit embarrassing.

The conversion narrative shifts to become an exploration of yet another possibility: Does he have a vocation to become a Jesuit? He is intrigued when the Jesuit fathers make the Spiritual Exercises around the time of

Corpus Christi. He is struck by the reputation of the Exercises as a transformative experience, so he joins them for the eight-day retreat. Here he experiences his first inkling—or as he says, God sparked in his heart the first seed of a religious vocation. But he has only been a Catholic for a few months. He has more to learn. He agrees to study Latin. He remarks upon his special fondness for Ignatius of Loyola. He does not say why, but perhaps it is because Ignatius, too, after his second conversion went back to school to study Latin, a grown man among boys.

Some letters come from Sweden. One friend mocks him, sending sarcastic felicitations on his sudden transformation into "a strong Spirit and a Man of Philosophy." Another friend writes with a more searing response, chiding him for first having become "a Man without fear of God and without Conscience" and now an apostate, aligned with "Jesuit wickedness." Thjülen should realize, the friend writes, that it is his Christian duty to dissolve such a friendship, and that Thjülen ought not have dared write to him. Thjülen reads these letters with a clear mind and considers his tranquility a good sign that he has chosen the right path. He writes back to his dwindling set of friends in Sweden, "explaining rationally" his decisions.

But Thjülen is less troubled by his old friendships than he is by a shocking falling out with a newer Jesuit friend. Thjülen now tells his readers that he had forged another significant friendship during his travels with the Mexican Jesuits. On the *Stockholm* he had become very close to a Jesuit coadjutor temporal who had a smattering of French. "He was in my ear," says Thjülen, encouraging him to convert to Catholicism, and was delighted by the idea that Thjülen was now considering a vocation as a Jesuit. In Ferrara they lived together in a house with other Jesuits. But Thjülen is thrown off balance by his friend's sudden change of heart. As he tells it, the unnamed Jesuit renewed his vows in the three-day ritual known as the Triduum. "After renewing his vows on the Feast of Saints Peter and Paul, the following morning he abandoned the Society, hanging up his religious vestments on a nail in his room." Thjülen is crushed. He feels manipulated. Hearing that the coadjutor has moved to Bologna, he writes a letter to rebuke him. Not unlike his own dismayed friends in Sweden, he reminds his friend of God's terrible punishment but also adds how deeply betrayed he feels and that he is reeling from this personally. This is a friend who had encouraged Thjülen to become a Catholic and then a Jesuit. Why? Thjülen asks. "Were you just trying to replace yourself?" He does not recall with any precision what he wrote in the letter, such was his fury. This is a dramatic episode in his continuing cycles of anguished rumination.

But the cycle continues. The fiery flashes, he says, of his desire to become a Jesuit would light up and then fade away. One such flash of clarity arrives in October 1769, and as we have come to expect, his moments of consoling clarity come while paying a visit to Iturriaga. The latter is now teaching at the Palazzo Ercolani, a villa in Bologna that has become a makeshift college for Mexican novices who are studying theology. Here Thjülen's observations of the Mexican novices play an important role in his decision making:

> The modesty, regularity, and fervor of these Youth, rejoicing in their Exile, in the life of poverty and discomfort that they lead, [this] awakened in my soul wonder, and then such an envy of their happy state, followed by a lively desire to be like them. Indeed, to be one of them. So, these longings grew. The many slanders and reprimands that I had heard and read against the Jesuits contrasted with such innocent living, it seemed to me that their persecutions were a mark, and a badge worn by true Children of God, true imitators of Jesus Christ, truly Predestined to Celestial Glory.

The Mexican novices provide the counternarrative to his friend's decision to leave the order. These young men who had not yet taken vows would have been allowed to remain in New Spain; therefore, these novices had in fact *chosen* exile.[58] Despite continued pressure from the moment of the arrest and through most steps of their journey to Italy, the novices continually refused to sever themselves from the Society of Jesus. He must see in them his own decision to remain attached to a Mexican Province under duress. Thjülen's vocation is clear to him now: He is set to join the Society, and here the story reaches its pinnacle of hope. His future is mirrored back to him in youthful possibility. Thjülen asks to join the Mexican Province. The young novices and Thjülen's hopes to be among them symbolize the onward march of the Mexican Province. About his aspirations to join the Mexican Province? No possibility. The Provinces of the Iberian Assistancy are all maligned. He must wait to join an Italian novitiate, for the Jesuit leadership in Rome has decided against his joining the Mexican Province.

While he waits to hear about where he will take his first vows as a novice, Thjülen enjoys a moment of peace that enables him to take in the sights in Ferrara. His tranquility, as we have come to expect, is momentary. He begins to take a second look at his vocation. Touring Ferrara, he becomes acquainted with members of the nobility. In the "Illustrious Citizenship of friends" his life is full of conversation and amusement, but his vocation is waning. Or, as he stated, "the Spirit dissipated, but the artifice of the infernal enemy was finer and more deceiving. This is because some solicitous friends who sought my advantage, made me the proposition of a Marriage, [the one] which awaited would be in all circumstances respectable, to a very civilized young girl." She was wealthy and had been "provided by nature with all the other personal qualities which are most appreciated in the world." He could have pursued this option. "The Lady was in utmost freedom to dispose of herself" and ardently desired a wedding.

> I thank the Lord who provides the strength not to let me use any word from this mouth to accept or at least accept that party; but I will also say to my confusion that the soul bowed mightily, and that I did not compose myself on that occasion with all the generosity that was appropriate for a young man called by God to Religion. So my mind and heart composed of one thousand fantasies, affections, and worldly desires, I had to do a little violence [to depart] from Ferrara, especially since my friends, and that Lady herself, at great insistence, prayed that I reside among them.

Thjülen returned to Bologna where Padre Iturriaga—"who had no idea of the changes I had undergone"—informed him that he had been accepted in the Venetian Province. That night he could not sleep, thinking about his vocation. His ideas about being a Jesuit were born of true admiration of those young Mexican theology students, who, like him, were choosing to stay on the battered vessel. His own transport to Catholicism had been peopled with Mexican Jesuits and he had imagined himself formally becoming a member of this association of religious men from the Americas. But in this moment of doubt, he worried again about his loss of liberty, with renewed doubts about living out his life "in a Nation that I did not know." He discussed his doubts with another spiritual director, but he was not consoled. He was compelled to turn to Padre Iturriaga.

Patiently, he told Thjülen that this was a matter that was between him and God, and that he should make the Spiritual Exercises again. He agreed. The first three days went well, but when he began to meditate on the Two Standards to make an election, "he was caught in a furious battle of contrary thoughts, such that he became desperate." He abruptly stopped the meditation and, frantic, ran to Padre Iturriaga's room. The latter simply reminded him to trust in Saint Ignatius, the protector of this day. "I am not sure how," Thjülen muses, again, with words that fail to register the characterize the distance he has traveled from his original quest for answers based upon "Reason." But his own "tender love of the Society, and the vocation, seemed evident." Thus, he adopted the name Ignazio. He was gifted a relic from the Father General, which he kept as a treasure. He signs off in 1771 by writing that this all transpired six months ago, and that he now lives in the Society as Lorenzo Ignazio Thjülen, a novice.

Monologue: Metamorphosis, Not Redemption

This narrative exists in large part because Thjülen had taken up the Jesuit General Ricci's prompting to write his account as a *counter* to the narrative of Jesuit demise. Accordingly, he submits his experience to the machinery of capture that is "the conversion narrative." He does perform "continuity" for the Society of Jesus because, as he says, he loves them and later in life, he comments once again, they were his friends and asked this favor. There is a friendly transactional quality hidden here: He tells their story within his own, highlighting both his quest as one of Enlightenment Reason as well as paying tribute to a Mexican Province of Jesuits who triumph over Lutheranism. His views are not always flattering to Catholicism.[59] But all Catholics rejoice at his conversion.

But another reality that threads its way through the narrative is Thjülen's situation as a traveler, an adventurer, whose adoption of Catholicism entails a conversion to statelessness. In considering this frame, Thjülen's testimony is a ritual akin to the demands made upon refugees and migrants by both government agencies and interested NGOs. That is, there is a demand for a narrative performance in exchange for support or status at the port of arrival. As his patrons, the Society of Jesus makes this same "request." In writing, he makes decisions about how much to expose about himself, to whom, and when. These choices, I imagine, add to the

ACT II: POSSIBILITY? 131

labor of the inventorying process that retrospectively lend an evaluative layer to the narrative. He is looking back at choices made. This evaluation reads as a list of "pros" and "cons." On the left, Thjülen writes cons: "mother, sister, Voltaire, the Enlightenment, Swedish friends." The cons also include the rosary and the Dominicans. His friend's choice to leave the Society interjects an uneasy question mark. He is also impeded by his worries about the Captain and the Swedish agent, and the woman he leaves behind in Ferrara. And on the right-hand side his list of pros includes "Mexican novices. Padre Iturriaga." Is that all? Perhaps that is enough. The Crown expelled the Jesuits, who in turn overwhelmed Thjülen, whose sense of self became a locational problem in which his affective turning points arrive and dissipate without the aura of *decisiveness* one might expect from a conversion narrative. Rather, his is a spatio-affective story in which the plot turns on his requirement to remain proximate to the father of his soul. This is a migrant love story whose relentless plotline is a series of pros and cons that circle around the primary migratory questions: Do I leave, do I settle? Stop here, go on?

What hides in plain sight, then, is that Thjülen does not fulfill the conversion narrative's demand for a story of sin and redemption. There is no ultimate transformation in Thjülen's narrative. We have established that he is overcome by a love that has no Reason, and he must be with Iturriaga, the man on the move. But the curious thing is that if he has a new relationship with the Catholic God, or with self through this God, he does not indicate this on the page. True, the Mexican Virgin is a new addition to the Lutheran's life. The altar figures into the conversion narrative as the scene of a solitary moment of despair in the abandoned church. But note that Thjülen says little about a new relationship with the Catholic God. The altar is "lively" only in that this decrepit ruin is overrun with mice: The body of Christ plays no role. In fact, what is clear is that the convert maintains doubts about the Catholic sacraments even when he is certain that he must remain with Iturriaga and wishes to become a Jesuit himself.

Metamorphosis? Much has changed outside the pages of his conversion narrative. My off-the-page interventions worked to bring the Mexicans more fully into the story, but also to sound some dissonant notes in this triumphal narrative. Throughout, the Mexican Jesuits have struggled to collect themselves in the few books and things that, maddeningly, were continually confiscated from them. They are losing members. Some secularize. Many others die. "Jesuit survival strategies" arrayed against real-time, are relentless dismantling. The men struggled to survive as "the Mexican Province." And it didn't work. The Spanish Crown clearly operated according to a practical theory of social formation that is almost Latourian in its ongoing moves to strip the men of any kind network that would allow actors to maintain connectedness, to replicate themselves as a community of religious men.

When Thjülen makes a few edits to his conversion narrative in 1778, he does a bit of wordsmithing (I have remarked on these in the endnotes), but little else in the narrative changes. The most telling change will be found in his signature. He signed his first narrative with the words "in obedience." But in 1778 he rewrites those words but then draws a line through them. He is no longer a Jesuit because the Society of Jesus no longer exists, having been dissolved in 1773, just two years after he took vows as a novice. Yet he signals his attachment to the losing cause by continuing to sign his name, Lorenzo Ignazio Thjülen, "ex-Gesuita." Disappearance is not antithetical to remains.

Change of Scene

Thjülen sits at the desk that is in the back corner of the stage. He finishes writing, then dramatically draws a line through the last bit that he wrote. He looks out at the audience, then stands up and exits the stage.

Dim to blue lights.

Curtain remains up.

Stagehands move the desk, chair, and writing implements to the front of stage but turn it around, backward, so the back of the chair is facing the audience.

CURTAIN DROPS

SOUND: Footsteps, the squeak of the chair being pulled from the desk. A cough. The sound of matches being lit. A smoky smell.

CURTAIN RISES

Man in a black robe is squatting near the desk, back to audience. He is lighting a little brazier, fanning the flames. When it is sufficiently lit, he sits at the desk. We never see his face.

Act III   Ruination

> They stand poised between the forms they were and the formlessness to which, in the absence of restoration, they are destined. They lose their original purposes and have the singularity of artworks, yet they are severed irremediably from their contexts of production.
>
> Susan Stewart

An inventory of things. An inventory of self. Now we turn to an inventory of the dead to analyze what it means to inhabit the "ex" in ex-Jesuit. What remains?

"Each was admired for his good death," José Felix de Sebastián (1736–1815) writes in the preface to his *Memorias de los padres y hermanos de la Compañía de Jesús de la Provincia de Nueva España*.[1] Sebastián's nine-hundred-page unpublished manuscript commemorates 389 Jesuits from the Mexican Province who had died since the first day of the arrest in late June 1767. "Never had they seen men die who enjoyed such great peace.[2] He hopes that his short descriptions of the men "who have died gloriously in exile" would ensure against the loss of the memories of the members of the Society of Jesus "from my Province of New Spain." The task he has undertaken is difficult, he notes. The number of Jesuits in the Mexican Province made it impossible to write a complete *vida* for each man. "I have written here what I have been able to learn about them, and much of what I have observed myself in their regular proceedings. [To that] I add what I say is the pure truth that has been told to me by trustworthy persons, and that which in great part, I have experienced myself." His introduction states that the deaths of his Mexican brethren were admired not only by Italian doctors and priests but were also remarked upon by those who had witnessed Jesuits die during the navigations over land and sea, and during the long delays in port towns. Although Sebastián died in 1815, his final entry is dated 1796. For twenty-nine years he keeps to the task of recording what he insists were "well-regarded" deaths. "Never," he writes, "had they seen men die who enjoyed such peace."[3] His inventory of dead Mexican Jesuits offers accounts of men whose virtuous lives were followed by good deaths; one might characterize his work as elegiac in the sense that he attempts to transform mourning and loss "into something of use for the survivors."[4]

No doubt his work has been useful to modern scholars. The *Memorias* has served as one of the bedrocks of Jesuit biobibliography in Mexican historiography. Consistently utilized as a source of "facts" about Mexican Jesuits, one cannot say that the work has been forgotten. But the original struggle that drove his storytelling has been lost to view. In pillaging the *Memorias* for names, dates, and places, historians have overlooked the simple architecture that orders the manuscript: the death date. In keeping the entire manuscript in view, we see that one at a time, at different ages, in different places, the Mexican Jesuits fall, the death-date chronology linking them together as if by a string. The rhythm to these entries, following one after the other, insist upon the fact that the task at hand is a dead-end because the question—"What survives?"—haunts this text that trails after dying men, first in Mexico, at sea, in Spain, in Corsica and then in the Papal States. The question becomes even more pressing in 1773 when, by papal decree, it is declared that the Society of Jesus no longer exists. In the years that follow, Sebastián stays with the task of documenting each death through 1796, when he stops recording, abandoning his own project well before all the dying is done.

From his preface, we understand the inventorying process—the counting and naming of the dead—as its own form of mourning. As I will discuss shortly, the structure blends the efficiency of a finding aid (numbered, chronological, with an index) with laudatory storytelling. He makes no appeal to any specific readers, but if he is writing for the Mexican Jesuits themselves, his audience is disappearing. The structure of the project is fragile, too. What is clear from the start is that the *Memorias* has a problem common to religious storytelling: Sebastián has taken up the task of bearing witness; he sets out a structure but then squirms under these constraints when stories structured as models for virtuous living are out of sync with the unfolding present. In this sense, his labors fit David Kennedy's description of the work of elegy as "a structure for mourning and consolation that is always on the verge of breaking down and whose efficacy is therefore in perpetual doubt."[5]

Doubt arises with Sebastián's very first entry. Following on the heels of Sebastián's prefatory claim about "peaceful deaths," it is jarring to find tranquility completely absent in the account of the troubled life and terrible death of the young student *hermano* Pedro Arenas (#1).[6] Once a promising Jesuit, Arenas had for a time taught grammar at the Colegio de Valladolid in Michoacán. But by the time of the arrest, he had already been suffering from a "great martyrdom" that was inflicted in the form of scruples, that is, he harbored obsessive thoughts about sin and salvation. In Sebastián's words, "he held scruples, [which] made him lose all sense, leaving him as if drunk, and out of himself in total dementia." He was sent to Mexico City to be cared for at the Colegio Máximo, but "all medicines were useless," and Arenas continued in an agitated state. Sebastián described his behavior as "nothing *furioso*, but rather very timid, no longer able to speak of anything but the fears that troubled his conscience." At the time of the arrest, he was left behind at the Colegio Máximo, "where he saw no one other than soldiers and weapons, so given his great timidity, together with the horror of his solitude and the noise of the soldiers, he was completely out of himself (*fuera de sí*) and in such a state, he threw himself out of a window." Sebastián provides no commentary about the stance of the Catholic Church on the mortal sin of suicide. Instead, his narrative is about a good man whose immense "fears of conscience" caused him to disappear. "Out of himself" is the phrase that Sebastián uses, repeating a variation on the phrase again: Pedro Arenas was "lost to himself" before he then threw his body out the window. Hollowed out, ruined, the Jesuit was gone before he died.[7]

If the first memorial is jarring in a collection that purports to describe peaceful deaths worthy of emulation, Arenas's death is nonetheless a fitting beginning to this repository of facts that tells of the slow and relentless ruination of the Mexican Province, a tragedy without finality. Each entry offers a false sense of closure: While the occasion for writing is the end of a life, Sebastián has taken up a task for which there is no real end in sight. The finality represented in each "good death" is an illusion that is quickly revealed in the continuing sequence of deaths. The Mexican Province survives, but as a narrative about unmitigated ruination, demise, and eventual disappearance.

A handful of Sebastián's "monuments" have taken on a monumental existence in Mexican nationalist historiography. So far from home, the ex-Jesuits of the Mexican Province, as we know well from existing historiography, shake a defiant fist at Europe's enlightened armchair anthropologists.[8] These American Jesuits are intimately acquainted with the continent, its people, its natural history, and its original source materials. Writing from Bologna, the exiled ex-Jesuits are the first to forge the imagined community that gives birth to the nation state. Well, some of them do just that. But the *Memorias* provides the basis for such a story only if one is extremely discerning, culling a handful of "nation-making" writers from the nine hundred pages of Sebastián's unfinished manuscript.[9] In what follows, I do not push ahead to the nation (1821) or to the restoration of the Society of Jesus (1814). But if there is a burgeoning democratic sensibility to be found, it is a byproduct of the death-date structure. The Jesuits, whether the lowly temporal coadjutor or the fully professed, are documented side by side. The more notable dead—Abad, Alegría, Campoy, and Clavigero—take their places alongside those who were never very remarkable in their lives.[10] As we have seen, even those whose deaths are considered notorious due to suicide are included in Sebastián's manuscript. Like alphabetical order in the new encyclopedias of the eighteenth century, attention to chronology is a flattening move: *All* men of the Mexican Province who died from the moment of the arrest in 1767 are memorialized alongside one another, with no attention to rank.

"Ruins images" have been productive meaning-making vectors in Western Christian culture, as Susan Stewart has explored in her study of how Renaissance and Enlightenment writers and artists engaged with material ruins. Sebastián's *Memorias* demonstrate little interest in ruined buildings, whether the empty colleges and abandoned mission stations left behind in Mexico, or the famed Roman ruins he no doubt encountered in Italy. Rather, the poignancy of the *Memorias* is in his descriptions of ruined men. Each entry first constructs a monument to "a good Jesuit life" before sketching the breakdown, disintegration, and disappearance of these individual monuments. Yet subtle shifts in the features of these monuments offer clues as to the transitions to life in the "new worlds" of Bologna and Ferrara. Slowly, the entries shift from descriptions of tireless work undertaken in New Spain, the arrest, and the ensuing hardships and deaths during the brutal migration. In time, the "Mexican" details are truncated, and the entries shift to offer some fragmentary accounts of lives patched together in Italy.

Note, however, that these accounts of survival are rarely triumphant. This is not only because each one ends with death, but also because he describes the diminishment of men, the decline of bodies. With the suppression of the Society of Jesus (for Sebastián, it is primarily the "abolición"), ruination has reached a scale he never imagined. Stripped of their black robes in 1773, the ex-Jesuits suffered another blow in 1775, when they were forbidden to live in groups larger than three persons. By the time Sebastián makes his last entry in 1796, we see how the Jesuits of the Mexican Province live an unstructured life in Italy that would have been unintelligible to their former American selves. Here he often describes an ex-Jesuit as someone who "lived for some time dying," neatly capturing how they lived through the breakdown of their former way of being as if in a mode of extended decay. The only place where the Mexican Jesuits remain together as an entity is on the pages of the *Memorias*.

NOTES ON LIGHTING AN INVENTORY OF THE DEAD

To light a close reading of a text, a soft desk lamp should illuminate the handwritten manuscript. The manuscript's author sits with his back firmly turned to the audience for most of these scenes. He keeps a magnifying glass on hand to revisit some of the notes he made in a very tiny hand.

There is a second desk. There the light comes from the computer screen because the pages of Sebastián's manuscript have been scanned by the archivists at the Bibliotheca Archiginassio. Now the historian reads Sebastián's manuscript on an iPad at home. The historian, as usual, remains in brown light, remaining at the edges of the stage, face illuminated only by the light emanating from the reading device.

So that the audience can see what is happening, project the computer screen on the back wall, like wallpaper. To give the textual feel of linen-cotton paper with brown ink, use a sepia-toned light.

When the story turns to "off the page" scenes, the wall-text should fade but not disappear, revealing cut-out shapes in profile that represent people walking under cover of an eighteenth-century Bologna portico. The light should now be colored, perhaps the yellow-orange of Bologna walls, but these scenes should always be accompanied by a light humming sound to give a sense that the still cutout figures have some life within them, even though their exact words are not available.

On the rare moment when we hear something of Felix de Sebastián's voice, he should step into a spotlight, but only in profile. He never looks directly out to the audience.

What is to be conveyed throughout is that attempting to find Sebastián himself is an eerie experience. In any search engine, he comes up everywhere but always as a footnote to biographical data about another Jesuit. Sebastián is everywhere, yet he himself is nowhere to be seen.

Scene I: The Transatlantic Culling of the Mexican Province

Each entry contains the name of the Jesuit, the date and place of birth, the date he joined the Order, in what capacity he served, and each place in which he served. The Jesuits are "Mexican" because they are members of the Mexican Province, whether they are born in Spain or Germany or, like most of the men, in New Spain. Sebastián always describes some "exemplary" characteristics. The pivot point in each entry is the Jesuits' precise location at the moment of the arrest. The entry is punctuated with a death date and, when possible, the location where the cadaver was buried. The first death, already discussed, provides a case in point in which Sebastián is silent on what happened to Arenas's body, probably because he does not have this information. But in most other entries, he will note whether there has been an appropriate funeral and where the Jesuit cadaver found its final resting place.

Indeed, any absence of rituals marking Jesuit deaths are noted with alarm. The second Jesuit death, for example, is ignominious due to the indignity of his burial. P. Pedro Blanco (#2),[11] a sixty-nine-year-old Jesuit, is described as an "angel in the flesh" who had taught grammar at the college in Querétaro for most of his life. At the time of the arrest he was too ill to travel, so he was transferred to a Franciscan convent in Querétaro. He died on July 11, 1767, and according to Sebastián, Blanco's cadaver was treated like simple rubbish to be disposed "with none of the honors to which priests are accustomed in that land, even though an Official who saw this sordidness paid the Friars the wax and enough necessary for his funeral."[12] A better sendoff was given to the elderly Jesuit P. Joseph Redona (#14), who, when left behind in Mexico City, was taken in at a hospital run by the Bethlemites. He died in early September, and Sebastián states approvingly that the Bethlemites gave Redona a "sumptuous funeral" that brought together all the city of Mexico.[13] It is hard to imagine that such a gathering was possible, given the Crown's efforts to restrict any public response to the departure of the Jesuits. But the Bethlemites are dependable: They provide yet another worthy sendoff to P. Antonio Salas (#24). Many "retired" Jesuits had been convalescing on a hacienda. Unable to travel, P. Joseph Elvillar went to the Hospital de la Santísima Trinidad de Pobres Sacerdotes, where he died on December 15, 1767. "His cadaver was buried privately," Sebastián explains, "so as not to renew the weeping of the Mexicans." The private ritual is lamentable, but a quiet gathering is better than the absence of ritual, which troubles him deeply in these early entries.

The causes of some deaths, too, are described as particularly appalling. The third death marks the beginning of a series of dreadful yellow fever deaths. H. Manuel Joseph Oyarzún (#3) is lauded for, among other things, his work at local hospital for *los dementes*—the mentally ill—where he worked in the kitchen "to ensure that all [meals] were well-seasoned and presentable."[14] His own death was anything but tidy. After having made the trek to Veracruz, he was the first to exhibit the "mortal symptom of black vomit that in little time took his life." A dark vomit—the color and consistency of coffee grounds—is the signature of yellow fever in its advanced stages, when coagulated blood caused by internal hemorrhaging is ejected from the stomach. This viral infection, transmitted by mosquitos, usually reared its head in humid tropics of coastal regions like Veracruz during the wet summer months. Most susceptible were those without prior exposure. Jesuits who had spent most of their lives in the cooler climes of the central valley of Mexico or the dry arid northern missions would not have been exposed to the yellow fever virus.[15] Hermano Oyarzún is the first Jesuit to die of this disease, exhibiting "great resignation" as he left this world." The term "resignation" signals a "good death," yet he was likely denied communion prior to this peaceful passing, as the ignominious black vomit prevented priests from placing the body of Christ into such a precarious position.[16]

Yellow fever made August and September difficult months. As the Jesuits awaited transport to Havana, yellow fever deaths took them down, one after the other. Father Berrios (#7) dies on August 9. Brother Joseph

Palacios (#8), who had been a nurse at the Colegio de San Ildephonso in Mexico, and who cared for many of the sick Jesuits, dies the same day. Brother Joseph Jordan (#9) dies three days later on August 12. "El Ynocente" Padre Joseph Calderon (#10) dies on August 18, and four days later Father Miguel Gonzales (#11) succumbs to the disease. A Jesuit well known to all, Pedro Reales (#12), a former provincial of the Mexican Province, dies on August 23. Everyone, he writes, mourned this *"grande Jesuita."*

These Veracruz deaths result from what Sebastián begins to refer to as "the infirmity" and only secondarily as the *"vómito prieto"* or the *"vómito negro."* Like Hermano Palacios, some Jesuits are marked out as succumbing to yellow fever because they had worked "tirelessly" to care for the sick. A German Jesuit named Hermano Jorge Schulz (#18) is among these. This brother was a botanist who had run the infirmary at the Colegio Máximo in Mexico City with skills that made him "a most useful subject" for all of the community, especially as he had constructed *"una preciosa Botica."* At this college pharmacy he had concocted "the most exquisite medicines." Sebastián describes him as "sacrificing himself" in his efforts to assist the many Jesuits who fell ill in Veracruz, before falling ill himself and dying on September 15, "a victim of the ardent Charity of his heart." Another German Jesuit, Hermano Juan Intereger (Hinterger, #13) had been a surgeon. He dies on August 29. The Irish Thomas Arsekín (#21), also a temporal coadjutor, is another who assisted the sick before dying himself on October 8. These were the Jesuit "first responders" and note that many of them were temporal coadjutors, a status that denotes men whom Sebastián lauded for operating in a serving capacity, about whom more will be said later.

By October 1767 sufficient ships had been requisitioned, and some Jesuits begin the next leg of the journey to Havana. But departure from Veracruz provides little respite from the grim reaper, who continues to cull this herd of religious men. P. Francisco Iguerategui (#22) is the first to die shipboard on the approach to Havana. He is buried on the island. Others do not have as secure a resting place. Sebastián marks several November and December deaths as taking place shipboard. Corpses, like that of Padre Marcos Gonzalez, (#25), are "buried in the waves of the sea," or like Hermano Pedro de Torres (#30), "his cadaver thrown into the waters of the Mexican Gulf." In fact, a cartography of the locations where Jesuits have been thrown overseas charts their piecemeal progress across the

Atlantic. By January 1768, bodies are no longer thrown in the waves of the Gulf of Mexico. H. Vicente Vera (#59) went into "el Golfo de los Yeguas a la altura de la Bermuda" marking the fact that this ship is past mid-Atlantic and closing in on the port of Santa María in southern Spain.[17]

But Sebastián cannot trace the deaths of Jesuits across the Atlantic without turning a backward glance to note the slow-paced travels and miserable deaths of the *padres* from the California missions in northern New Spain. A botched journey on every front, these men are described as suffering ill treatment and the most ignominious deaths, as can be seen in the lengthy description of the death of P. Sebastián Cava (#72). Born in Spain, Cava came to the Mexican Province as a novice. After his studies, he was sent to work on the Misión de Vaca in Sinaloa, "a country on fire [*todo del Fuego*] in which he brought together a great flock." Following an order to transfer to the mission of Santa Cruz, he arrives only to hear news of the arrest, after which he is conducted to the port of Guaymas, where missionaries from Sonora and the Pimería have gathered. Here Sebastián states in parenthesis that because Cava was the first to die on this journey, he will paint a detailed description, just this once, to not have to repeat it for each Jesuit who died on this particular journey.

> [Cava] was badly treated by the Commissioners who believed each Jesuit possessed some great treasure, threatening each with his life to indicate where it had been hidden. Was there no value in reason, in saying 'I don't have more than what is seen? Can't you see?' They would be satisfied with nothing, which procured their mistreatment as [the Commissioners tried] to make them confess to that which they did not have.
>
> Finally, after many days of painful travel through undergrowth in depopulated lands, he arrived at the Port of Guaymas. Guaymas is a high desert plateau, where there had once been a Mission that was desolated by the Barbarous Seri Indians. Here there was nothing else, but a few shacks that had been fabricated for the Soldiers. From there they would go to Mexico. Being a very warm climate, the poorly maintained shelters were close to the guards, who did not permit them to communicate among themselves, and [they were] maltreated with work invented for the purpose of cruelty.
>
> He was in this unhappy situation for nine months, at the end of which they embarked on small boats, all packed together, unable to move, to be taken to Puerto de San Blas. It is indescribable, their

laborious suffering from hunger, thirst, and misery, all of them lacking in strength, decayed by scurvy, having consumed the few very poor provisions. They arrived at *Puerto Escondido de la California*, where they were gathered in shacks on the beach that had been made by Missionaries of the Province, [where] those charitable *Californios* gathered around and gave them all that they had, which was but a little maize.

They took up again the journey and, after ninety days of navigation (a trip that is commonly made in five days) they arrived at Puerto de San Blas. Here they found *Comandante* Don Manuel Ribero, a native of Ayamonte, who treated Padre Cava, and all his *compañeros* with great charity and generosity. They left here on horseback riding from morning until evening through swamps, marshes, and quagmires (being the time of the rains) where the beasts added up, always fearful of the caymans that are in abundance in those lakes, losing the larger part of their clothes and their breviaries that fell into the mire; they passed the nights on the hard ground, completely soaked. In this way they continued on the road, sometimes on foot, sometimes on horseback, until reaching Tepique where, with the great charity of the *naturales*, they regathered a bit of their strength.

They departed for Tetitlán, but without the natural strength to stand up to such labor and misery, they began to become sick with *tercianos* [tertian fever]. Father Cava deteriorated, and there being no cure, and he so destitute of strength given the great trials he had suffered, upon arriving at the town of Aguacatlán, he gave up everything, handing his spirit to God on the 18th day of August [1768].[18]

In quick succession, over a two-week period from late August until September 14, 1768, thirteen worn-down Jesuits die in the towns of Aguacatlán and Ystlán.[19] An additional six men die before finishing the journey to Veracruz.[20] And from 1770 forward, whenever Sebastián documents the deaths of those who survived the notorious journey, all will have died in southern Spain, still imprisoned in the port town of Santa María.[21] He notes that part of the suffering of the survivors was a great sense of powerless experienced as they buried one Jesuit after another. "Martyrdom" and "*via crucis*" have been used—largely by the Jesuits themselves—to describe this well-known episode of extended misery. By the year 1773, his terminology shifts: He uses the term "inhumane" to document the death of Padre Carlos Rojas in January 1773. He adds that Rojas and the rest of his *compañeros* imprisoned in Santa María were treated like "prisoners of war." In sum, the "martyrdom" of the Californians becomes paradigmatic of the generalized suffering during the migration that follows the arrest of the Jesuits from the Mexican Province.[22]

But Sebastián describes martyrdoms in many forms and includes mental afflictions among those. Arenas, the first dead Jesuit in 1767, is one among several Jesuits whom Sebastián described as suffering from "troubles of conscience." Sebastián characterizes the intense agitation and distress of scruples as a "continuous martyrdom." Sebastián not only shares these mental struggles experienced by some of his brethren but also shows how serving the mentally distressed was among the ministries that some Jesuits undertook. Recall his descriptions of *hermano* Oyarzún's ministry to ensure that palatable food was served at a hospital for *los dementes*, or that special arrangements were made for mentally troubled Mexican Jesuits, many of whom were cared for at the Colegio Espíritu Santo. Padre Joseph Ignacio Calderon (#31) is among those described as requiring special care.[23] He had been born in Puebla de los Angeles in 1710.

> The great capacity that nature endowed as well as his great desire to take advantage of this to be useful to Religion, was made almost useless by the continuous martyrdom of scruples with which he was tormented all of his life, in such a manner that he was made useless for anything at all, arriving at a point where he lost his judgment. One knew him by his exterior torments, that followed the same suffering, he was always with the most modest posture and completely enclosed within himself (*todo recogido en sí*). In this mode he lived at the Colegio [Espíritu Santo] in Puebla de los Angeles.

The Jesuits struck out for Veracruz, but "following a few days at sea he became sick and surrendered his spirit to the Lord in the Gulf of Mexico, in whose waves he was buried, dying on November 4, 1767."[24]

Padre Joseph Urtasun (#33) is described as "virtuous from the cradle." Urtasun is affable and charitable, but "always suffered with himself (*padeció siempre con sigo mismo*) from scruples that tormented him continuously." From the outside, Sebastián observes, he appeared to be a reserved novice "dedicated to Apostolic Ministry when his strength was sufficient." He had described Arenas as "out of himself." Here he describes Urtasun as "suffering greatly with himself." He, too, died on the passage from Veracruz to Havana and was buried at sea on November 7, 1767. Similarly, Padre Joseph Guerrero (#37) is described as a Jesuit with promise—"gifted with a sharp wit, great talents, and an excellent ability" but also "very timid of conscience and tormented by the martyrdom of scruples,[25] an angelic man in his habits, and a martyr to himself" (*Hombre Ángel en costumbres, y mártir de sí mismo*). He died in Veracruz, "here, tormented by his scruples, anguished, and exteriorly [tormented] by the rigor of the climate, he gave up on life [*dejar de vivir*], dying a holy death on November 12, 1767."

The importance of the determination "holy death" becomes all the more apparent when he notes the unholy death of Padre Francisco Morales (1711–1767).[26] Morales is described as "very humble and of timid conscience." Despite that fact that he was a "prim and fearful subject," he remained "very useful" as a great *operario*. But the arrest horrified him and "his faintheartedness increased." Any time he heard or saw soldiers

> he trembled and went out of himself (*salía fuera de sí*). There are no few examples of [how] his *Compañeros* cheered him and demonstrated fearlessness in the face of these outbursts [in order] to root out the fears that sent him outside of himself. He was taken to the Port of Veracruz where it was determined he was out of himself with such apprehensive foreboding (*fuera de si en aquella tan timida aprehensión*) and his heart so imprinted, he was declared insane.

Havana, it must be noted, is usually described as a terrible stop. "When Jesuits arrived [in Havana] they entered into a rigorous imprisonment in a house until they could be offered passage to Europe. They are surrounded by Soldiers, day and night, and under the care of the most ignorant Commander who made everyone suffer greatly over ordinary matters."[27] Sebastián notes that although his fellow Jesuits assisted Morales "with great care" on the passage to Havana, the arrival on the island took a singular toll on him. Morales is housed at

> the prison of Regla, where all day and night, the house was circled by Soldiers passing word, on guard, as if guarding a fortress with the fear of assault. Seeing the Soldiers continuously and hearing the thunder of the drums, these things made him lose his judgment/mind (*juicio*), he went out of himself (*salió fuera de sí*). Throwing the band of some white breeches around his neck, he suffocated himself, dying this way on March 22, 1768. His corpse was buried at the Hospital of Havana.

When historians write about the expulsion of the Jesuits from New Spain, none have noted these cases of mental anguish and suicide. It is the harrowing trip from Guaymas that is the cause célèbre. Yet Sebastián does not paper over death by suicide; they did not "disappear" from Sebastián's archive.[28] In fact, one might venture to say that those suffering terrible scruples are, indeed, "celebrated," as he described them as enduring martyrdom, a form of suffering that ranks high in the Catholic pantheon of saints. The standard martyr dies for a purpose. But with suicide death is to be explained. So, he describes these cases as men who are "lost" to themselves, so they killed . . . themselves? Consciously or unconsciously, Sebastián handles the vexed problem of their salvation by sketching a scene in which men first disappear before our eyes. Suicide is committed, not by any stable "self," but rather by a ruined shell of a person. And in this, the "ruination" of the mentally ill is not so different from Sebastián's monuments to the ruined lives of many "true" Jesuits who populate his inventory of holy deterioration. Worn down to shells of their former selves, they become "useless."

Monologue: Performing the Dead

As he continues to collect the dead, Sebastián is something of a performance artist who crafts temporary monuments and then stages their disintegration. He puts a time stamp on each appearance—with the names and the dates that mark birth, vows, ordination, and various forms of employment—followed by the story of each Jesuit's denouement, before he moves to deftly stage the next performance of life, disintegration, and death. As Susan Stewart writes so poignantly, ruins "have the singularity of artworks, yet they are severed irredeemably from their contexts of production. . . . They call for an active moving viewer—often a traveler, with a consciousness distinct from that of a local inhabitant—who can restore their missing coordinates and names."[29] Such is Sebastián's creative, artful labor to grapple with ruination in his presentations of the Mexican lives whose truth lies less in the singular coordinates and names, and more in the ongoing descriptions of decay. The result is a layered, multitemporal series comprising "monuments" to different types of Jesuits who had lived and worked in the Mexican Province. The termination of each life provides the momentary "end" that anchors Sebastián's backward glance. But there is no single perch of memory, where we might imagine him looking back to sees all at once. Rather, each death is but a temporary resting place. Sebastián's project is ongoing; he must trail after the next dying man and situate him according to the next "present" moment.

If he never writes from a stated vantage point it is, in part, because for several years there is no fixed place for the Mexican Jesuits. We can imagine him as something of a reporter whose information is gathered at a series of unstable assembly points. These shifting forms of temporary community spring up in a variety of locales: carriages, encampments, boats, mule caravans, makeshift prisons, makeshift housing, makeshift hospitals, and makeshift colleges. By June 1768 the majority of the Mexican Jesuits begin traveling from Cádiz to Corsica, the intended "final" destination, until the Genoese cede the island to the French, provoking the Corsican revolt and the ensuing violence that Jesuits had witnessed shipboard. The Papal States provide the next possible future, and the Mexican Jesuits begin to trickle into Bologna and Ferrara by late 1768. But note that this same summer of 1768 finds the Sonora Jesuits still in New Spain and about to enter the autumn of back-to-back deaths in Aguacatlán and Ystlán.

His subjects are on the move. So is he. And are not the Jesuits known for their mobility? The Jesuits had understood themselves (and promoted themselves) as men on a worldly mission. They were busy, so much so that there would be no monastery to which to return after a long day, there was no hard and fast schedule of prayers to be sung in unison. The world is our home, they insisted. Accordingly, they called themselves "contemplatives in action" and they insisted that God could be found in any of the wide variety of worldly tasks they undertook.[30] So what is unique about this new situation in which they find themselves, again, on the move?

The telos. There isn't one. They are no longer building the Universal Christian Empire once represented by the Horoscopium Catholicum that showed how the sun never set on the Jesuit global order. They have been decisively removed from mission and ministry. Now their Empire is shrinking, one man at a time. Sebastián's *Memorias* offers a new cartography of the Mexican Province as a series of burials stretching across the Atlantic. When they arrive on a smaller stage, the strange new world of the Papal States, they are disoriented, less busy, and finding God in fewer and fewer things. Jesuits remain mobile but now, untethered from the college and

FIGURE 7. Photograph of a painting of Francisco Javier Clavigero, SJ, from Ronan Archive, Courtesy of Loyola University Chicago Archives & Special Collections.

hacienda, and released from enforced proximity shipboard, their ability to gather hits hurdle upon hurdle. Without the reiterative action of place-making, any future-oriented transmission of Jesuit culture becomes a problem for the Jesuits in Italy. Accordingly, we turn next to these descriptions of prior Jesuit mobility that, I argue, form an elegiac retrospective cartography, a nostalgic evocation of the rhythms of the now-lost hustle and bustle of the Mexican Province in New Spain. He is performing endings.

HOW TO LIGHT THE PERFORMANCE OF JESUIT ENDINGS

Sebastián sits at the desk with his back still firmly turned to the audience. Leaning down, he places a piece of coal into the brazier and waits while it heats, rubbing his hands over the tiny blaze.

Then he holds up engravings of individual Jesuits that he has stacked upon his desk. The audience can see the image that he is examining, usually the black-and-white bust of a Jesuit posed in three-quarter view. He examines each man's face, individually, carefully. He puts the image back down on the desk while he takes the time to write notes on his pages.

When he is finished writing, he leans back toward the fire to place the image on the burner. Made of paper, the image curls up quickly along the edges then disappears, making a small flame.

He picks up another image.[31]

Scene II: "True" Monuments—The Ruination of *el Verdadero Jesuita*

The structure of each entry is relatively simple. Sebastián sets up the "good life" and the good ministries that each Jesuit was undertaking. The arrest halts and upends this work. The Jesuit suffers a decline. But not all Jesuits are the same. While Sebastián always finds positive ways to eulogize each dead Jesuit, it is his laudatory adjective—"*verdadero*"—that sets some individuals above others. These monuments to authentic or true Jesuits are further differentiated based upon the individual's rank (*hermano* or *padre*) and the types of ministries in which he engages. There is the *verdadero* Jesuit intellectual who is lauded with descriptors like "erudite" (*docto*), the true Jesuit missionary often called *Apostolic*, and the Jesuit *hermano* or temporal coadjutor who is lauded for his *verdadero hu-*

mildad. But beyond these additional descriptors, these "true Jesuits" all labor tirelessly at "useful" tasks. The authentic Jesuit is indefatigable. This model travels to Bologna and Ferrara, where the *ways* for Jesuits to become an admirably tireless laborer shift, then decline, before diminishing altogether. The model of "true" as "tireless" is pitched against the new reality that, for many, there seems to be nothing very "Jesuit" to do.

Character Study: The Verdadero *Intellectual*

Let us begin with his monuments to tireless Jesuit intellectuals of the Mexican Province. These Jesuits are portrayed as having a certain kind of urban cachet. Every Jesuit went through a rigorous training process that included the study of philosophy and theology, but the ideal-type Jesuit excelled in these topics, while also having a good personality, a strong religious sensibility, and a love of work. In Sebastián's mini-eulogies, Padre Miguel Benfumea (#51) is one such *"verdadero Jesuita"* who is described as having *"un genio vivacissimo"*—his intellect was incredibly vivid. Benfumea's "love of work" is underscored in Sebastián's account of the wide variety of tasks assigned to him, from professor of philosophy and theology to college *operario* and as prefect of various Marian congregations and as minister at the Colegio Máximo. "Tireless in the confessional and at the pulpit," Benfumea was so indefatigable that "it seems that his rest was found in work (*pareciendo en el ser su descanso, el trabajar*)." Benfumea was dedicated to Our Lady of Sorrows, whose devotion he promoted, tirelessly. At the time of the arrest, he was the prefect of the Congregación del Populo (which he notes was also known as Nuestra Señora del Dolores) at the Colegio Espíritu Santo in Puebla. He died on December 4, 1767, in Havana, "the laborious course of his life, crowned by dying with great resignation to Divine Will."[32]

Puebla de los Angeles is "the Patria" (birthplace) of Padre Joaquín Rodriguez Calado (#139), another spiritually and intellectually gifted Jesuit who worked without cease. This *"hombre de costumbres innocentissimas"* is described as having great piety and virtue, and his excellent talents were on display for all his life throughout the Province *en las Cathedras y Púlpitos*. "*Cathedras*" refer to professorships or "chairs" held at Jesuit colleges, and "*púlpitos*" to the pulpits from which they gave sermons. The phrase is often coupled in Sebastián's descriptions of the Jesuit intellectuals who excelled in both teaching and preaching. But Calado's intellectual prowess did not prevent him from being "a charitable operator" who was of service to his neighbors and assisted in the confessional. For Sebastián, the *verdadero* Jesuit intellectual must get his hands dirty—or really, his ears—in hearing the confessions of common people. "Now, in his old age, he continued working, as his strength allowed, when he was arrested." He survived the journey to Bologna, where he lived outside of the city in the town of Castel San Pietro. But in Italy he does not continue working. "Here he lived very *recogido*. He always had a fire going in the chimney because he could not live in another way in a climate so contrary to that in which he had always lived. He commended himself to God, aggravated by the years, the fatigue, and the abandoned houses that were not made for Religious men to inhabit. He became sick and crowned the long course of his life on August 19, 1772." If the afterword is an indication, Sebastián had fond feelings for the man, as he laments the loss of the man who had purity of heart, of words, and of work. Work is crucial. In New Spain, even in old age, his strength allowed him to continue some of his ministries. Not so on the other side. In Italy his task is to stay warm in a house that is, fittingly, an uninhabitable ruin.[33]

"His great potential and his Religiosity made him a true Jesuit." Here Sebastián praises P. Antonio Paredes (#47), a "learned scholar"—*docto en las Cathedras*—who was also "eloquent in the Pulpit, indefatigable in the confessional, and a charitable Superior." He taught, wrote, and governed the Mexican Province, and, as Sebastián attests, in all he was loved by the Jesuits. "He was always hardworking." He also founded a *beaterio de las Teresas* in Querétaro, which Sebastián described as an "exemplar of sanctity and a reliquary of virgins." At the time of the arrest, he was slowing down. "Already old, he worked with the vigor of a Youth" hearing confessions at the Colegio de San Andrés in Mexico City, where he also wrote "learned and holy instructions for devout souls." He died in Veracruz, "consoled in the Lord while dying in a prison."[34] At San Andrés, Paredes had likely been hearing confessions for the laity who made the Spiritual Exercises at the Casa de Ejercicios at San Andrés. There he would have been working with Padre Agustín Márquez (#99), who also had excelled at the sciences but "refused" this path. Márquez chose instead to work at Colegio San Gregorio, the Jesuit college dedicated to the education of sons of elite indigenous leaders or, "that downtrodden nation (*aquella abatida nación*)" as Sebastián notes here.

"I can say"—here Sebastián breaks into the text—"without exaggerating anything" (tacit admission that he exaggerates everything?) "that he was the epitome, the model of Christian and Religious perfection." Márquez's life is a monument to those who *could* have had a life as a theologian and preacher but, Sebastián implies, he made the holier choice of devout simplicity: "His room was dedicated to devotion and poverty, with only some paper prints and a crucifix to adorn it." His résumé includes ministries to Mexico City's Indians, the opening of a house near the Casa Profesa to care for those afflicted by the *peste* that hit Mexico City in 1762, the promotion of devotion to the Santíssima Madre de la Luz, and the retreats he ran for the laity at the Casa de Ejercicios, which he had begun to expand in 1767.[35] "When he was arrested the fruit [of his labor] was also arrested." Upon arriving in Havana, he received "the poor treatment that was common to those who put their feet on that Island." He withstood the journey to Spain but arrived sick and destitute of strength. *Destituto de fuerzas* is a phrase that will become common in Sebastián's accounts of Jesuits who survive overseas travels but arrive completely spent. With no "fruit" to cultivate, the trope of the "tireless" worker beings to lose its tight focus. Where does one put this energy, if one has any? This is not a question for Márquez, as he has none. Depleted, he is sent to the prison hospital at the Puerto de Santa María, but as he lay dying, many of the Jesuit prisoners note his suffering and "put to work" to sing to him the *Stabat Mater* as he died.[36]

In Act I we met one of these tireless (*incansable*) workers or more precisely, we encountered the things on his desk. Padre Francisco Aramburu (#100), born in Puebla in 1706, had spent most of his life in that city where he taught philosophy and theology, became minister of the College of Espíritu Santo, was an instructor for those who came to make the Spiritual Exercises, and ultimately was the prefect. Sebastián weighs this busy subject down with adjectives: prudent, affable, charitable, humble, most obsequious, and a good director of souls. "He was given all the gifts that could be desired in a Wise Religious Jesuit." As we saw in the first chapter, Aramburu was devoted to Madre Santísima de la Luz. Sebastián confirms that he wrote various novenas for her fiesta that were "filled with a fervor to make known his hidden love for the Mother of God." Following an arduous journey over sea and land, he arrives at the Papal State of Ferrara "sick, unable to find any relief for his ruination (*su estragado*). Aramburu's death is the first occasion that Sebastián uses the word "ruination." He died on February 5, 1769, his cadaver buried in the Colegio de Jesús in Bologna.[37]

Character Study: The Verdadero Missionary

The second type of Jesuit ceaseless indefatigability is found in Sebastián's monuments to the *verdadero* Jesuit missionary, an ideal type modeled upon the frenetic pace established in the sixteenth century by Francis Xavier.[38] Padre Joseph Iranzo (#49) served in the Tarahumara region at a mission "in the high and lofty Sierra Madre" where often there was insufficient food to sustain the population. When provisions dwindled, the mission's indigenous inhabitants "easily absented themselves." Sebastián depicts Iranzo's rugged life, in which he traversed the ravines of the Sierra Madre

> cutting wood and making *carbón* (coal) which he sent to the Reales de Minas (the mining camps) where he sold it, and with the proceeds bought maís and some clothing to assist his flock. He reduced a good number of the gentile families that were scattered through those *barrancos*, in little time he already had baptized sixty families, and grouped them into a town (*hecholes un pueblo*) where he cared for them with great tenderness.

The word *reducido* in the Spanish Catholic colonial context is a complex term indicating "civilized living" whose definition includes a spatial semantics specifying something well-ordered or properly arranged, whether referring to the logic of an urban grid, a mission station, or that of a well-structured grammar (i.e., a language "reduced").[39] When Sebastián says *hecholes un pueblo* he means that they were formed and shaped, that is, "civilized" by living in the structured town and thus made into a "people" on recognizably Spanish Catholic ground. Sebastián is impressed by Iranzo's heroic labor but also laments its ultimate futility because Iranzo's reaction to the arrest is described not only in terms of the "long and dangerous trip across the vast continent with such great sufferings" but also expressing missionary anxiety about "the pain of seeing his Neophytes forsaken, those who [will] so easily return to their *gentilidad* (their gentile ways)." In his view, the Jesuit civilizing mission is soon to fall into ruin. Yet Iranzo's own "super missionary" status endures in the description of his death. He died on board the ship from Veracruz to Havana "commending his spirit to his creator in the Gulf of Mexico, the same day that the Apostle of the Indies S. Francisco Xavier died on the Beaches of Sanchón (Shangchuan), on December 2, 1767." Unlike Xavier's remains, which are preserved in the Basilica de Bom Jesus in Goa, Iranzo's cadaver was "thrown into the waves of the sea."[40]

"His spirit was so joyful," Sebastián says of the "*fervorissimo*" Padre Bartholome Braun (#53) when he learned that he would be a Tarahumara missionary. At the Mission of Temotzachic, he learned "that barbarous language" to dedicate himself "to the instruction of the natives" who loved him like "a true Father." "The fatigue of working to produce fruit in those uncultivated lands was infinite." He had been rector and visitor to the Tarahumara region and with his "great devotion, great labor, great affability in his business dealings, great humility and great charity" he was *un verdadero misionero*. After the arrest he was "conducted through all of America" but died while crossing the Gulf of Mexico and was also buried at sea on December 5, 1767, missing Xavier's feast day by just a few days. The "joy of living among the barbarous Indians" is a theme that Sebastián used to great effect in his description of Padre Manuel Clever (#54).[41] Clever died on December 8, 1767, but the never-ending joy of infinite labor was imprinted upon the body of this "*grande Jesuita*." Sebastián gives voice to a sailor who declaimed that he had never before seen such a holy priest, as the cheerful visage on Clever's cadaver called the attention of all on board.

The ideal missionary is not always the priest who roams the remote *barrancos* of the Sierra Madre. Life in Mexico City could also be called "an uninterrupted Mission," which is how Sebastián describes the tireless labor of P. Miguel Castillo (#55). Castillo "began his course in philosophy "in obedience"—that is, he did as he was told by his superiors, but at the first opportunity renounced all the honors of the *Cathedras* to apply all of his talents to apostolic ministry with "the poor and unhappy," first in Parral, then in Mexico City. "He was such a holy man that the Archbishop Manuel Rubio y Salinas kissed his hands. Died on Dec 12."[42] Here we can see that while Sebastián conceives of all Jesuits as tireless workers, he applauds Jesuits like Castillo (and earlier, Márquez) for choosing "humility" over theology and philosophy.

The bias in Sebastián's account in favor of the *verdadero* Apostolic missionary no doubt resides in the fact that this category applies to him. He signs the title page of the *Memorias* "José Felix de Sebastián, of this same Province, Missionary of the Tubára Nation." Although he was born in Spain, his primary loyalty is to the Mexican Province, and the labor of memorialization reinforces this identity. While he rarely positions himself as an eyewitness, he does so in writing about the ruination of Padre Pedro Diez (#89). After noting the place and date of Padre Diez's death, Sebastián makes an uncharacteristic move. His voice breaks through and, in first person, he pushes past the death date and continues his prose:

> This was the life of P. Pedro Diez, told here in compendium. If I were to innumerate all of his virtues, this would be very extended, as I have been his *concurrente* for some years, walking in his Company more than 300 leagues into the interior of America. I conserve vividly in my memory his angelic life, of great edification to mine. Unattached to the things of this world and given to know the interior castle in which he had to make, [understanding] that he was soon going to move to heaven.

All at once, it seems, the structure he set up for himself proves inadequate to properly mourn the death of his friend, Diez, who had died with the Sonora junket at Ystlán on Sept 14, 1768. Sebastián goes on to relate that when Diez was selected to be a missionary, his expression of great joy "edified everyone." We have already seen that the *verdadero* apostolic missionary wears his joy for all to see. But Sebastián's close friendship with Diez enables him to render this missionary's humanity with some additional strokes of the pen. Notably, he puts some chinks in the armor of missionary bravado when he describes Diez' feelings about the assignment: "His scruples together with his weakness of health were enough to terrify him."[43] The model proves inadequate to the task of accounting for a missionary's fear when taking on a "monumental" lifestyle.

The intrusion of Sebastián's first-person perspective is momentary, but from this point forward, the "afterword" becomes a device that Sebastián draws upon occasionally to add some details, likely about someone he knew well.[44]

Character Study: The Verdadero Hermano

In stark contrast to the labors of the erudite fourth-vow urban intellectuals and the restless missionary, the *hermano* or brother is lauded for taking up menial tasks with profound humility. The *hermano* is a special grade of Jesuit called *coadjutor temporal*, a member of the Society of Jesus who did not take final vows. While he could teach, the brother most often ranked among those tasked with the occupations of cook, nurse, or doorman. In New Spain, *hermanos* frequently ran the botanicas. Many had arrived at their vocation later in life, having been "secular" for much of their lives and usually not schooled in Jesuit institutions. Many had been born outside of the Spanish empire, as was the Bavarian Juan Laudner (#48), who is described as having undertaken "the tasks of his status with true humility." Hermano Francisco Villar (#52) had been born in France and came to New Spain "secular." He is noted to have been "a very obedient subject who worked in the ministries of his status with great punctuality." When he landed in Havana, he promptly "leapt to the ground to serve with great tenderness" the many Jesuits who were detained in what now is always described as the "rigorous" Casa de Regla. Similarly, Hermano Antonio Urroz (#94) is extolled for a "very particular virtue that always shone in him, namely, the Holy Humility with which he always served, quickly and willingly in the work of his grade."[45] The birthplace of Hermano Manuel Sánchez (#117) is left blank. He had overseen the dispensary at the Colegio de Zacatecas, and a sense of duty follows this "true" Jesuit coadjutor across the Atlantic. In Ferrara he served as a cook in one of the Jesuits' houses before he was sent to Bologna to serve at a house functioning as a makeshift hospital.[46] Finally, as we have seen in Act I, to be a hacienda administrator was among the "exercises" or tasks appropriate to the coadjutor's "station" in the Society. Shortly, we will examine how Sebastián describes this class of Jesuit when, about fifteen years after the expulsion, the hacienda administrator emerges as an important model for men living outside of the routines of the Jesuit college. For now, it suffices to say that Sebastián's many references to the humility of the coadjutor indicate that a *verdadero hermano* accepted his "humble" place on the totem pole.

Character Study: Angelic Youth and True Mothers

It must have been difficult for Sebastián to watch so many young men roughly his own age die. Perhaps that is why he shaped some of his monuments into angels. The "angelic youth" appears with greater frequency as he memorializes the lives of young men who die in Italy. "*El Inocentisimo*" Padre Ramon Rivero (#102) was born in 1731, roughly contemporary to Sebastián—did he know him? Rivero lived in a shack in Ferrara, so he was glad when the plans came about for young men to live together in a large house that functioned as a makeshift college. But he did not have that chance. He became sick with an unknown illness "because he knew no doctors and did not have a bed." The day before he died, he called upon everyone "in their diverse houses of said City" to say his goodbyes.[47]

Padre Ygnacio Fano (#123) had been born in Cantabria, Spain, in 1743. He was in his third year as a novice at San Ildephonso in Puebla at the time of the arrest, and he is likely among the novices that Thjülen so admired for their decision to leave home to remain with the exiled men of the Mexican Province. Fano was ordained in Italy, but this "angelic youth" became ill just as he began to study theology in a house outside the walls of Bologna, another of the makeshift institutions meant to imitate the college structure considered key to shaping young Jesuits and maintaining Jesuit identity more broadly. Sebastián often sounds a note of dismay about a lost future, as in the case of the young scholar named Hermano Joseph Barragan (#140). He died of typhus (*tabardillo*) in Italy at the age of twenty-three. He had been very happy, Sebastián writes, studying in Italy and had great promise in sacred theology. He adds an afterword, stating that Barragan's death was premature and as such was felt deeply by those who saw him as having great promise.[48]

The categories of *verdadero* exemplarity continue to expand. The angelic exiled youth needed a "*verdadero madre*." Padre Dionisyo Perez (#143) had been just such a true mother, first for those studying at the Colegio Máximo. Dionisyo is lauded for ensuring that his children lacked for nothing. He continued to care for them "on the long navigation and the disastrous land voyages, and he cared for the young at Castel San Pietro, later in Bologna, making sure they would live, as they had lived, with great regularity, as in the colleges of the Province." This monument to the *verdadero madre* is brought down by a slow fever that he could not kick, despite a trip to Ravenna to recuperate. He died on December 2, 1772. There is a brief afterword: "His death was mourned by everyone, because lost in him was a charitable superior, and Angel of Peace, a Saint, and a *verdadero* Jesuit."[49]

We can see that life in Italy is changing the shapes of these monuments. As they settle into Bologna and Ferrara, they remain "tireless." Yet Jesuits are no longer ministering to others; they minister to themselves. The model Jesuit becomes the man who scrambles to keep the Mexican Province together in the face of great difficulty. Joseph Luis Aguirre (#115) had been rector at the Colegio de Guanajuato and now, in Ferrara, he was chosen to be Rector in "of one of the houses" where he worked to "find as much relief as he could" for the small scattered groups of exiles who lived in community.[50] Consoling other Jesuits is a task that Sebastián foregrounds, including Padre Vicente Gomez (#126) who is "*exemplarissimo*" (his Italian is creeping in now) for his hard work at Colegio San Xavier for indigenous elites in Puebla. Because he spoke the Mexican language, he was from the start useful in a college described as "*laborosissimo*" (another bit of Italian). In Italy he lived in a town outside of Bologna, called Castel de Bologna, where his labor entailed consoling the Mexican Jesuits, "alleviating them of the heavy weight of this terrible exile however he could."[51] Some Jesuits are trying to keep the ship afloat, with the makeshift communities, but for many others, there is just not as much to do any longer but pray and visit sick and ailing Jesuits. This is what an older Jesuit might have done in his retirement. The shift is subtle but noticeable: *All* the Mexican Jesuits who had once thought of themselves as "contemplatives in action" are described as having more time for "contemplation" than "action."

In Italy, Sebastián's deployment of the "afterword" becomes more frequent. He reaches for it again when describing the life and death of Padre Juan de Urrutia (#144), another young Jesuit who died at age of thirty-two. He had studied "science" at Colegio Ildephonso in Puebla de los Angeles, and then sacred theology at Colegio Máximo. In Bologna he "was completely occupied in serious studies" and would have ranked among the monuments to the Jesuit intellectual, had the Mexican Province remained intact. Instead, he is worn down and ruined by a fever (*calentura etica* [*hetica*]) that "little by little consumed him." In the brief afterword, Sebastián remarks in the first person: "This was the life of P. Urrutia written in brief, but his virtues require greater extension. He was a subject in whom there was never observed any fault. He always lived very loving of his Religion and his vocation. He had great talent but never vanity." He ends by saying that he was a *verdadero Joven Jesuita*—a true Jesuit youth—in whom there had been high hopes for the good of the Province."[52] Urrutía died in December, the last death commemorated in 1772. Sebastián's phrasing suggests that the Mexican Jesuits are watching their hopes dwindle as each Jesuit dies in exile, especially the young. The year 1773 would quash remaining aspirations, when Pope Clement XIV issued his papal brief announcing the end of the Society of Jesus.[53]

Sebastián refers to the *Breve de Abolición* in recounting the life and death of Padre Joseph Neve (#151) in October 1773. We know the story of the Sonora Jesuits in some detail already and usually Sebastián does not repeat the story in full. But in Neve's memorial, Sebastián restates each stop of the journey. Why does he repeat this? Quite likely he is ruminating on the total ruin of the Society of Jesus via this paradigmatic story of "martyrdom" by migration. Notably, he is not yet using the term "suppression" and will not for several years. Neve's is the first death that he is recording since hearing the Papal decree of July 1773. Sebastián describes how Padre Neve, sick and a prisoner at Puerto de Santa María, heard the terrible news that the Pope had dissolved the Society of Jesus from "an imprudent Royal Commissioner, believing himself heroic, barbarously announced this to the dying, while removing the Soutane that [P. Neve] kept draped over his bed." This is the death knell for Neve, who died of "this major pain" on October 24, 1773."[54]

Sebastián's own distress about the abolition of the Society becomes poignantly palpable when recording the death of Padre Salvador de la Zandara (#153), the Provincial of the Mexican Province at the time of the arrest. His is the last death to be entered into the *Memorias* for the year 1773. As we have seen, Sebastián occasionally puts a more personalized word in at the end of an entry. But here he is unable to suppress a brief outcry in the middle of his account. Sebastián is describing how Zandara was visiting Querétaro at the time of the arrest and had been escorted to Veracruz along with those fathers. Here Sebastián's voice interjects: "*I need here all of his great virtue not to falter under this great blow.*" The Mexican Province, shuffling along, already so broken, is now hit by a disastrous shock and, clearly, Sebastián is reliving the "first blow" in his re-telling of the arrest and expulsion of Zandara: "He watched a good number of his subjects die in Veracruz, treated like prisoners, disconsolate in the terrible climate." But he also lauds Zandara as a model of adaptation given his efforts to ensure that members of the Mexican Province would maintain a semblance of normalcy in exile. He describes how Zandara scrambled in Bologna "to congregate the young Jesuits in a Palace where they could follow with some formality their studies and be ordained priests. He wrote letters to everyone, consoling them and exhorting them to keep their Religious observances." Zandara's entry solidifies what we have noticed: These new monuments memorialize a novel form of tireless struggle to keep the members of the Mexican Province connected to one another in exile.

But Zandara was retired when he died and had passed the job of Provincial to another Jesuit before moving to a house in Bologna where "he was totally united with God in prayer when he received the last and most terrible (*sensible*) blow, which was the Abolition. This unthinkable, cruel work was such that he completely surrendered to it. At the point of feeling sick, and no longer able to resist the illness, he took to the bed, where even though assisted with much charity, he was being consumed."

Sebastián recalls Zandara's simple explanation for the events of 1767 to his *compañeros*: "We are in a time of suffering. God wants it so. Let it be his Divine Will."[55] To bear witness to this ruination, Sebastián ventriloquizes the ghost of Zandara to remind—his readers? himself?—that this is *holy* ruination. And here we see most clearly that marking death is a spiritual exercise: He is recording and meditating upon one man's exemplary past to understand and accept his own present. Writing, at this moment, constitutes his own struggle for resignation.

Monologue: Thinking about Ruins

Ruins are inherently full of tension, contradiction, as the worn down and useless are now valued and maintained *as broken*. Part of their beauty, Stewart points out, resides in a cathartic "indulgence in pain." We know so little about Felix de Sebastián that to say that in his writing he explores and laments suffering is not to offer any insight into the man or how he lived day to day. Yet it is clear that Sebastián's pained labor is to describe with precision something he thought beautiful, both in its original, as well as in its lamentable decay. The Society is important to him, but his *ekphrasis*—a painting in words—makes clear that curating the Mexican Province is his task. He is not (just) creating an archive; rather, he is engaged in a struggle for intelligibility that has its own aesthetic rhythm, one that he attempts to hold steady in the face of an indeterminate future.

Stewart also refers to ruins as boundary objects or "syncretic phenomena." She argues that their very appearance depends on an act of translation between the past and the present, "between those who have vanished and those who have survived." What we see next is how the Mexican Jesuits navigate Bologna as a contact zone between cultures, but also between past and present. But we discover that securing a place in Sebastián's artful inventory of ruins is in no way guaranteed. Indeed, there are some Mexican Jesuits whom he does not memorialize. Instead, he performs a disappearing act.

Scene III: Off the Page—Bologna

There is much about Jesuit life in Bologna to which Sebastián's *Memorias* alludes briefly or never mentions. For example, it is sometimes difficult to gather from Sebastián's accounts just how fully abandoned are the Jesuits. He never describes the Mexican Jesuits as stunned, after their arduous journeys, to stagger into Bologna and find the Italian Jesuits so very unhelpful. This view comes from the pen of the Spanish Jesuit diarist, Manuel Luengo, who notes how assiduously the Bologna Jesuits ignore the bedraggled Spanish and American Jesuits. Apart from two Italian Jesuit coadjutors who share some advice about where to live, the Bologna Jesuits share neither funds nor facilities.

Death is a topic that vitally concerns Sebastián, so it is surprising that he never hints that members of the Mexican Province receive no assistance from the Italian Jesuits when it comes to burying their dead. If we rely upon Luengo's reports, the Italians never speak to them: "It is a quite singular thing that none of them greet us, ask us where we come from and what we are looking for, they don't speak a single word." In contrast, Luengo notes that the Franciscans from "la Abadía" (the Abbey of San Stefano) are welcoming and that the Jesuits hear Mass there, but that the local archbishop, Malvezzi, a man who "serves the Bourbon court," is accordingly "committed to our mortification."[56] Even the Jesuit General, Lorenzo Ricci, tacitly endorses Italian Jesuit standoffishness when he points toward the surrounding countryside, suggesting that the Mexican exiles not seek housing in central Bologna. Sebastián does not comment upon the Jesuits exiled from other provinces, neither those from other American Provinces, nor from the Iberian Peninsula.[57] Sebastián is not a descriptive ethnographer.[58] His task remains narrowly confined to describing the exemplary lives and (not all of) the deaths of the men who served in the Mexican Province.

The exiles arrive sick, tired, and with a limited income. The Crown pays a pension to each Jesuit individually and continues payments to those who secularize, that is, those who choose to leave the Society, as many were pressured to do between 1767 and 1773. The problems with the pension are numerous. First, the Jesuits are paid in Spanish currency, which is on the losing end of the exchange rate. They receive between sixty-five and seventy-five pesos per each hundred granted. Meanwhile, the locals, hearing rumors of Jesuit "treasure," raise the prices on room and board, asserting that there is a "tariff for foreigners" to be added to the rents. The Jesuits need to earn extra money. Some families send money from New Spain, or sometimes funds are collected and sent from New Spain but distributed only among Jesuits who did not leave the order. After the Society of Jesus is dissolved in 1773, many take positions as tutors. They are in fact never financially secure and send letters to Spanish officials requesting that the pension be augmented, or that they be allowed to live in larger communities to offset costs.[59] But Sebastián never discusses the "hustle." When he does refer to their impoverished condition, this is largely to laud an ex-Jesuit for enduring such circumstances with grace.

By 1773 Sebastián has accounted for 153 of the dead. Here, as we step away from the pages of Sebastián's *Memorias* to examine some pages written by his contemporaries, we learn that Sebastián has not, in fact, been collecting the deaths of *every* man who served in the Mexican Province. In his study of the "work" that the dead do for the living, Thomas Lacquer notes that naming the dead keeps them among us, and that "to become nameless, to lose that by which the dead were known among the living, is a profound and deep kind of death: mortality in flesh and in memory."[60] So, who deserves to be erased?

Sebastián excludes those Jesuits who have "secularized," that is, those who in the aftermath of the expulsion chose to leave the order. Recall how Thjülen registered utter dismay upon seeing his confrere's soutane hung on the peg of the wall. Sebastián registers his dismay by excluding the secularized from among his monuments, his silence a ringing indictment of the men who had left the Society.[61] He is vocal, however, about those who refused an opportunity to leave. A case in point is Padre Gabriel Viedma

(#242, 1741–1782) whose plans for ordination were derailed by the arrest in 1767. He was among those eventually ordained in Bertinoro, Italy. Sebastián writes that Viedma had a "European uncle" who offered a "pathetic" example by leaving "the Religion" (that is, the Society of Jesus). The uncle invited Viedma to make a life with him in Rome, and made "fantastic promises and offering conveniences, to which he Religiously responded that he would not abandon the road upon which he had commenced for any goods of this earth."[62] Suicide is regarded with compassion, but secularization is a kind of self-inflicted death that excludes one from the necrocommunity that is taking shape in the pages of Sebastián's manuscript.

Scene IV: Displaced, or the Jesuit "College" in a New World

In Act I, we saw how the Jesuit college in New Spain served as a dense and busy hub within a local, transregional, and, ultimately, global Jesuit network. Functioning as networked launch pads, each man's assignment was associated with a college, a hub that was, in turn, linked to their neighbors, Jesuit churches, confraternities, jails, haciendas and distant mission stations. The college hub-and-spoke system had been central to the Jesuit way of proceeding. According to the Jesuit Miguel Venegas, an eighteenth-century historian for the Mexican Province, the system provided uniformity. Apart from some "accidental differences in style," he noted that Jesuit colleges were similar around the world and no matter where a Jesuit was assigned, he could easily orient himself.[63] But the Mexican Jesuits were not integrated into the Italian colleges. After the expulsion, the only Mexican Jesuits who lived in a college were the handful of sick and infirm men who never left New Spain and were imprisoned at the now empty Colegio Espíritu Santo.[64]

Sebastián's accounts do give a palpable sense of how, against ongoing disintegration, the men of the Mexican Province attempt to anchor themselves in a routine that approximates how space and place had once structured their lives in New Spain.[65] When they first arrived in Italy, the Mexican Jesuits scramble to find any available housing, for which they are gouged, paying higher rates due to the ongoing rumors about the great wealth of the Jesuits. At first, they rent homes in the rural areas surrounding Bologna. In 1770, the Mexican Jesuits produce a census that

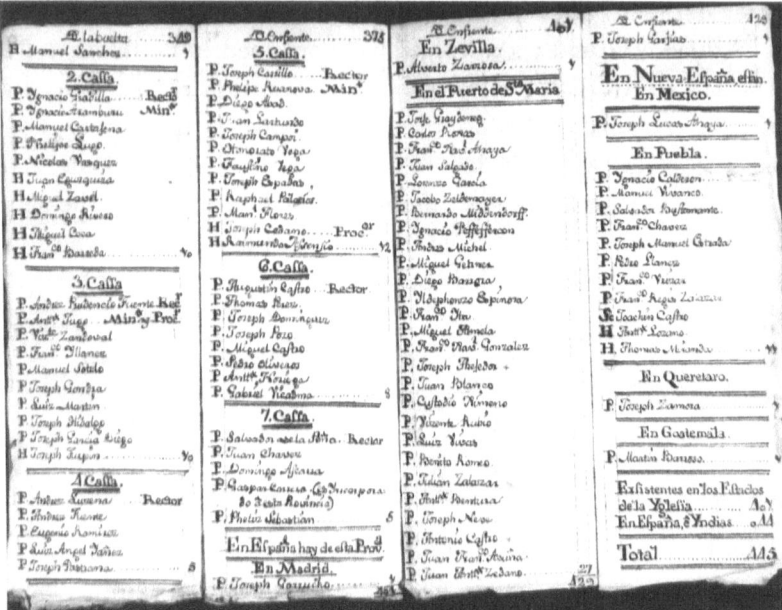

FIGURE 8. 1771 census of Mexican Jesuits in Bologna. This page shows Felix de Sebastián residing in "Casa 7." Courtesy of Loyola University Chicago Archives & Special Collections.

notes where their members reside, who has died, and who has secularized. This list indicates that although some Jesuits are housed in the surrounding countryside, by 1770 the majority have moved to houses inside or just outside the city walls of Bologna and Ferrara. In this way, they replicate a key aspect of their former lifestyle as men who lived and worked largely in urban centers. But they do not have a college and the absence is glaring.

In the scramble to recreate a semblance of past order, the results are as frenetic as the efforts. There are ten houses in Bologna and another seven in Ferrara. In these houses they mimic the college system: Each house has a rector, a minister, and a procurator.[66] One of the houses serves as a hospital, and the census notes that it is served by a doctor, a surgeon, and a pharmacy. The Spaniards are their literal neighbors, and the different Provinces are housed separately, except for the special case of two Mexican Jesuits, Eligio Fernández and Ignacio Maldonado, who are studying mathematics "with Padres from another Province" at a house in Castel Forli.[67] It is unclear whether the two Mexicans are with Jesuits from other American provinces or if they are studying with peninsular Jesuits.

We can see this effort to achieve a sense of normalcy in Sebastián's memorial of a man who was a Master of Theology. After concluding his description of the life *"en la América"* of P. Francisco Xavier Rodriguez (#359), Sebastián pivots to describe "the painful, and in these circumstances, laborious job of Master of Theology for our youth, who were divided into various houses that had been rented, to continue on the scholastic paths upon which they had commenced. From here he passed with all the school to a house in the country half a league distant from Bologna." The villa had been built for elites who escaped the heat of the summer; it was poorly equipped for the winters that Sebastián continually complains about as very harsh. "With everyone suffering a thousand inconveniences on top of the rigors of the seasons, [Rodriguez] continued this work, until the last year of the existence of the Religion, when he came with everyone to the City of Bologna."[68]

Sebastián's description of the life and death of Padre Vicente Rothea (#361) offers another example of how the Jesuits scrambled to recreate a sense of emplaced identity. In Puebla, as minister, Rothea had always paid special attention to the sick who had been sent to convalesce at the Colegio Espíritu Santo. He was also attentive to the servants and workers, a rare mention of those who worked for the Jesuits. "Just as our Padre Vicente proceeded in America, so he did in Italy." Sebastián's swift pivot simultaneously acknowledges and sweeps away the past in one fell swoop. Now, in Bologna, Rothea is the superior at a rented house that serves as a makeshift hospital, but he sounds more like a nurse attending the sick and then a servant in the kitchens, who is lauded for devising appetizing meals that alleviated some of the suffering of the sick. Sebastián writes, "Many gave their lives in his arms; he accompanied the deaths of each one with tenderness, and each one who died snatched a little piece of his heart."[69] From the Bologna infirmary, Rothea was sent to Ferrara to serve as the superior in a "large community," also located in a rented house. His task was to keep a rickety ship afloat: "[The Jesuits] found themselves in a foreign country, disconsolate and full of anxiety, and with little income, barely enough to eat poorly. The charitable Rector gave everything, although he was not able to assist them as would be the wish of his liberal heart, rather, he procured for each one according to his precise scarcity. He saw that the House was well arranged and devout, as if it had been a well-stocked college from the Province."

This is a rare moment when Sebastián openly acknowledges their dire situation, one that only gets worse with the abolition of the Society of Jesus. After "seeing his Religion destroyed" in 1773, Rothea moves back to Bologna to live with his two brothers (Pedro and José) where he continued to visit the sick "for the next twenty years." That he glosses over a twenty-year period in Rothea's life as one long bout of visiting the sick is telling. The lack of description indicates that after the dismantling of the Society, the semblance of order that the Mexican Jesuits had created in Bologna and Ferrara is disintegrating. Now instead of an expansive Jesuit network, they have been reduced to a few houses that are very *unlike* the colleges, with the occasional "hospital" as an annex.

In the first years after what Sebastián continues to note as the "abolition" or the "extinction," the ex-Jesuits continue to live in small groups of six or ten, but also sometimes on their own, renting rooms with local families. Some ex-Jesuits remain in the Papal States; some move to Rome. But in 1775 the Spanish Crown moves to extinguish any remnants of Jesuit corporate identity. Groups of men larger than three persons could not live together. Older men cannot live with and train the younger men. There will be no transmission of Jesuit culture. This decree is a blow to men who have scrambled to ground collective morale in this semblance of college life. It also hits hard on the pocketbook. Once again, they are compelled to move, but now from houses for which they have paid rents months in advance. The decree is enforced with the threat that they will lose their pensions if they do not comply.[70] Sebastián does not describe how some men had more time to work on a variety of academic projects and how, in the years after the Suppression, they made use of Ibero-American intellectual networks to do so.[71] Rather, the accumulated details in Sebastián's account add up to a scene in which the men are becoming closed in upon themselves. Once connected to a dense local network of men and women that kept them busy, by Sebastián's account, there is no longer any corporate entity whatsoever.

Scene V: The Hacienda, Another Model

Now that the ex-Jesuits are prohibited from living communally, the college is no longer a viable organizational model for the Mexican Province. It cannot be a coincidence that, soon after the Suppression, Sebastián expands his descriptions of Jesuits who had worked as hacienda administrators in New Spain. In these idealized accounts, Sebastián mentions, but minimizes, the administrator's role as an overseer of free and enslaved laborers who worked on farms, ranches, or sugar haciendas. Rather, he details how, in the absence of the Jesuit college, the hacienda administrator had conducted himself *as if* living in a Jesuit college. An example is Hermano Thadeo Rosales (#64), who was born in Chalco and, like a good brother, "worked hard in the exercises of his state and with great edification to the Province, being truly obedient, and prompt when ordered by obedience." Rosales had been the administrator of many different haciendas, and his ability to care for some of these properties, Sebastián notes, "in no way diminished his being a true Religious."[72] In other words, the life of a hacienda administrator offers a model for what it is to live a religious life outside of college routines.

As we saw in Act I, the hacienda administrator's life was lived largely among laypeople, which had been a source of concern for Jesuits whose assignments took them away from the rhythms of life at the Jesuit college. We saw how the eighteenth-century anonymous manuscript titled the "Instructions that the Brothers Administrators of the Haciendas Must Observe" had been written precisely with this issue in mind. In this directive the hacienda comes into focus not only as an extractive economic institution, but also as one that was tied to an individual Jesuit's devotional life.[73] At the hacienda—and "there more than in other places"—administrators needed to demonstrate that they are "true religious men in the fervor of their spirits and in their observances." On the hacienda, there is no superior to keep a watchful eye, no bell to call him, no visitor to keep a record, no eyes that observe, nor censors that note the life of "*un religioso campista*"—a country Jesuit, who must (in a small twist on the Jesuit phrase "God in all things") demonstrate that God is present *everywhere (en todo lugar)*.[74]

These aspects come through quite clearly in Sebastián's descriptions of the ideal hacienda administrator, *hermano* Francisco Xavier Yarza (#68):

> He lived for many years as Administrator at the Hacienda de San Geronimo that belonged to the Colegio del Espíritu Santo of Puebla, and here he always comported himself as if he were a Novice. His house was like a very tightly run College, to the edification of all of the domestic workers, who venerated him, each one, as if he were a Saint. He

never felt diminished by the variety of tasks he had, rather he embarked upon them with great novitiate fervor. Continually in prayer and meditation, he procured that he was always in the presence of God, which was evident in his comportment and his dealings.[75]

This new monument to the hacienda Administrator who lives "as if" at a Jesuit college is unambiguous in the obituary of Hermano Miguel Sabel (#158).[76] He had been a merchant in Cádiz, Spain, but after arriving in New Spain, he "renounced what he possessed and all of his worldly hopes to embrace the Cross of Jesus Christ." Like most Jesuits who came to a vocation later in life, he was admitted as temporal coadjutor. His business savvy was put to good use in administering the Hacienda de Chicomozelo, which he did for the remainder of his life *"en la América."* In describing Sabel's spiritual life on the hacienda, Sebastián appears to rip a page straight out of the eighteenth-century directive.[77] As Sebastián notes: "In the countryside, he ran a schedule as tight as that of the most observant college." Sebastián extolls him in the same way he does other monuments to life as a coadjutor, that is, he has "singular modesty" and "profound humility." And yet, in his life as a Jesuit hacienda administrator, the Jesuit "brother" transcends his humble status because his duties are described as like that of the Rector who runs a Jesuit college. He models the way one can manage one's spiritual life while living away from the tempos of the Jesuit college.

> He woke up early every morning and immediately fell to his knees before the crucifix, and the Holy Virgin Maria where he had his hour of prayer, when finished he passed to the Chapel to assist in the Mass given by an elderly Padre, once that was finished, he went to undertake the work of his Office. All the workers and persons who depended on him venerated him, and without ever getting upset by their occasional faults, he rebuked them with such love and charity that they obeyed him happily and without fear of punishment.

These last words about his relationship with his laborers and dependents, again, echo the guide for running a hacienda, wherein the ideal administrator is a patriarchal figure who never punishes his subordinates in anger. Sebastián describes Sabel as caring for an older Jesuit who "retired" and lived in the hacienda. "There a great silence was observed, and a great punctuality in all of the schedule (*distribuciones*)." He is exemplary for diligently examining his conscience and never neglecting his spiritual reading. He repeats more than once that the house resembled a very observant college more than a country house. He returned every year to the Colegio Máximo in Mexico City to make the Spiritual Exercises "and in this time he was always akin to a very devout (*recogido*) novice." In Ferrara, he remained an exemplar of virtue, for everyone. He continued as soon as he regained his strength, to give everything to prayer, meditation, and reading, the rest of the time he passed in the churches, whenever he could, but an obstinate sciatica detained his steps. When the fatal blow of the abolition fell, he remained "unchanged but in clothing" and continued to follow "his accustomed tenor of a holy life."[78] Sabel died on September 5, 1774, a model of how to remain true to the Order when distant from the tempos that had structured life at the Jesuit college.[79]

These models of hacienda administrators become more prominent in the years after 1775, the year that the Crown prohibited ex-Jesuits from living with one another in groups larger than three. The hacienda administrator seems to have served as an example of virtuous maintenance of the Society's precepts. When we looked at the guide for hacienda administrators in Act I, we saw how the overextended Jesuit used charts and lists to manage his very busy schedule. In contrast, the *Memorias* emphasizes the hacienda as a place of contemplation more than tireless action. Hermano Pedro Sobrino (#187) worked as procurator and caretaker for the haciendas that belonged to the novitiate at the College of Tepotzotlán. The haciendas flourished under his care, and he was able to remodel the church magnificently. Sebastián states clearly that his religious schedule "was never interrupted by his tasks as an administrator." He was, Sebastián writes, "like a holy novice." "The people who served him at the hacienda did not fear him, but loved him, and venerated him like a saint."[80]

When "perfect hacienda administrators" are described as running a utopian Catholic community, Sebastián is glossing over the hacienda's hierarchical and exploitative labor systems. But in the context of ex-Jesuit reality in 1780s Italy, the invocation of the model hacienda administrator has an amplified meaning. We see this in 1783, when he lauds P. Andrés de la Fuente (#250) as a model administrator of an hacienda that belonged to the Jesuit Colegio de Querétaro. Here Sebastián's words ring like a warning to his dispersed comrades: "He never forgot what he owed to his Religious vocation, nor to the ministries of his Institute, and with holy humility he maintained a firm rule over all his actions."[81] The words are an admonition of self-control for men who have no Order.

Scene VI: "*La América*" and Nostalgia for Tepotzotlán

In the 1780s, Sebastián's entries begin to demarcate a decisive split between life in *la America* and life in Italy. In his earlier entries, he simply announced the place where the Jesuit had been arrested and then proceeded with a few details about the migration to Europe or sometimes skipped ahead to note where the Jesuit found his home, usually in Bologna or Ferrara. But in the 1780s, he often comments explicitly about an end to a former way of life by announcing "such was his life in *la América*." The phrases alternate slightly. "This series of a life dedicated to serving God and neighbor was that had by Our Padre Piedra in *la América*."[82] This interruption is followed by a brief, if repetitive, summation of the Jesuit's virtues as exemplified by his track record in New Spain—a first death—before he moves to the Italian scene. This new elegiac interlude demarcates a clear separation of "before" and "after," making explicit that American possibilities have perished. The invocation of "*la América*" conveys a clear sense of loss.

But Sebastián is not a protonationalist or a creole patriot.[83] We can see this in the way he deploys the term "México." México is the city, or it is the "Mexican" language, Nahuatl. When he deploys the term "*patria*"— homeland—he refers to a Jesuit's birthplace and always specifies a city, as in "his patria was Puebla." Or Mexico City, or Veracruz, etc. If there is a "country" (*país*) it is "that country" (*aquel país*)—distance implied—as in "that country" of the uncivilized "*naturales*" of northern New Spain. Mission-station subjects are not often referred to as "Indians," but have names: the Pimas, the Seri, sometimes modified with the word "barbarous," especially when the Jesuit missions have been disastrous failures. The term "Indian" is, for the most part, reserved for urban natives, some of whom attend Jesuit colleges or attend Jesuit churches. "*La América*," then is an expression of nostalgia that refers not to a place or a people, but to a temporality, to a time when Mexicans—that is, the Jesuits of the Province of Mexico—were confident in their mission.

As Sebastián begins to invoke "*la América*," the appearance of the term "innocent" becomes ubiquitous. Every third Jesuit is "so innocent" or "the most innocent." The word is intended to describe a man's simple or childlike faith in God. But in this last decade of record-keeping, Sebastián's amplified use of the term works in tandem with his expressions of spatiotemporal rupture. Accordingly, he paints a picture of la América in the past tense as a place that had once been so busy and full of possibility. In the 1770s, he had pivoted to note how men, in a rather vague Italian present, find a somewhat desperate purpose in efforts to find shelter and routine. But this "busy-ness" has largely disappeared in Sebastián's presentations in the 1780s, when he constructs monuments to lives passed in prayer and contemplation. "Innocence" refers to a time when these same men had yet to go through the upheavals that he now describes as the "total dismemberment" (*desmembramiento*) of the Mexican Province,[84] unimaginable to Jesuits who in "*la América*" had held an innocent faith in the continued order of things.

In this era of complete decline, he anchors his nostalgic backward glance in a moment in which each Jesuit had looked *forward*: "Novitiate fervor." Here Tepotzotlán, the Jesuit novitiate in New Spain, rises to the fore as a prominent symbol for a now lost innocence. The novitiate is not quite a paradise; the hand of human labor is too prominent in his metaphors. Rather, Tepotzotlán is the orchard that had produced tender trees, or alternatively a seedbed or a garden where virtue had once taken quick and firm root. Sometimes he draws upon metaphors of human-made delight: a theater of innocence, or a palace one could visit to rekindle "novitiate fervor." For example, P. Joseph Vallejo (b. 1718–1785) (#277) is described as "the sum total of innocence" (*innocencia suma*). In 1741 he was "transplanted to the Orchard of Religion in Our Novitiate of Tepotzotlán, where he applied himself with all of his spiritual zeal, gave himself over to prayer and meditation and worked to accumulate numerous virtues, which shone in him all of his life."[85]

When describing the life of P. Pedro Vaquera (#320) Tepotzotlán is memorialized as "a garden of perfection and a palace [*alcazar*] of virtues, one breathed nothing other than the ambience of devotion and piety that one encountered upon entering. Nothing seemed difficult, and all the minutiae that comprises the spiritual life and the religious life, was adjusted such that one seemed to have been born religious and rooted in such an exact virtue that in only a few years one was left in a state of perfect self-understanding akin to that of an old man."[86] In collecting a past,

Sebastián is writing against disappearance, and perhaps with some urgency, because the past that appears on his pages is no longer found in his world. But we cannot forget that he is also cognizant of his "now" and this is why his monuments change: He shapes them to meet his moment. His memorialization strategies do little to change the fact that the Mexican Province no longer has the material density to replicate itself. Is he attempting to write models geared toward *seeding* a collective future? For him, the value of the story of the ex-Jesuit resides in how the life of the individual refers back to the collective experience, distant in time and space. Nothing seemed difficult in *la América*. In fact, if measured in terms of virtue accrued, time was accelerated in wondrous ways, especially at Tepotzotlán.

Scene VII: To Live Dying—Mourning in an Etiological Mode

Time moved very differently in Italy where, as Sebastián says so often, they "lived dying." Sebastián's Imagistic phrase—"he lived dying"—captures well the drastically changed existence for Jesuits who are now absent a mission. But the men he wrote about also went through an actual process of dying. In *The Work of the Dead*, Thomas Laqueur argues that the dead body works to organize our societies. "This thing—this inanimate thing—that is always more than a thing has been the stuff of our imaginations since the beginning. We need it. It does massive work for the living."[87] The dead body is "powerful, dangerous, preserved, revered, feared, an object of ritual," say Laqueur, and we can learn much by studying how different cultures care for the dead body.[88] Now we turn to the final moment, that is, the last section of each entry in which Sebastián marks individual deaths.

When we consider how elaborate early modern Catholic deathbed and public funerary rituals could be,[89] it becomes clear that Sebastián gives very cursory attention to the deathbed scene and the ultimate disposal of the dead body. Yes, he will characterize a death as "good," but apart from some words on holy resignation to God's will, he does not offer a blow-by-blow description of the moment of passing. He records virtually no last words; he never describes the signing of final testaments. Following the death, he is concerned to mark that a burial took place and, as we will discuss shortly, he is keen to obtain the precise date of death and the location where the cadaver is buried. But his brevity on these topics holds even when, in the 1780s, his obituaries grow steadily in length.[90]

Rather than the dead body, it is the *sick* body that most often takes a moment on stage in the *Memorias*.[91] The cause of death, as we have already observed with deaths by suicide and yellow fever, are consistently noted. Sometimes Sebastián describes the cause of death rather bluntly, as in the obituary of Padre Joseph Carillo (#161) who died in 1774: "Little by little he was consumed by a *molestissima* diarrhea." Padre Laureano Bravo (#162) was "struck" with an apoplectic attack, a stroke, "that left him babbling" and he remained this way, praying the rosary and attending mass, until a second attack killed him in 1775. Padre Miguel Ybarburu (#236) died from a "black jaundice" (*ycterizia negra*). Padre Lorenzo Echave (#239) was "overcome by *un grande hidropesia*." Some causes of death are rather vague, as in the obituary of Padre Miguel López, who "became completely debilitated in his health, placed all in God and in the arms of his beloved Holy Mary whose heart he loved and venerated, and within three days he was reduced to bed, where he died angelically."[92]

Other causes of death took up more space on the page. Among the last entries, we find the memorial to Tomás Pérez (#383). Pérez is described as suffering a very painful long-term physical ailment but then experiences a swift and unexpected death. Padre Pérez is paradigmatic among monuments to that lost possibility of an American life filled with "tireless" labor. In the first half of his life, Pérez served the destitute (*los desvalidos*) in jails and in hospitals, where he sat with them during their own processes of dying. He was "indefatigable" in the confessional. In his last years in New Spain, he returned to his place of birth, Veracruz, where he was charged with serving as prefect of Christian doctrine, preaching to *negros* and mulattos. "So far, this was his life in la América when the common storm shipwrecked all of his people on the stormy reef of Exile, to which he was condemned." After this dramatic segue, his short eulogy to Pérez's life in America circles back to reiterate the Jesuit's zeal for ministering to those in jail, to enslaved persons, and to the maligned *plebe*, "all of whom he searched out to offer caring instruction."[93]

And then the reader is informed of the nature of Pérez's excruciating malady. Once he made a mission to the towns of "that burning coast." He rode a poorly appointed horse, and the constant movement on what must have been a terrible saddle caused a tumor to form near his anus that he ignored, which augmented its growth, and he suffered great pain. But he did not want to abandon his mission "to confess those destitute inhabitants." The return trip made matters worse. He was advised to "put himself in the hands of Surgeons who, recognizing the great danger he was in, cut off large pieces of flesh, which left him forever with a deep fistula that served continuous torments all the days of life, but never did anyone hear him complain of the sharp pains he suffered, living in extreme discomfort."[94] Perhaps this is the reason that, at the time of the arrest, Pérez had a manual on surgery on the desk in his room. Had he been reviewing the details of his fate?[95] Sebastián's point is to highlight Pérez's capacity to labor while suffering in "the most frequented port in America." Sebastián repeats himself: "He lived in this manner in la América, so saintly were his occupations in his Patria [Veracruz] when suddenly he was ejected and sent to Italy."[96] Pérez lived in Ferrara until forced to remove his soutane in 1773, after which he moved to Rome, since he had never adapted to "the frigid weather of Ferrara." With access to financial support from America, Sebastián testifies that Pérez paid for many of the necessities of his exiled compañeros. He never tells us much about what Pérez did in Rome, but for the fact that, despite failing vision, he wrote *alabanzas* to the Virgin Mary. He says Mass in the mornings, reads and rereads his holy books, and writes about the Virgin Mary. In the afternoon he visits the Holy Sacrament at church and after he would visit "Our sick"—consoling ex-Jesuits who had moved to Rome, and distributing alms but no longer the man of action, the *verdadero* Jesuit martyr who suffered to be on the road, preaching the word.

And his martyrdom in Italy? Death by the wheel:

> One late afternoon, he returned from a Church near his house. Now almost night, he did not see the carriage that was coming down the street, he stepped out in front and fell to the ground, and with the wheels passing over the middle of his body, he was left for dead. The Surgeons and the Doctors arrived and declared that there was no remedy, for his bones were broken, and his intestines injured. He revived long enough to insist that it was his own fault, due to his failing vision. He died on January 10, 1796. He is buried at the Gesu, as he had asked, wishing to his remains to rested in the place where those of his Holy Father Ignacio rested.[97]

This is an example of how Sebastián was much more concerned to detail the illnesses or accidents that precipitated death. Similarly, Padre Juan Villamil (#160) was employed as a tutor, likely served to supplement the pension provided by the Spanish Crown. He lived at the family's country house. He met his untimely death—or, rather, a very precisely timed death—when, on a return trip to Bologna, he passed by a building at the very moment that a servant threw a straw pallet out of a window. He was thrown violently to the ground and injured his leg. He was carried to a hospital, where he was examined by surgeons. Surgeons never get good billing in the *Memorias*. These surgeons judge that the injury was not grave, but "after a short while" (we wonder how long) they discovered gangrene that "in a few hours robbed him of life and offering this to his Creator with great resignation and conformity to the Divine will, he died with the signs of predestination at the Hospital of Santa María de la Vida in Bologna."[98]

We get a sense of how some Jesuits lived in quite dire conditions when Sebastián describes a series of deaths in which "*un recio tabardillo*," that is, a severe case of typhus fever, killed many ex-Jesuits. Padre Phelipe Ruanova (#212), described as "irrepressible, and much loved by everyone," had moved from Ferrara to Bologna after the suppression. Once the illness hit, he was taken quite suddenly, to everyone's deep regret, Sebastián added. He died "with great peace" on May 17, 1779. About ten days later, Padre Luis Angel Yanez (#213) died "from charity" as he had taken care of Ruanova day and night, but after preparing the funeral, he fell ill himself. Yanez died on May 29, 1779. In his wake followed the death of Padre Pablo Robledo (#214). Only in Robledo's obituary do we learn that the three men lived together. The doctor determined that he had typhus, and that this had also taken the lives of his companions. The doctor attempted to bleed him "in order to weaken it [the typhus]" but Robledo died on June 2, 1779. Padre Salvador Davila (#229) also died of typhus. He had rented a room from a very poor family after the Suppression. Sebastián says Dávila was asked why he remained living in such poor conditions, to which he replied, "What can I do? In my house there is no more than what I bring with my pension. If I leave, they die of hunger, better that I suffer like this."[99] Typhus is a disease that, passed by infected body lice, strikes people living in unsanitary cramped conditions.[100] These last deaths offer a glimpse of the poverty that many Mexican Jesuits experienced in Italy.

The attention paid to the cause of death gives us a sense of how they died, but also how some men's bodies were ruined. The diseases, long-term maladies, or brutal accidents could have been the cause of death among any number of people living and dying on either side of the Atlantic in the eighteenth century. But the lasting effects of scurvy that afflicted many Mexican Jesuits was particular to the terrible conditions than many experienced when crossing the Atlantic. Padre Manuel Guraya (#171) is described as having never fully recovered from the scurvy that afflicted him when crossing the Atlantic. He died in 1775, living many years as a "martyr to scurvy." Another Jesuit is described as *"picado de escarbuto"* (#217), that is, pocked or bitten by the disease. Padre Andres Soriano (#271) suffered from a seemingly incurable scurvy. He lived in Medicina, and studied geometry, algebra, and astronomy, "without failing to study the Sacred Scripture" but he had a "weak complexion and he had been assaulted by scurvy" on the transatlantic journey. Sebastián writes that the disease exasperated Soriano "little by little until it fell into his esophagus causing an internal inflammation, which the Doctors declared to be incurable."[101] He clearly "lived dying," surviving only on liquids for about four months. At first his diagnosis "caused him great horror and terrible fears, but he put himself in the hands of God" on March 18, 1785. He had lived for eighteen years with the ramifications of contracting scurvy on his overseas trip.

But if scurvy made a ruin of the human body, so did the surgeon's knife. As we have seen with Padre Pérez's fistula, the surgeon's handiwork appears in many of the most gruesome descriptions of suffering and death. Sebastián never describes how Padre Nicolas Peza (#190) died, but in the afterword he details how the angelical Peza wore down his own body over the course of his time in Italy. "His continuous mortification treated his innocent body with great rigor. In the town of Castel San Pietro, even in the middle of the most unbearably frigid weather, he would go to a secluded orchard belonging to the house where he tore his flesh to pieces with bloody disciplines (*se despedazaba sus carnes*); this would have occasioned his death, if his Superiors had not prohibited it. But the wounds that he made on his innocent body became gangrenous, and he had to suffer another martyrdom at the hand of a Surgeon, who cut away pieces of corrupted flesh."[102] In this gruesome bloodbath, Peza's body was subject to both devotional and scientific torment.

P. Joaquin de Tapia (#231) suffered his "*martirio*" at the hands of surgeons who cut away "the growths that came out of his neck and face." These interventions caused to him to suffer severe fevers. Sebastián does a little maneuvering here. He says that Tapia was not cared for properly but then moves to clarify in a parenthetical aside that assistance is never lacking among the Jesuits "as this has been exercised to the utmost among all of Ours in exile." Everyone made their best efforts, he states vaguely, yet there were problems that he blamed on a general sense of lack ("in the absence of all things") and on the weather ("in this country whose rigorous cold has made most of [the Jesuits] useless for everything." Then natural forces intervened to tip the balances for Tapia. "In the last earthquakes of the years 1779 and 1780, the city and territory of Bologna suffered, and [Tapia] was so frightened that for much of that time he took leave of himself (*fuera de sí*)." This last bout of melancholy "changed his manner." Tapia takes to his bed in hopes of being granted salvation, given all that he had gone through "with great resignation." Sebastián states that "it was Divine Will that he was continuously martyred by these troubles for almost the entire course of his life." On March 7, 1781, he died in peace, says Sebastián. But it is perhaps more accurate to say that peace came in the form of death for Padre Tapia.[103]

In memorializing Tapia, Sebastián continues his pattern of frank description of what we now consider mental health issues. The phrase *fuera de sí* captures a "taking leave" of oneself, or a "loss" of self, that become crucial issues of agency: Is one who has lost himself responsible for his actions? P. Manuel Arenas (#363) provides a case in point. "He studied continuously," Sebastián remarks, "and occupied many moments of insufferable idleness of Italy in making Poetic compositions, translating some excellent and pious Italian authors, which were read by Ours, as they served to pass the time, and the praise was unanimous, they were excellent compositions." Here we have another hint about the ways formerly "tireless workers" now fill gaps in time, in this case, with translation projects. But Arenas becomes destabilized by the end of the Society of Jesus in 1773, and his "decomposition" is among the more dire responses to the Suppression reported by Sebastián:

> For several days he did nothing but cry, and then, as if alienated from himself (*como enajenado de sí*), he found no comfort in anything ever

again. His vivid fantasies vexed him continuously, and he spent the rest of his life dazed, without knowing how to govern himself in anything, nor could he find rest anywhere. [But] even in the middle of this decomposition, he tried to celebrate the holy Sacrament of the Mass and to follow in his old devotions to the Virgin Dolorosa, Saint Joseph, Our Padre San Ignacio, and San Juan Nepomuceno. Finally, he moved to Ferrara and here his great devotion to the Virgin of Sorrows, called there vulgarly, "de la Raqueta." There he passed [the time] until little by little, suffocating under the melancholic humor that was predominant, he came to be as if insulted (stricken by stroke), and without being able to move from bed.[104]

He is beyond reach. Yet note how Sebastián works to keep Arenas spiritually active and mobile on paper. Despite decomposition, Arenas "celebrates" the Mass, and "follows" some very familiar Jesuit devotions. Yet he is also described as stripped of his power to act, immobilized under the weight of a great depression. Sebastián writes, it is *as if* Arenas has suffered an *insulto*, a word that usually indicates a sudden stroke, but here underlines Arenas's absolute inactivity.[105]

Agency is critical to proper preparation for death, and this becomes an issue for those who are "lost to themselves" or "as if" already dead. In a similar mode, Sebastián uses the phrase "*fuera de sí*" to refer to the way P. Juan Joseph Muñoz (#360) is disempowered by a stroke.[106] This Jesuit had taken the arrest and subsequent exile in stride—"he received these crude blows with the greatest resignation to Divine will." He adjusted, becoming "like an anchorite"—a denomination we will discuss shortly. Little by little, he was "deprived of all power and left like a [tree] trunk. . . . Remaining out of himself (*fuera de sí*), without the power to speak or to move, he was assisted by his charitable Compañeros, and he had received very much in advance the Sacred Viaticum."[107] Here *fuera de sí* indicates an absence of agency that has implications for receiving the Eucharist on his deathbed. Sebastián's "very much in advance" seems to point to a time prior when he had been capable of receiving it. Muñoz's inability to actively will explains why it became pointless to give him the Eucharist: He cannot accept it. Similarly, absence of "judgment" is the stated reason for refusing the Eucharist to another Jesuit, Vallarta (#328) on his deathbed. Having suffered from scruples all his life, Sebastián is careful to note that although Vallarta had lost his judgment, he did not say anything untoward in his "ravings." He spoke only of "holy things." But he could not receive the sacrament. "Few were the days that he lay in bed, and they did not dare to give him the Viaticum, due to his lack of judgment (*juicio*); but they administered the Extreme Unction, and he was left in great peace, as he calmly surrendered his innocent spirit into the hands of his creator."[108]

Monologue: The Liveness of the Litany of the Dead

I have established that Sebastián is not an ethnographer. So how to explain that he describes illnesses in such detail? Two formalities merge here: the list and the litany. The result is a numbered litany of the dead following the death-date chronology that is also a litany of the *dying*. The attention to the details of the affliction and death has the effect of breaking the litany and recalling these men to individuated "liveness." The illnesses emerge as among the most personal or personalized details he offers about each man. In dying, each man is facing his own constellation of aging and illness, mental decline, the occasional sudden accident. On one hand, Sebastián continues to rely upon the language of exemplarity, for example, when describes their suffering as forms of martyrdom. But on the other hand, the particularity of his descriptions interrupts his literary mode, and is the place in his *Memorias* where we get the closest to what historians would call reliable facts.

Is this a humanizing move, an homage to individuality that he wished to emphasize? I wonder, how do the wasting bodies generate value? Perhaps these stark sketches of contingency in death circulate among and accrue to the ex-Jesuits of the Mexican Province, allowing them to continue as a kind of necrocommunity. Whether his manuscript circulates, we do not know. But we do know that Sebastián himself circulates. We catch a rare glimpse of this in his effort to share mournful facts in the next scene.

Scene VIII: Necrocommunity, or a Mournful Mode of Sociability

Sebastián's task of counting and marking the dead may seem a solitary task, but his efforts point to an existing scaffolding of sociability that took place in a mournful mode.[109] Each ex-Jesuit's death is a literary occasion for collecting and telling stories that, in turn, depends upon and reinforces connections among the scattered ex-Jesuits. Distance from home requires precise details to be relayed to those who were absent, whether family, friends, or other ex-Jesuits. We have some indication that some long-distance Jesuit networks were maintained—connecting the ex-Jesuits living in Bologna to those who had moved to other Papal States or Rome, as well as to those few who died in Spain and to those who never left New Spain—but there is little evidence as to how Sebastián collects his information.

We know that he requires some stories from each man's life, and we have seen that he always reports with some detail the cause of death. Dates are important, as is the place of death. In fact, Sebastián expresses frustration at the lack of documentary information about the final days of the California *padres* who die in prison in Spain: He finds it something of a struggle to maintain a precise chronology and garner a few details about the death of each man. The California Jesuits were held in Puerto de Santa María and eventually transferred to monasteries across Spain to live out their lives, still imprisoned. Padre Francisco Ita (#240) was sent to a monastery in Córdoba, not freed, Sebastián clarifies, but merely moved to "a better prison." He is scandalized by the lack of details he has about P. Yta's last days: "I wish I knew and that it were possible to have known the circumstances of his death, and in which convent it happened, but there is no one to communicate this to us."[110] As we have seen, describing the disease and other "circumstances" of an ex-Jesuit's death is almost of more importance than imagining his soul properly commended to God.

When Sebastián wraps up the year 1785 (and with it finishes the first volume of the manuscript), he takes a moment to backtrack and add more biographies of men who died in Spanish monasteries over the years. He writes that Juan Lorenzo Salgado (#287) died in prison in in a Spanish monastery of discalced Franciscans. "It is the most natural thing," he rails,

> to give notice to one's own people about the death of relatives and friends, so they can commend them to God. This courtesy, this Christian piety is extended from hospitals, ships, and armies, yet it is not to be found among the Spanish Regulars; thus the Jesuits who have died among them, we come to know about it very late, and not through them, but through some Secular [priest], who charitably has notified us. Because of this, not until four years after have we come to know about the death of P. Juan Lorenzo Salgado in Tabladilla in the Convent of

the Discalced Franciscans, we can conclude, in 1781, without knowing month or day.[111]

We rarely hear about his information gathering or how he succeeds in collecting the stories of the sick, aging, or mentally ill Padres who were unable to travel and who died in New Spain under house arrest at the Colegio Espíritu Santo. Yet Sebastián describes the decline of Juan Francisco Regis Salazar (#165) and informs the reader that he resided "in the prison for the infirm at Espíritu Santo, where he lived with holiness and humility until one day, when he was dressing himself to say Mass, he was assaulted by an attack (*un insulto*) that in a few hours took his life."[112] How does Sebastián get these reports about the circumstances surrounding the deaths of distant brethren? His tirade about the feeble information to be garnered about many of the men who died in prison in Spain offers evidence that he must usually have dependable networks of communication.

There are few clues as to his "writing process" on the pages of the *Memorias*, but we catch a glimpse of how Sebastián's litany of the dead fostered a network of necrosociability.[113] A rare and informative letter from Sebastián to the ex-Jesuit Eligio Fernández offers clues as to how translocal and transatlantic ties were maintained in part through sharing information about a Jesuit's "good death."

> Bolonia. 16 de Agosto de 88
> My esteemed Don Eligio, you have already learned of the death of Don Joseph Sánchez,[114] that took place in the town of Medicina on the seventh day of this month at two thirty in the morning, we say today seven hours Italian.
>
> I went to assist, and he died with all the signs of predestination. He already had the Holy Oil administered to him on the fifth day [transcription problem].
>
> He received one [a letter] from you, with the letter from the dear nun, your sister, which I return here, I did not want to read it [to him], because I could not judge his state [*por que no lo juzque en estado de esto*]. On his behalf, I appreciate the fineness in her that it demonstrates.
>
> He was poor, but was always very generous, and he comported himself with great honor, but thank God he did not lack anything and had enough to make the funeral arrangements there, paying everything to the Ecclesiastics, paying everything, and leaving with honor without asking anything under pressure.

I deliver this blow and, having been a great friend, you will have the Consolation that he was very assisted and that he lacked for nothing for his relief in life, and honor in death.

To the dear nun, you can write her that I commend her to God, and tell her that he died in great peace and completely full of consolation in the Lord.

All that occurs I wrote to you, you already know who I am, you know me well, and as such your wish is my command, surely, I live without changing in anything, and I am as I have always been. Greetings to Pancho Alegría, and to Hilario, and I remain your

Most affectionate friend.

Feliz de Sebastián.[115]

This letter puts Sebastián, for a moment, in the spotlight. It is worth bearing in mind that he is brought into view by a different kind of document altogether, wherein he is less concerned with universals, focusing instead on conveying some of the particulars of Sánchez's death. He confirms that he received last rites; he reports firsthand from the bedside of the dying ex-Jesuit; the funeral arrangements have been made by the dead man himself. Had that not been the case, it is possible to imagine a different letter that asked for assistance to bury him properly. Sebastián is not writing to collect information for his *Memorias*, however. He is reaching out to friends and in so doing, we have a tantalizing clue as to the way that collecting the dead also keeps transatlantic communication alive. There is a "home" audience in the offstage presence of Eligio's sister in Puebla de los Angeles. All the men mentioned are from Puebla and know one another well. Eligio Fernández has moved to Rome and has remained close with other ex-Jesuits, Pancho Alegría and Hilario Ugarte, who were with Fernández at the Colegio Espíritu Santo at the time of the arrest, and now live together, postsuppression, in Rome. The letter taps into and reinforces this transregional network of ex-Jesuits. But here the connection is *patria*, that is, the hometown.

Scene IX: *Verdadero* Anchorites

Now that they are no longer contemplatives in action who take sail under the banner of God in all things, the "late-Sebastián" shifts to valorize the contemplative life. Implied for years, Sebastián finally makes an unequivocal statement about the absence of a Jesuit mission. When Padre Juan Torija (#243) dies in 1782, Sebastián writes: "Finding himself deprived of his Apostolic work, he was dedicated completely to Prayer, passing the days in the Churches, in front of the Holy Sacrament."

After the *abolición*, Sebastián often described men with the phrase "he took off his soutane but remained unchanged." He insists upon this for himself in his letter to Eligio Fernández: *I live without changing, I am who I always have been.* Yet his monuments cannot avoid showing that, despite great efforts to remain "unchanged," the Mexican Jesuits are disappearing. This is not simply a natural progression in which aging men get sick and die. The reality is that Jesuit ways of being are not actively replicated. Jesuits cannot teach, preach, live together, or train novitiates. Absent these mechanisms for recruiting and training Jesuits, the Spanish Crown has been incredibly successful in dismantling both formal and informal infrastructures that had once made male religious reproduction possible. Further, the Society of Jesus and their institutions are no longer central to the buzzing "swarm" of activity that anchored people, devotional practices, and publications to places like the Jesuit college. The indefatigable Jesuit is gone, there is little action, or really, no action in which "the Jesuits" are at the center of things. The "mobility" model is in ruins, thus the stories they tell themselves about themselves are no longer anchored into embodied systems of mimetic reproduction.[116]

In the late 1780s and the 1790s, the word "anchorite" enters Sebastián's lexicon. The *verdadero* Jesuit is, indeed, anchored in quiet and stillness. This is a representational issue, to be sure, a solution to the problem of what Sebastián should now privilege in his descriptions in this era. Sometimes, despite himself, Sebastián hints of how, individually, men did move on with their lives. We know that men earn money as tutors and can earn a double pension if they write works that fight the proliferation of the Spanish black legend.[117] Padre Hidalgo (#324) is described as "never losing time," so he turns his energy toward painting. "He was making great progress in painting," Sebastián reports, when he developed "some large obstructions and had a low fever that lasted months without cease, there was no relief to be found in Doctors nor Medicine [until] full of merits and virtues, he gave his spirit placidly to the Lord in Bologna on the 7th day of May [1781]."[118] Padre Joachim Truxillo (#163), born in 1726, was a Tarahumara missionary who had always fantasized about writing literature.

Now he had the time.¹¹⁹ As did Sebastián, whose entries have now extended well beyond his original half-page comments to six pages in length, written in a smaller hand, on larger paper. He has time to compose.

Nonetheless, the emergence of the term "anchorite" in his lexicon offers a striking contrast to the original Jesuit sensibility of being men in the world whose contemplation would be found in action. Value is now found in leading a life much more cloistered. The *verdadero* "anchorite" describes men who rarely left their dwellings and, if they did, went only to "visit"—either to call on other ex-Jesuits or to pray before the body of Christ exposed at a local church. For example, when Padre Juan Joseph Muñoz (#360) was commanded to leave the company of his fellow Jesuits after the suppression, he "retired" to a little rental house "where he lived the life of the most austere Anchorite. He did not leave the retreat but to go to Church and to offer the bloodless (*incruendo*) sacrifice at the altar, or to sweeten [the suffering] of some brother going through a sickness. In his home, he was always occupied with thoughts of God, reading spiritual books, and praying." When Padre Manuel Muñoz y Barba died in 1793, he was described as having lived the remainder of his life after the suppression in a little rental house, wherein he passed this period of twenty years as a *verdadero Anacoreta*. The sensibility is even applied retrospectively to a more "active" era in the case of Francisco Xavier Gonzales, who is described as making the transatlantic journey "as if he were on a silent retreat." Upon arriving in Ferrara, he lived his life as in ecstasy in front of the divine sacrament. After the suppression, he lived with some poor "but very honorable" people among them he "lived like an Anchorite."¹²⁰

Monologue: Abandoning the Stage

For twenty-nine years Sebastián collected the dead; he built and decomposed his monumental men on the pages of his lengthy manuscript. And then he abandoned the project. There was no third volume, even though Sebastián lived another nineteen years. The project was itself a ruin. In considering the whole of the *Memorias* as a kind of monument, it is useful to think about the work that humans do when attempting to maintain physical ruins. Ruins are marked out, Stewart reminds us, "curated to

ACT III: RUINATION 185

FIGURE 9. An unidentified anchorite praying in the desert. Etching by seventeenth-century Italian artist, Bellavia, Marcantonio. Open access, courtesy of The Trustees of the British Museum.

resist the encroachments of rain and wind and vegetation over time. Being given a name, becoming a place, is a means of vitality and protects a form from indifference and inevitable destruction."[121] In this work of collecting and curating his dead ex-Jesuits, Felix de Sebastián inscribes a kind of restoration on the pages of this monument to the Mexican Province.

His memorialization—dependent upon literary replication of moments when Jesuits once wielded sacramental power—is nostalgic for *la América*, a place, yes, but more so, a *time* when the Mexican Province was unified.

But the text is only ostensibly about preserving the past. The manuscript reveals how Sebastián makes sense of his own shifting *present* in the face of an unknowable future. He projects no afterlife for the Society of Jesus.[122] Reading him, we cannot foresee the formal "Restoration" of either the Society of Jesus (1814) or the Mexican Province (1816). Sebastián does not see those dates on the horizon; his writing conveys no sense of destiny. Against an indeterminate future, his memory work might be considered akin to a making seed bank. Laqueur writes about the way a relationship to the future is mediated through the dead who have "[a] right to be written in death, to be mourned as a name that is filled by a person; the right to have a denouement. Or put differently, since the dead have no rights, the right of the living to the stories of the dead, which comes down to keeping them until 'we need them.'"[123] For Sebastián, absent any clear idea of which specimens from this dying Order will be useful, he saves them all, or almost all, exercising a historicist faith that words will outlast the inevitable decay of the human form. With only this vague sense of future, the inventory entails blind trust, or a Kierkegaardian "leap of faith"—against the odds, you can have what you have lost.

Like ruins, his monuments have fallen out of use. Even when still existing in the center of a hustling and bustling locale, ruins are no longer central to the bustle of daily living. They play an aesthetic role. In the eighteenth-century especially, as Susan Stewart notes, the "decline, fall, destruction [of] ruins are beautiful to paint." The aging and dying men of the Society of Jesus are rendered here as lovely ruins, once active men now anchored in place, quiet and prayerful. The skeleton that remains is an idealized life of prayer and contemplation, thus exposing an older form, a simple structure that, in fact, the Jesuits had bombastically rejected in the sixteenth century. John O'Malley, lauded historian of the early Society of Jesus, once issued a corrective to Jesuit historiography that I cannot help but read as a warning about how we ought to interpret the appearance of Felix de Sebastián's "anchorites." O'Malley wrote, "But we still must be on our guard to prevent scholarship from falling into the fallacy that would treat the spirituality of the Society of Jesus independent of its commitment to ministry."[124] Independent from mission and ministry, one is not really talking about "the Jesuits" any longer.

Or we can take our cues from Aristotle, who wrote that without action, there is simply contemplation, and that alone should bring the curtain down.

We end.

Concluded
The Mexican Province

Suddenly the setting in which reality unfolded had become completely, dizzyingly different.

Laurent Olivier

What happens when change is sudden and dramatic, making clear that what you had staked your life upon is no longer out in front of you? You can no longer gear into the same future.[1] You are history. Or you *might be* history. This is how the poetics of transformation underwrites history as a gamble. A fragment from your story—an object, a book, or some ink on a page—might provide a trace of a lost way of being. And within this struggle to stabilize the ever-shifting present by documenting what is passing, it is the eye to the future that proves most anxiety-provoking.

In writing about inventories of things, of the self, and of the dead, I have presented "change over time" as a mobile story of the initial durability, waning strength, and ultimate disintegration of knots of relations among people and things that had once formed a group of men as "the Mexican Jesuits." Act I established the complexity and density of Jesuit-styled knots of active relations among people and things that had formerly moved, buzzed, and ignited in relation to the space of the altar. In the Acts that follow, these knots fray as dispersed Jesuits find themselves anchored to fewer people, places, and things. This is not to say that individual men do not become actants and conduits in other kinds of networks. But my study has shown how "the Jesuits" can no longer consistently light up in any reliable way. Their former connectivity is undone by the Spanish Crown's offensive, which bears an uncanny resemblance to the Latourian insight that "there is no group, only group formation." To foreclose Jesuit futures, the Crown's inventorying processes not only accounted for their holdings but also worked to immobilize the things that had once moved within Jesuit orbits and had been central to how they formed and sustained themselves as mediators of divinity.

In trailing after Castillo, and subsequently the sacramental silver, what has become clear is that he and the anonymous notaries had been tasked with inventorying each and every item. Anxious to locate Jesuit power, *everything* is under scrutiny. But the silver trail is particularly telling about the nature of Jesuit loss. The Society of Jesus, a group of men who had the audacity to name themselves as with Jesus, find themselves summarily dismissed from the network of colonial power fueled by Christ's appearance in the Eucharist.

In Act II, the shipboard encounter with the Swedish youth has provided a unique angle on the unfolding demise of the Mexican Province. This story began with the young man's quest for answers about "True Religion" in a world challenged and galvanized by Enlightenment ideas. But Thjülen is confounded and then transformed by the black-robed men. He follows a hunch that the Mexican theologian, Iturriaga, paves his path toward a new self. His spiritual transformation is affirmed by the Virgin of Guadalupe and further buoyed by Iturriaga's assurances that, if necessary, Thjülen can take refuge with Iturriaga's family in Mexico. Thjülen might become a Mexican himself, for he hopes to join the Mexican Province as a Jesuit.

But Thjülen has attached himself to a losing cause. Each port is a new resting place, but none provides the Mexican Jesuits with the certainty that they will be able to firmly root themselves as a community. The fraying threads begin to show in the chaos that marks their travel from Cádiz to Corsica, when the Vatican is compelled to step in at the last moment to fend off disaster by offering the Papal States as a refuge. Accordingly, Thjülen's soul-searching unfolds in fits and starts not only because he is a seeker but also because he anchors himself in the Jesuits whose sense of order is fragmented. In 1773, when the Order is formally disbanded, they no longer have a future to offer him.

In Act III we have found the Mexican Jesuits settling into life in the Papal States, their desire to persist evident in the way that they seek to replicate their former lives in the makeshift colleges scattered across Bologna. These ad-hoc situations are dissolved with the abolition of the Society in 1773, after which the men are prohibited from living together. No group formation. Even while keeping them together in his ever-growing manuscript, his Jesuits ultimately lose themselves in prayer and contemplation. Sebastián might perform group formation in his inventory of the dead, but when he begins to put the men to death as "Anchorites," he has moved far away from the collective identity that had once so thoroughly shaped the members of the Society of Jesus as contemplatives in *action*. In the end, if the knot of relations that is "the Mexican Province" remains, it is only in quasi-fictionalized form in Sebastián's twenty-nine-year project of inventorying the dead.[2]

We already know that "disappearance is not antithetical to remains."[3] Clearly, we see that some Jesuit "things" continue to circulate in the wake of this dismantling. The contested devotion to our Lady of the Light is under attack but does not disappear. Images, prints, and cutouts of the Sacred Heart of Jesus also continue to circulate. Yet this symbol takes on a new valence in nineteenth-century ultramontane theopolitics. Even when the Society of Jesus is reinstituted in 1814, the Jesuits never again establish their primacy as *mana* workers, in part because the material relays in the sacramental networks are limited and only partially operative. The Jesuits at no time manage to fully reestablish a thriving network of missions, colleges, haciendas that had served as dense nodal points for people-thing coherence. So even if some devotional symbols persist, scholars need to understand them in semiotic terms.[4] How do these objects signify in new nineteenth-century webs of meaning and practice in which, if "religion" dominates, it is because it has emerged as a deeply contested category?[5]

On Finding and Losing, and the Intervals Between

That Sebastián depicts Jesuit loss in this particular way is ironic because self-formation as *worldly* missionaries had been at the heart of Ignatius of Loyola's Spiritual Exercises, which itself served as the bedrock of their communal formation. This process of becoming was a lifelong practice of continued searching in order to fine-tune the passions and attain God's love through worldly ministry.[6] The meditative practice had taken geographic mobility and change over time into account. In remaking the Exercises each year, the Jesuits were asked to reaffirm individual vocations not in terms of an authentic originary point but rather, they were charged by its meditations to consider anew, each year, *who am I now?* This method required narrating oneself as a sinner with a past, but in relation to an unfolding present and geared into an imagined future. For the mobile Jesuits, this type of reevaluation considered questions of temporality, space, and place: *Where* might he be *now*?[7]

This logic, as we have seen, would define the way a Jesuit ought to shape himself as an ethical subject, whether teaching at a Jesuit college, preaching at a remote mission station, or administrating the lives of servants and slaves on a hacienda. Spatiotemporal change was a manageable part of his vocation as long as the telos of global Christian mission remained relatively uniform. In other words, selves are forged in a present, but one is not "lost" if changing circumstances can be rendered comprehensible within a relatively unchanged telos. To be a Jesuit is itself a process of becoming, but one that is geared into a shared vision of a *collective future*. Their problem after the expulsion is this telos. They no longer have one. Ruination, then, is a spatiotemporal argument about the dissolution of material relations that render Jesuit futures radically different or impossible to imagine. The ex-Jesuits continue to scramble to remake and to repurpose, and in doing so, many individuals carved out individuated futures.[8] But the "Society" is fragmented, broken down, a relic of a former way of being that is aestheticized in writing, but increasingly difficult *to live*.[9]

Staged this way, Sebastián's *Memorias* is a gamble. He has pitched memorialization of the Mexican Jesuits against an unknown future. How will they be found? If the inventory of the dead is a future-oriented container of stories that belongs to humans in an unforeseeable future, this turns out not to have been the best bet on "having" a future that Sebastián would recognize himself. The great irony is that manuscript has been much consulted, yet his monuments are no longer valued on the same terms. I wrote about his project in part because I do not think *his* Jesuits have ever seen the light of day. In modern hands, Sebastián's Mexican Province has been fragmented into minimal biographical facts, primarily dates, places of employment, and bibliographical information. In other words, historians have pillaged his *verdadero* monuments for basic data that, like so much *spolia*, has been repurposed to build different historical edifices. Today a handful remain legible. These few are lauded for having foreseen glimmers of the new collective: the nation-state, an entity built upon a modern sensibility that values collecting archival "facts."[10] But that is a very different memorializing project. Most of Sebastián's *verdadero* facts about "good deaths" are no longer relevant to the new imagined community.[11]

The fact is, *having* a history is always an indefinite project. As we have seen in these accounting processes, memorializing is subject to correction. Consider the additions, modifications, cross-outs, and complete erasures, whether in Thjülen's efforts to wordsmith subsequent versions of his conversion narrative, Mary's miraculous remake of the painting of her likeness, the notaries' various corrections of the mismarked "classes" of silver, or in Sebastián's refusal to memorialize the secularized ex-Jesuits in his pages. This is the theater of history which, as Elin Diamond says so well, is a "perpetual dialectic of the visible and the invisible, of appearance and disappearance."[12] Diamond's insights propelled me to characterize these three texts as machineries of capture, but whose holding capacity could reach limits, making the resulting inventories very rich but also full of lacunae.

I have insisted on keeping in view both the *forms* and the *processes* of memory-making as a method for reading historical texts. I have wanted to shed some light on how matters of concern and contestation appear *and* disappear. This syncopated rhythm becomes increasingly off-beat because these texts were produced across an ocean world. We have trailed after historical subjects who cross geographical borders. In lining up three inventories to track demise across different scenes of encounter, we have also run into the "borders" of texts, genres, and historiographies. The resulting gaps between these archival sources can be a cause of anxiety: How do we get these disparate sources to "line up" with one another? Should we creatively "paper over" the gaps? The shape of this book is intended as a performative contrast to historical trends that valorize synoptic history, an approach "invested in identicality."[13] My own instinct has been to carefully consider those gaps without finding ways to dissolve dissonances. I have paid close attention to the structural demands of each genre, finding some continuities in a story line shared across them, but ultimately, I have allowed the gaps to remain.

Here Laurent Olivier's meditations on archaeology and memory have guided my thinking. "History is memory creation. What is to be deciphered is located between the fragments."[14] Olivier notes how our historical perspectives in "the now" are shaped by a process analogous to how the "shot-reverse-shot" functions in visual storytelling.[15] The way that the film editor juxtaposes images determines the mood and meaning of the scene, so too does a director rely upon lighting to set moods and convey meaning on the stage. In Act I the notary's labor gave us access to the moment of the arrest, but it also offered a view of the wide variety of objects that accumulated in and around Jesuit spaces. To illuminate the shape of the inventory itself is to outline its inherently dramatic contours, forged as it was in the thick of the action.

But instead of sorting those inventoried items to slot Jesuit power as variously "economic," "political," or "religious," I utilized lighting schemes that illuminated a trail of silver that pointed toward the body of the Christ. The mood and meaning evoked in that staging decision gave affective weight to an incarnational theology grounded in material and relational networks. In the colonial Mexican world, God took up space and appeared in time. Christ appeared most regularly according to liturgical time, where his flickering presence found some permanence in the silver altarware that, in Alfred Gell's words, performs as an artifactual presence.[16] Silver provides a case that, following Massimo Leone and Richard Parmentier, is double in the "sense of *standing in place* of something that is absent and *making present again* that which was previously absent."[17] When touched by the body of Christ, silver remains, resonates with sacrality, even when the Eucharist is absent, yet another disappearance that is not antithetical to remains. Thus, a certain uncertainty animates theopolitical position-taking around that altar that, in turn, indexes how competing sovereignties vied for power in a world in which theological practices animated material sacramental networks that reverberated outside of church walls.

Note that when "sacramental logics" take center stage, "religion" exits the scene. The term is too imprecise in character. Like Latour's critique of how the "social" can become vacuous in its explanatory overdeployment, so too can the use of the descriptor "religious" be flabby and tautological. All too often "religion" names in advance the subjects and objects that will be found, telling us what we already know.[18] Can we use more specific descriptive language? My attempt to trace a sacramental network is just such an aim for granularity. I have found objects both mundane and holy situated within a sacramentally driven network that implicates how all colonial subjects across this hierarchical Catholic society might grab power if situated near the body and blood of Christ. Even the Crown is compelled to account for the shape-shifting power of the God-made-man. But the state's own desire for a granular sense of Jesuit power does not confer a sense of *certainty*.[19] Thus, the minions of the state are tasked with documenting and sorting *everything* because, apart from the sacramental silver of the first and second degree (and even this was subject to bureaucratic deliberation), one is never absolutely certain which among the remaining books, things, and buildings has the potential to channel the power that circulated around the transforming and transformative body of Christ.

Across all of these scenes, I have been tracing experiences of anchoring into unknowable futures through list-making. Inventorying entails slotting embodied experiences into categories, degrees, types, models—all of which are but temporary resting points. In all cases mobility has been a plot driver as these writers' quests for stability, meaning, and history became more complex because of their shifting locations. If there is any constancy, it is "change," the historian's watchword. When genres prove inadequate to the shifting realities of life on the move, new iterations are composed to make something new or to shut something down.

In sum, the pen was taken up with a desire to captures selves, to know others, and sometimes to constrain them. Reading with attention to space, place, and affect brings into sharp relief how textuality is a product of embodied experience, the existential ground from which they took up writing as locational labor: Castillo, Thjülen, and Sebastián crafted inventories as waymaking devices.

Acknowledgments

Northwestern University, with its faculty in religious studies, has proven a congenial environment to think and write. Almost everyone in the department has read bits and pieces of this book, but I am especially grateful to our fantastic cohort of graduate students many of whom, over the past few years, have read and chatted about this work in some of my seminars. Special thanks to colleagues Kevin Buckelew, Beth Hurd, Sarah Jacoby, Brannon Ingram, Richard Kieckhefer, Mark McClish, Robert Orsi, and Barry Wimpfheimer, who have laid eyes on various pieces of this book. I have presented in the workshop on religion and global politics organized by Beth and Brannon, which has been an ideal audience for thinking through issues pertaining to Catholicism and colonial sovereignty. And I cannot forget Mira Balberg, now off teaching in the sunny climes of southern California, but who is in no way a "former colleague" when she continues to read and comment upon the bits that I have sent her way.

Outside of the department, I have been supported by Latin American and Caribbean Studies (LACS) under the supportive leadership of Paul Gillingham, Mark Hauser, and Jorge Coronado. I have also very much enjoyed working with an informal workshop of early modern scholars who are true GEMs (Global Early Modern scholars). Thank you to Lydia Barnett, Caroline Egan, Rajeev Kinra, Paul Ramírez, Claudia Swan (now at SLU), and Rebecca Zorach, who have all read various segments of this work. Across campus, over in Radio, TV, and Film, Dave Tolchinsky generously read versions of the introduction, offering excellent advice about playing with play structure and how to think about lighting. Northwestern University helped fund research and time off from teaching through the Alice Kaplan Humanities Fellowship, as well as the Provost's Faculty Research Grant.

In the Chicago area, the Newberry Library is a local treasure, the source of my best manuscript find in this book. Special thanks to Lia Markey and

Jessica Keating for including me in the wonderful workshop Captured Objects: Studying Premodern Inventories in 2022. I have also presented portions of this work at UIC's Catholic studies workshop under the leadership of Laura Dingeldein. I am always grateful for Matthew O'Hara's sharp eyes, which he leant to an early draft of the entire manuscript.

Thank you to for the assistance of staff and archivists at many archives, especially Dario Scarinci at the Archivo Romanum Societatus Iesu (ARSI), and to Camilla Russel from breaking away from her work at the journal to find time for lunch or a glass of wine, but always an illuminating chat; to the staff at the Archiginassio in Bologna (one of whom was so kind as to tap me on the shoulder to stop my furious note taking; she let me know that Sebastián's work had been digitized, and I could have a copy of the whole thing!). Thanks to all the staff who assisted at the Faenza municipal library; the Archivo General de Indias (AGI); the Archivo Histórico de Loyola in Azpieta; the Archivo Histórico in Madrid; the Biblioteca Histórico José María Lafragua in Puebla; and of course the Archivo General de la Nación (AGN) in Mexico City. Special thanks to Patricia Vargas Gallardo at the Galeria Mariana in Guanajuato and to Tania Vargas Díaz for her assistance with access to the Biblioteca y Acervos of the Museo Franz Mayer.

As this work took shape, I benefited immensely from conversations across the United States. Special thanks to Jonathan Sheehan and Diego Pirillo for inviting me to present at the Renaissance and Early Modern Studies workshop at UC Berkeley; to Chad Seales for organizing the conference on Material Religions in the Americas at University of Texas, Austin; to Karen Graubart for her invitation to present a chapter at the Kellogg Working Group on Latin American Studies; and to Elaine Fisher for her invitation to participate in the Global Reformations conference at Madison, Wisconsin. I developed the first inkling of this book at a workshop on conversion in Bloomington, Indiana, at the invitation of Christopher Wild and Hal Puff in 2015. But the ideas really took shape when thinking with and writing for Valentina Napolitano and Carlota McAllister's special edition on theopolitics. Conversation with Carlos Manrique about religion, sovereignty, and popular culture provide new terrain for thought. I am delighted to have a new conversation partner about Reform Catholicism in Rachael Johnson, while Pam Voekel's insights remain crucial. Ongoing conversations with Kristin Bloomer, Jennifer Scheper Hughes, Florence Hsia, and Karin Velez continue to be inspiring.

Thank you to John Seitz and Jessica Delgado for including this book in the Catholic Practices in the Americas series. I have enjoyed working with John Garza at Fordham University Press and am grateful to the anonymous reader, and deeply indebted as well to Pamela Voekel for the critically engaged reading of the manuscript. Thank you so much, Timothy deBold, for the excellent index.

Ryan Dohoney deserves a special shout out not only for having read through the entire manuscript at least twice, but also for having the best suggestions for reading, for both work and fun. He is an incredibly supportive colleague and friend, not to mention an incredible cook. Bryan Markovitz is an excellent writing partner. I am grateful for the cross-fertilization of ideas that has included detailed discussions about performance studies, theater, aporias, the stock market, and Farrel and Ball paint colors. Mary Weismantel always has a good reading suggestion but also super practical advice, whether about academics or life. This home team counts on Nathalie Bouzaglo's dry humor to cheer us all upward and onward, or at least we raise the glass up before we move on home! Debra and Dave Tolchinsky are treasured friends whose hilarity and immeasurable kindness make our lives better, as does sharing a meal with Sandra Binion and Lou Mallozzi, whether in their garden or anywhere they happen to be in Italy. Pam Lui and George Bucciero are wry, funny, and beloved family. This entire crew has been a solid support for me here in Evanston. Ana Maria Apodaca, my Altadena rock, remains foundational in my life.

What has been lost, what has been gained?

In the time since I published my first book, my father, my mother, and now, one of my sisters, have all left the planet. My hometown, Altadena, California, has for the most part burned to the ground. Hard losses, to be sure.

But as I have insisted throughout this book, disappearance is not antithetical to remains. Suzanne Watkins Molina died quite suddenly in August 2016. She didn't hear much about this project because it was just getting off the ground, and as she was dying she was far more intrigued by stories about my dating life. What remains is my mother's smile, as well as her laugh, which inhabit my body and thus pave the way toward my very social existence. I carry on my father's sense of humor (I'm sorry!) and his appetite for digging into politics. My father died in April 2024 after two years of losing him a piece at a time to dementia. But I prefer to remember how, after fifty plus years of marriage, he knew he needed to keep moving even without my mother, so he was a frequent visitor in Chicago. Most memorably he came along with me on a research trip to Bologna in 2017 when I was tracking down some of Lorenzo Ignazio Thjülen's more obscure writings. The Italian librarian at the tiny municipal library in Faenza kindly admitted him into the special collections reading room, where he kept his eyes on his *Atlantic* magazine while I read Thjülen's anti–French Revolution fantasy novel about a boy falling into the center of the earth. But more than anything else, we both remembered the incredible lunch afterward. Italy! I treasure these memories of my parents who hit the road with me to Spain and Mexico when I went on research trips, especially how keen they were to help with Sam and Theo, who were lucky to grow up feeling so unequivocally loved by them.

I honor the memory of Johanna Molina and am grateful for the years of sisterhood and friendship that, after some very fun years together at UC Berkeley, included almost daily long-distance phone calls where we mostly chatted about the kids we were raising. She passed down to her own children the "Molina" sense of humor as well as the deep appreciation of conviviality over a great meal. Olivia and Gabe, you are so clearly your own people, and yet it is through you that Joh lives on. I'm grateful.

What has been gained? Since I have published my first book, I have gained an entire new family! I met Dave Dunne in 2017, and I thought, damn it, Mom really would have liked not only this man but also his two wonderful children, Maureen and Augie. She would have enjoyed the entire Dunne clan, who have been so supportive of me in these recent difficult years. She would have thrived at any one of the family parties. And It is in no small part due to Mary Katherine Avery's open door policy and her sincere love of Sam and Theo that our genuinely blended family has come into being. Luckily my father, Charles Molina, got to know and enjoy my new family in his last years. Remarkably, in the last days of dementia, he continued to ask about everyone: me, my husband, my kids, and my stepkids.

These kids! They are all in their early twenties and they are truly friends to one another. I admire each of them for their determination to do what they love in this life. They find their individual paths, each through different mediums that combine structure and beauty: Sam, with his technical genius in oil and watercolors creates abstract mystery, Maureen merges political activism and stringed instruments, Augie hikes, tracks, hunts, cooks, and chats his way toward preserving rugged nature, and Theo creates cloudy worlds in code. Sam and I compare notes on the agonies and ecstasies of our respective crafts: painting and writing. Special thanks to Theo for engaging in conversation about Hadot and Bourdieu, some of my go-to thinkers. But he hasn't gotten hooked on Merleau-Ponty. Yet.

Dave Dunne! He gets his own paragraph now. I am so lucky to wake up to music every morning. Any place that I go with him feels new. How did I grow up in Altadena and never go to the Bunny Museum? He has made a tennis addict of me. His love of adventure makes me do things like walk across tiny bridges with no railings in the Dades Gorges in Morocco. He is my biggest fan, forever encouraging: Do it, go for it, try it, why not? He knows what makes me tick. Sam and Theo feel their lives enriched by the stories told by this former PD, whom they admiringly accuse of maneuvering the Chicago streets like a taxi driver. When I ask if they want to join on a trip, they always ask, is Dave coming? Translation: Will it be fun? I dedicate this book to Dave.

Notes

Introduction

1. J. Michelle Molina, *To Overcome Oneself: The Jesuit Ethic and the Spirit of Global Expansion* (Berkeley: University of California Press, 2013); Angela Barreto Xavier and Ines Županov, *Catholic Orientalism: Portuguese Empire, Indian Knowledge (16th–18th Centuries)* (Oxford: Oxford University Press, 2014); Ulrike Strasser, *Missionary Men in the Early Modern World: German Jesuits and Pacific Journeys* (Amsterdam: Amsterdam University Press, 2020); Karin Velez, *The Miraculous Flying House of Loreto: Spreading Catholicism in the Early Modern World* (Princeton, NJ: Princeton University Press, 2019); Luke Clossey, *Salvation and Globalization in the Early Jesuit Missions* (Cambridge: Cambridge University Press, 2008); Markus Friedrich, *The Jesuits*, trans. John Noel Dillon (Princeton, NJ: Princeton University Press, 2022).

2. For an overview of this still emerging field of study, see Robert Maryks and Jonathan Wright, eds., *Jesuit Survival and Restoration: A Global History, 1773–1900* (Leiden: Brill, 2015). Thomas Worcester asks scholars to look more closely at the difference between a "restored" or "new" Society of Jesus. I argue here for a "new" and very diminished one if compared to its former global power.

3. For an approach that emphasizes "continuity" over time despite radical changes, see José Casanova and Thomas Banchoff, eds., *The Jesuits and Globalization: Historical Legacies and Contemporary Challenges* (Washington, DC: Georgetown University Press, 2016).

4. In his account of issues ex-Jesuits faced throughout Europe from 1767 to 1814, Niccolò Guasti concludes his essay with the words, "And so the Order of St. Ignatius rose again in the shadow of an internal conflict and at the same time as a new expulsion." His rising phoenix language is simultaneously undercut by the phrase that points squarely to the real-world problems that made Jesuit cohesion quite difficult to maintain in most parts of the world. Niccolò Guasti, "The Age of Suppression: From the Expulsions to the Restoration of the Society of Jesus (1759–1820)," in *The Oxford Handbook of the Jesuits*, ed. Ines Županov (Oxford: Oxford University Press, 2017), 936. John McGreevy's argument is

that an embattled Society of Jesus struggled through the first half of the nineteenth century and found new institutional strength in the United States in the latter half of that century. "Global" in this work indicates US reach into the Philippines. John McGreevy, *American Jesuits and the World: How an Embattled Religious Order Made Modern Catholicism Global* (Princeton, NJ: Princeton University Press, 2016).

5. For the "death" of the Catholic Enlightenment's global movement in the wake of the French Revolution and Napoleon's rule and the beginnings of "papal Catholicism" or Ultramontanism, see Ulrich L. Lehner, *The Catholic Enlightenment: The Forgotten History of a Global Movement* (Oxford: Oxford University Press, 2016).

6. For a short account of narrative responses to the expulsion, see Karen Stolley, "East of Eden: Domesticating Exile in Jesuit Accounts of Their 1767 Expulsion from Spanish America," in *Jesuit Accounts of the Colonial Americas: Intercultural Transfers, Intellectual Disputes, and Textualities*, ed. Marc André Bernier, Clorinda Donato, and Hans-Jürgen Lüsebrink (Toronto: University of Toronto Press, 2014), 243–62.

7. I am riffing on Diana Taylor's concept of embodied "repertoires," which she conceptualized as having an ongoing life never found in "the archive." Her scholarship also helps me read for the quasi-ritualistic gestures that underwrite knowledge production, and her work can clue scholars into the performative dimensions that undergird (and sometimes undermine) the authoritative language captured on the page and filed away in archives. Diana Taylor, *The Archive and the Repertoire: Performing Cultural Memory in the Americas* (Durham, NC: Duke University Press, 2003).

8. Rebecca Schneider, "Performance Remains," *Performance Research* 6, no. 2 (2001): 100–108, at 105.

9. Taylor, *Archive and Repertoire*. See also B. M. Watson, "Please Stop Calling Things Archives: An Archivist's Plea," *Perspectives* 59, no. 1 (2021), https://www.historians.org/perspectives-article/please-stop-calling-things-archives-an-archivists-plea-january-2021/.

10. Alex Woloch, *The One vs. the Many: Minor Characters and the Space of the Protagonist in the Novel* (Princeton, NJ: Princeton University Press, 2004); Rebecca Schneider, *Theatre & History* (London: Bloomsbury, 2014); Schneider, "Performance Remains."

11. Schneider, "Performance Remains," 103.

12. In what follows, Dale Van Kley provides the European outlines, while Mörner and St. Claire Segurado provide the American details. Dale Van Kley, *Reform Catholicism and the International Suppression of the Jesuits in Enlightenment Europe* (New Haven, CT: Yale University Press, 2018). Magnus Mörner, "Los motivos de la expulsión de los jesuitas del imperio español,"

Historia mexicana 16, no. 1 (1966); Eva María St. Clair Segurado, "Difusión en América de la polémica europea en torno a la Compañía de Jesús: Literatura propagandística pro y antijesuita en Nueva España, 1754–1767," *Dimensión antropológica* 10, no. 27 (2003): 7–45.

13. William Doyle, *Jansenism: Catholic Resistance to Authority from the Reformation to the French Revolution* (New York: St. Martin's Press, 2000).

14. Luis de Molina, *Liberi Arbitrii cum Gratiae Donis, Divina Praescientia, Providentia, Praedestinatione et Reprobatione, Concordia* (Caesar Joachim Trognaesius, 1595); Juan de Mariana, *De rege et regis institutione* (Toledo, 1598).

15. Van Kley, *Reform Catholicism*, 103.

16. Andrea Smidt, "Bourbon Regalism and the Importation of Gallicanism: The Political Path for a State Religion in Eighteenth-Century Spain," *Anuario de historia de la Iglesia* 19 (2010): 25–53.

17. Karen Melvin, *Building Colonial Cities of God: Mendicant Orders and Urban Cultures in New Spain, 1570–1800* (Palo Alto, CA: Stanford University Press, 2012).

18. For a collection of essays that captures the global nature of these debates, see Ines Županov and Pierre Antoine Fabre, "The Rites Controversies in the Early Modern World: An Introduction," in *The Rites Controversies in the Early Modern World*, ed. Ines Županov and Pierre Antoine Fabre (Leiden: Brill, 2018), 1–26.

19. A detailed account of this is Smidt, "Bourbon Regalism."

20. Pamela Voekel's scholarship has been key to understanding how reform Catholicism reshaped colonial politics. Her first book situates Mexican Jansenist reformers as promoters of new notions of individualism and virtue, and her second takes a deep dive into how theologically-informed stances taken by reform Catholics influenced the emergence of liberal politics in Mexico and Central America in the late eighteenth and first half of the nineteenth-century. Pamela Voekel, *Alone Before God: The Religious Origins of Modernity in Mexico* (Durham, NC: Duke University Press, 2002); Pamela Voekel, *For God and Liberty: Catholicism and Revolution in the Atlantic World, 1790–1861* (Oxford: Oxford University Press, 2022).

21. Eva María St. Clair Segurado, *Expulsión y exilio de la provincia Jesuita Mexicana (1767–1820)* (Alicante: Universidad de Alicante, 2009).

22. Stephen Greenblatt, "A Mobility Studies Manifesto," in *Cultural Mobility: A Manifesto*, ed. Stephen Greenblatt (Cambridge: Cambridge University Press, 2010), 250–53.

23. Tamar Herzog, *Defining Nations: Immigrants and Citizens in Early Modern Spain and Spanish America* (New Haven, CT: Yale University Press, 2003).

24. Leo Cabranes-Grant, *From Scenarios to Networks: Performing the Intercultural in Colonial Mexico* (Evanston, IL: Northwestern University Press, 2016).

25. I have drawn inspiration from Matthew O'Hara, *The History of the Future in Colonial Mexico* (New Haven, CT: Yale University Press, 2018).

26. During the era of abolition, one island of Jesuit possibility remained in the Jesuit Province in Russia supported by Catherine the Great.

27. Alessandra Russo, "Cortés Objects and the Idea of New Spain: Inventories as Spatial Narratives," *Journal of the History of Collections* 23, no. 2 (2011): 229. For an excellent study of inventories that discusses how they can be deceptive and with suggestions for methodologies to apply to understand them, see Jessica Keating and Lia Markey, "'Indian' Objects in Medici and Austrian-Habsburg Inventories: A Case Study of the Sixteenth-Century Term," *Journal of the History of Collections* 23, no. 2 (2011): 283–300.

28. Aposento del Padre Thomas Perez: Libros que son del Colegio HM 15000–15003, 1771, Veracruz, Huntington Library, San Marino, California.

29. Alfred Gell, *Art and Agency: An Anthropological Theory* (Oxford: Oxford University Press, 1998), 96.

30. See William Mazzarella's highly productive rethinking of Durkheim's "mana." William Mazzarella, *The Mana of Mass Society* (Chicago: University of Chicago Press, 2017).

31. Joy Palacios and Richard Reinhardt were early interlocutors and copresenters who prompted me to think more deeply about these flows of power. See their own subsequent publications: Richard Reinhardt, "Francis of Assisi's Perfect Jouissance: Theorizing Conversion through Objects and Affects in Early Franciscan Fragments," *Material Religions* 18, no. 2 (2022): 228–49; Joy Palacios, *Ceremonial Splendor: Performing Priesthood in Early Modern France* (Philadelphia: University of Pennsylvania Press, 2022).

32. Robert Orsi, *History and Presence* (Cambridge, MA: Harvard University Press, 2016), 4, 8.

33. Amira Mittermaier, "Beyond the Human Horizon," *Religion and Society: Advances in Research* 12 (2021): 28.

34. For transactional struggles over physical and mystical agency that shape asymmetries of power in a colonial context, see Florence Bernault, *Colonial Transactions: Imaginaries, Bodies, and Histories* (Durham, NC: Duke University Press, 2019).

35. Cabranes-Grant, *From Scenarios to Networks*, xi.

36. J. Michelle Molina, "Technologies of the Self: The Letters of 18th Century Mexican Jesuit Spiritual Daughters," *History of Religions* 47, no. 4 (2008): 282–303; Molina, *To Overcome Oneself*; Mary Carruthers, *The Craft of Thought: Meditation, Rhetoric, and the Making of Images* (Cambridge: Cambridge University Press, 1998). Also important are Pierre Hadot, *Philosophy as a Way of Life: Spiritual Exercises from Socrates to Foucault* (Malden, MA: Wiley-Blackfield 1995); Brian Stock, *Augustine, the Reader: Meditation, Self-Knowledge and the Ethics of Interpretation* (Cambridge, MA: Harvard University Press, 1998).

37. Carruthers, *Craft of Thought*; Stock, *Augustine, the Reader*.

38. Bruno Latour, *Reassembling the Social: An Introduction to Actor-Network Theory* (Oxford: Oxford University Press, 2005); Cabranes-Grant, *From Scenarios to Networks*, preface and introduction. See also Thomas Tweed, *Crossing and Dwelling: A Theory of Religion* (Cambridge, MA: Harvard University Press, 2006).

39. See José Saramago, *All the Names* (New York: Mariner Books, 2001). See also Lacquer's insightful discussion of Saramago's novel in Thomas W. Laqueur, *The Work of the Dead: A Cultural History of Mortal Remains* (Princeton, NJ: Princeton University Press, 2015). For an account of nineteenth-century restored French Jesuits who labor to compile bibliographies written by the "Old Society," see Adina Ruiu, "French and Canadian Jesuit History Writing: A Bridge between the 'Old' and the 'New' Society," in Županov, ed., *The Oxford Handbook of the Jesuits*, 974–1003. I think her research demonstrates how worries about a future can animate the desire to inventory the past.

40. See Woloch, *The One Versus the Many*.

41. Lauren Berlant, *Cruel Optimism* (Durham, NC: Duke University Press, 2011).

42. Maurice Merleau-Ponty, *Phenomenology of Perception* (Englewood Cliffs, NJ: Routledge, 2012), 16.

43. Antoinette M. Burton, *Archive Stories: Facts, Fictions, and the Writing of History* (Durham, NC: Duke University Press, 2005); Arlette Farge, Thomas Scott-Railton, and Natalie Zemon Davis, *The Allure of the Archives* (New Haven, CT: Yale University Press, 2013); Carolyn Steedman, *Dust: The Archive and Cultural History* (New Brunswick, NJ: Rutgers University Press, 2002); Michel-Rolph Trouillot, *Silencing the Past: Power and the Production of History* (Boston: Beacon Press, 1995).

44. Elin Diamond, *Unmaking Mimesis: Essays on Feminism and Theater* (Englewood Cliffs, NJ: Routledge, 1994), v.

45. For a fictional inventory whose objects are placeholders for moments of affective intensity, see Leanne Shapton, *Important Artifacts and Personal Property from the Collection of Lenore Dooland Harold Morris, Including Books, Street Fashion, and Jewelry* (New York: Strachan & Quinn Auctioneers, 2009).

46. Elin Diamond, *Unmaking Mimesis: Essays on Feminism and Theatre* (Englewood Cliffs, NJ: Routledge, 1997), 104, 98.

47. My approach to "gaps" differs from how Saidiya Hartman's has practiced critical fabulation precisely to imaginatively address how archives have suppressed voiced of enslaved and maligned black historical actors. Saidiya Hartman, *Wayward Lives, Beautiful Experiments: Intimate Histories of Social Upheaval* (New York: W. W. Norton, 2019).

48. Ryan Dohoney, *Saving Abstraction: Morton Feldman, the de Menils, and the Rothko Chapel* (Oxford: Oxford University Press, 2019). In Feldman's

practice, he sat at his piano, an anxious participant in creating the appearance and disappearance of sound. Personal communication with author.

49. Diamond, *Unmaking Mimesis*, 104.

50. Deniz Gökturk engages a methodology of "dynamic frame adjustment." This is a flexible and combinatory methodology that addresses human "mobility" through a scholarly approach that is itself dynamic and mobile. Deniz Göktürk, *Tracing Complicity through Personal Archives and Machine Learning: On the Art of Border Trouble* (Berkeley: Center for Interdisciplinary Critical Inquiry, UC Berkeley, 2023).

51. J. Michelle Molina, "Making a Home in an Unfortunate Place: Phenomenology and Religion," in *Anthropology of Catholicism: A Reader*, ed. Kristin Norget, Valentina Napolitano, and Maya Mayblin (Berkeley: University of California Press, 2017), 257.

52. Schneider, "Performance Remains," 105.

53. Caroline Walker Bynum, *Dissimilar Similitudes: Devotional Objects in Late Medieval Europe* (New York: Zone Books, 2020), 53.

54. Schneider, "Performance Remains," 104.

55. Diamond, *Unmaking Mimesis*, xvi.

56. William Hanks, *Converting Words: Maya in the Age of the Cross* (Berkeley: University of California Press, 2010), 94–96.

57. Latour, *Reassembling the Social*, 30, 49, 68–74.

58. Benedictus de Spinoza et al., *The Ethics; Treatise on the Emendation of the Intellect; Selected Letters*, 2nd ed. (Indianapolis: Hackett, 1992); Susan James, *Passion and Action: The Emotions in Seventeenth-Century Philosophy* (Oxford: Clarendon Press, 1997); Gilles Deleuze, *Spinoza: Practical Philosophy* (San Francisco: City Lights Books, 1988).

59. Laurent Olivier, *The Dark Abyss of Time: Archaeology and Memory*, trans. Arthur Greenspan (Lanham, MD: Rowman & Littlefield, 2015), 9.

60. Latour, *Reassembling the Social*, 35.

61. Merleau-Ponty, *Phenomenology of Perception*, 50.

Act I. Arrest

1. Karen Melvin, *Building Colonial Cities of God: Mendicant Orders and Urban Cultures in New Spain, 1570–1800* (Palo Alto, CA: Stanford University Press, 2012); Pilar Gonzalbo Aizpuru, *La educación popular de los Jesuitas* (Mexico City: Universidad Iberoamericana, 1989); Gerard Decorme, SJ, *La obra de los Jesuitas mexicanos durante la época colonial, 1572–1767* (Mexico City: Antigua Librería Robredo de José Porrúa é Hijos, 1941).

2. Markus Friedrich, *The Jesuits*, trans. John Noel Dillon (Princeton, NJ: Princeton University Press, 2022).

3. Lindsay Jones, *The Hermeneutics of Sacred Architecture: Experience, Interpretation, Comparison, Vol. I* (Cambridge, MA: Harvard University Press, 2000).

4. Ingie Hovland, "Christianity, Place/Space, and Anthropology: Thinking Across Recent Research on Evangelical Place-Making," *Religion* 46, no. 3 (2016): 331–58.

5. Ernst Kantorowicz, *The King's Two Bodies: A Study in Medieval Political Theology* (Princeton, NJ: Princeton University Press, 1957).

6. Paul Johnson, Pamela E. Klassen, and Winnifred Fallers Sullivan, *Ekklesia: Three Inquiries in Church and State* (Chicago: University of Chicago Press, 2018), 3.

7. James D. Riley, "The Wealth of the Jesuits in Mexico, 1670–1767," *The Americas* 33, no. 2 (1976): 226–66.

8. For the history of the transition from slavery to a predominantly freed black Catholic community in eighteenth-century Puebla, see Pablo Sierra Silva, *Urban Slavery in Colonial Mexico: Puebla de los Ángeles, 1531–1706* (Cambridge: Cambridge University Press, 2018).

9. Jennifer Scheper Hughes, *The Church of the Dead: The Epidemic of 1576 and the Birth of Christianity in the Americas* (New York: New York University Press, 2021).

10. Croix, Carlos Francisco de Croix et al., *Documents concerning the expulsion of the Jesuits from Mexico in 1767–1781*, Ayer 1128, 14, Newberry Library. Hereafter Ayer 1128.

11. Kathryn Burns, "Notaries, Truth, Consequences," *American Historical Review* 110, no. 2 (April 2005): 350–79, at 351.

12. Ibid., 352; Tamar Herzog, *Mediación, archivos y ejercicio: Los escribanos de Quito (siglo XVII)* (Frankfurt: V. Klostermann, 1996).

13. *Colección general de las providencias hasta aquí tomadas por el gobierno sobre el estrañamiento y ocupación de temporalidades de los regulares de la Compañía que existían en los Dominios de S. M. de España, Indias, e Islas Filipinas* (Madrid: Imprenta Real de la Gazeta, 1767).

14. The resulting inventories of books and liturgical items are the historical sources that scholars have utilized, to various ends. Some examples include the scholarship of the eminent art historian Clara Bargellini, who has put inventories to work to undergird her longue durée history of the aesthetic impact of Jesuits' missionary enterprise in northern Mexico. She studies various items on the inventories to better understand the impact of Jesuit missionary labors on aesthetic and religious sensibilities. Clara Bargellini, "El arte de las misiones del norte de la Nueva España," *História, histórias* 1, no. 2 (2013): 123–66. Other scholars of Jesuit inventories have been guided by a bibliographic sensibility. Manrique Figueroa takes this approach in his study of the inventories of Jesuit books and libraries in New Spain to study the contents of certain college's

library collections. César Manrique Figueroa, "Arsenals of Knowledge: Reconstructing the Contents and Purpose of the Lost Jesuit Libraries of Northern Mexico," *Journal of Jesuit Studies* 10 (2023): 520–36. He wants to know what the Jesuits read. Specific studies of Jesuit silver altarware are few, but a good example would be Alma Montero Alarcón's essay, which takes a cultural heritage approach to Jesuit inventories. She evaluates the importance of these catalogues within the framework of historical patrimony. She wants to know what happened to Jesuit things, lamenting that much of ecclesiastical material history disappeared in the tumults of the nineteenth century. Alma Montero Alarcón, "Platería en el antiguo colegio jesuita noviciado de Tepotzotlán, año de 1767," in *El tesoro del lugar florido: Estudios sobre la plata iberoamericana—Siglos XVI–XIX*, ed. Juan Haroldo Rodas Estrada (Mexico City: El Forastero, 2017), 487–518. As will become clear here, my approach differs in that I am keen to trace the *process* of inventorying.

15. For the spatiality of affect in an entangled material world, see Carlos Manrique, "Spiritual Memory, Spatial Affects, and Churchstateness in Popular Uprising in Afro-Columbia's Pacific Littoral," *Political Theology* 25, no. 3 (2024): 261, 268.

16. See the special edition on theopolitics in *Social Analysis*, especially the introduction by Carlota McAllister and Valentina Napolitano, "Introduction: Incarnate Politics beyond the Cross and the Sword," *Social Analysis* 64, no. 4 (2020): 1–20. See Charly Coleman, *The Spirit of French Capitalism: Economic Theology in the Age of Enlightenment* (Palo Alto, CA: Stanford University Press, 2022).

17. Charly Coleman, "Vagaries of Disenchantment: God, Matter, and Mammon in the Eighteenth Century," *Modern Intellectual History* 14, no. 3 (2017): 881.

18. Coleman, *The Spirit of French Capitalism*, 22.

19. "Introduction," in Zvi Ben-Dor Benite, Stefanos Geroulanos, and Nicole Jerr, *The Scaffolding of Sovereignty: Global and Aesthetic Perspectives on the History of a Concept* (New York: Columbia University Press, 2018), 6, 10–11; Lauren Benton, *A Search for Sovereignty* (Cambridge: Cambridge University Press, 2009).

20. Bruno Latour, *Reassembling the Social: An Introduction to Actor-Network Theory* (Oxford: Oxford University Press, 2005). William Hanks writes brilliantly on this topic in *Converting Words: Maya in the Age of the Cross* (Berkeley: University of California Press, 2010).

21. Jennifer Scheper Hughes captures this beautifully in her rethinking of the meaning of the maps of the Relaciones Geográficas. See Hughes, *Church of the Dead: The Epidemic of 1576 and the Birth of Christianity in the Americas* (New York: New York University Press, 2021).

22. For a succinct evaluation of the mixed fate of remote mission stations after expulsion, see Olga Merino and Linda A. Newson, "Jesuit Missions in Spanish America: The Aftermath of the Expulsion," *Yearbook, Conference of Latin Americanist Geographers* 21 (1995): 133–48.

23. *Instrucción*, 15, 6.

24. Ayer 1128:14.

25. Ibid., 14v.

26. Ibid., 16. This statement is worth exploration. The secret is the king's secret, which he keeps in his royal heart (see *Instrucción*). It is inscribed in the documents as a royal secret, the act not to be made public until it occurs, but also the reasoning is explicit: In this performance of power, he has no need to justify his dominion.

27. Ayer 1128:17v, 18.

28. Johnson, Klassen, and Sullivan, *Ekklesia*, 7.

29. *Instrucción*, 2.

30. Ayer 1128:7.

31. Ibid., 21.

32. Ibid.

33. Ibid. On charitable dowries for unmarried women, see Jessica L. Delgado, *Laywomen and the Making of Colonial Catholicism in New Spain, 1630–1790* (Cambridge: Cambridge University Press, 2018).

34. Ayer 1128:21v.

35. Ibid.

36. This was common practice, as Zumáraga, the first bishop of Mexico, established an episcopal library that was supported by Crown funds and had extensive Renaissance holdings. J. Gabriel Martínez-Serna notes that even the small Jesuit college at Parras had several hundred volumes that included "books in Portuguese, Italian, Latin, Nahuatl, and authors such as Ovid, Cicero, Quevedo, Suárez, Vieira, and Cervantes." J. Gabriel Martínez-Serna, "Procurators and the Making of the Jesuits' Atlantic World," in *Soundings in Atlantic History: Latent Structures and Intellectual Currents, 1500–1830*, ed. Bernard Bailyn and Patricia E. Denault (Cambridge: Cambridge University Press, 2009), 96; Ignacio Osorio Romero, *Historia de las bibliotecas novohispanos* (Mexico City: SEP, 1986); Stuart M. McManus, "The Art of Being a Colonial *letrado*: Late Humanism, Learned Sociability and Urban Life in Eighteenth-Century Mexico City," *Estudios de historia novohispana* 56 (2017): 40–64; María Cristina Torales Pacheco, "Los jesuitas novohispanos, la modernidad y el espacio público ilustrado," in *Los jesuitas y la modernidad en Iberoamérica, 1549–1773*, ed. Manuel M. Marzal and Luis Bacigalupo (Lima: Fondo Editorial de la Pontificia Universidad Católica del Perú, 2007), 158–71.

37. M. Isabel García-Monge Carretero, "Inventarios de las bibliotecas de Jesuitas en la colección Biblioteca de Cortes de la Real Academia de la Historia," in *La memoria de los libros: Estudios sobre la historia del escrito y de la lectura en Europa y America* (Salamanca: Cilengua, 2004); Manrique Figueroa, "Arsenals of Knowledge."

38. Ayer 1128.

39. J. Michelle Molina, *To Overcome Oneself: The Jesuit Ethic and the Spirit of Global Expansion* (Berkeley: University of California Press, 2013).

40. Mónica Díaz, "The Education of Natives, Creole Clerics, and the Mexican Enlightenment," *Colonial Latin American Review* 24, no. 1 (2015): 60–83; J. Michelle Molina, "Technologies of the Self: The Letters of 18th Century Mexican Jesuit Spiritual Daughters," *History of Religions* 47, no. 4, (2008): 282–303; Susan Schroeder, "Jesuits, Nahuas and the Good Death Society in Mexico City, 1710–1767," *Hispanic American Historical Review* 80, no. 1 (2000): 43–47.

41. Ayer 1128:22.

42. Ibid., 27.

43. Joseph Och, S.J., *Missionary in Sonora: The Travel Reports of Joseph Och, S.J., 1755–1767*, trans. Theodore E. Treutlein (San Francisco: California Historical Society, 1965), 52.

44. Ayer 1128:26v.

45. Ibid., 27.

46. For discussion of debt in colonial Spanish Americas, see Regina Grafe, "An Empire of Debt? The Spanish Empire and Its Colonial Realm," in *A World of Public Debts: A Political History*, ed. Nicolas Barreyre and Nicolas Delalande (New York: Springer, 2020), 5–35.

47. Ayer 1128:27, 27v.

48. Ibid. Note that soldiers, then, are not surrounding haciendas, if the commissioner divided up that labor on the morning of the arrest. Gravina is likely Giuseppe Maria Gravina, *Trattenimenti apologetici sul probalismo*, vols. 1–3 (Palermo, 1755). Raccolta is Italian for "collection" and could refer to any Italian collection of sermons, selections from scripture, or poetry, among other options.

49. Ayer 1128:28. The introduction of this luxury item in New Spain is connected to its strategic position on the Manila Galleon trade route, as was the fashion for other "Asian" items including porcelain and lacquerware, and the Japanese screen. In the early seventeenth century, Mexican Jesuits incorporated kimonos into celebrations of the canonizations of Ignatius and Francis Xavier (1622), worn by participants who represented Asia as one of the "four corners" of the world in which the Jesuits were stationed. The seventeenth- and eighteenth-century history of the garment in New Spain parallels

the adaptations of the Armenian or Indian "robe" or dressing gown in European fashion for both men and women, the latter being a mode of dress that by the eighteenth century in New Spain was considered on par with "Parisian" styles, though the name *quimono* and its connection to Japan were retained in local accounts. See Andreia Martins Torres, "El quimono en la Nueva España: Una manifestación local de una moda global en los siglos XVII y XVIII," *Conservar património* 31 (2019): 79–95.

50. Ayer 1128:28.

51. Ibid., 28, 28v, 29, 29v. The next room belonged to Padre Augustín Arriola, who had nothing to declare. The "Calancha" refers to a work by Antonio de la Calancha, perhaps his *Corónica moralizada* published in the 1630s. Despite paralysis, Diego Vargas did leave New Spain with his fellow Jesuits but was secularized in Puerto Santa María and died in Genoa in 1769. He is not included in Felix de Sebastián's *Memorias*. Louis de Blois was a Flemish monk and mystical writer. The next room belonged to Padre Joaquín de Tapia, who declared that nothing in his room belonged to anyone else. Hermano Baltasar de Porras, and Hermano Mariano Coca similarly claimed all items belonged to them.

52. Ibid., 30. The next room belonged to Hermano Manuel Ciorraga, who had nothing to declare.

53. Ibid., 30, 30v, 31. The next rooms belonged to Padre Enriquez Alvaros, Hermano Antonio Ramirez, Hermano Francisco Xavier Gerardi, and Padre Juan de Chavez, who had nothing to declare. Neither did Padre Ignacio Guben, Hermano Magdaleno Osio, Hermano Manuel Velasco, Padre Laureano Bravo, Padre José Bueno, Hermano Juan Francisco Ponse, Padre Miguel Baqueda (Vaquera?), and Padre Narciso Gonzales Ayer.

54. Miguel Angel Pascual, SJ, 1644–1714, wrote *Operario instruído, El oyente remediado*, and *El missionero instruido. Speculum amoris et doloris in sacratissimo ac divinissimo corde Jesu Incarnati, eucharistici et crucifixi orbi christiano propositum: et nunc ex occasione celeberrimae Congregationis sub titulo SS. Cordis Jesu authoritate Summ. Pontificis Clementis XI*, opera & studio a R. D. Antonii Ginther (Anton Ginther). Ayer 1128:32. Also note that Narciso and Eligio, who appear briefly in Act III, have rooms right next to each other.

55. The commissioner interviewed Hermano Salvador Rodriguez, one of two Jesuits tasked with door duties, who said he had nothing alien but noted an uninhabited room above. "In the same act, the Lord Commissioner collected the key of said high Chamber." They examined a false door. They asked additional questions of the second doorman, Hermano Francisco Xavier Gerardi. This *portero* claimed to nothing had been given to him, but added that he held an additional key to the unnumbered room on the higher floor explaining that is where he waited for the arrival of the Fathers after he woke

them up. He also informed them that certain *aposentos* had, in essence, been overlooked, because Hermanos Pedro Inchaurrandieta and Juan Antonio de Aguirre, assistants to the procurator, made their room in the *procuraduria*. He added that a Jesuit named Bernabé Pozo had yet to arrive from Guatemala. Ayer 1128:32, 32v.

56. Leora Auslander, "Beyond Words," *American Historical Review* 110, no. 4 (2005): 1027.

57. Zvi Ben-Dor Benite, Stefanos Geroulanos, and Nicole Jerr, *The Scaffolding of Sovereignty: Global and Aesthetic Perspectives on the History of a Concept* (New York: Columbia University Press, 2018).

58. Auslander, "Beyond Words," 1015.

59. James Duncan Gentry, *Power Objects in Tibetan Buddhism: The Life, Writings, and Legacy of Sokdokpa Lodrö Gyeltsen* (Leiden: Brill, 2017), 16.

60. This is not so different, in some respects, from modern evangelicals who make use of a wide variety of places to launch their local and translocal evangelization. Hovland, "Christianity, Place/Space, and Anthropology."

61. Michael Marder, *Dust* (New York: Bloomsbury, 2016), 74.

62. *Instrucción*, 8–10.

63. Ayer 1128:36.

64. The Jesuits from Puebla had a peaceful departure. This was not the case in Guanajuato, where there was a popular rebellion followed by swift and very violent reprisal. See Felipe Castro Gutiérrez, *Nueva ley y nuevo rey: Reformas borbónicas y rebelión popular en Nueva España* (Mexico City: Colegio de Michoacan/UNAM, 1986).

65. *Instrucción*, 13, "para responder y aclarar exactamente, baxo de deposiciones formales, quanto se le preguntare tocante a sus Haciendas, Papeles, ajuste de Cuentas, Caudales, y régimen interior."

66. Martínez-Serna, "Procurators and the Making of the Jesuits' Atlantic World," 198–200.

67. Ayer 1128:38.

68. Ibid., 54, 58.

69. Ayer 1128:54, 58, 41, 47, 60v, 61. Zelís lists Sarmiento as an administrator at San Andres in Mexico City.

70. *Collección*, 8.

71. Ayer 1128:49.

72. Dale Van Kley, *Reform Catholicism and the International Suppression of the Jesuits in Enlightenment Europe* (New Haven, CT: Yale University Press, 2018).

73. Pamela Voekel, *For God and Liberty: Catholicism and Revolution in the Atlantic World, 1790–1861* (Oxford: Oxford University Press, 2022), 30–31, 37.

74. Pamela Voekel, *Alone Before God: The Religious Origins of Modernity in Mexico* (Durham, NC: Duke University Press, 2002), 42–76.

75. Debates about theological worldviews grounded the new political order in postindependence Mexico and Central America—that is, competing views about the Church's role in guiding a proper human relation to God were the religious grounds of nineteenth-century political battles. Voekel, *For God and Liberty*.

76. Ayer 1128:50. P. Francisco Arámburu, b. 1706, Puebla–d. 1769, Ferrara, Italy, was a prefect and confessor. Rafael de Zelís, *Catálogo de los sugetos de la Compañía de Jesús que formaron la Provincia de México el día del arresto, 25 de Junio de 1767* (1871), 113, 45. http://hdl.handle.net/2027/nnc1.0037123319. See also José Felix de Sebastián's *Memorias de los padres y hermanos de la Compañía De Jesus de la provincia de Nueva España difuntos despues del arresto acaecido en la capital de Mexico el día 25 de junio del año 1767* (Archiginnasio), 135–39.

77. San Jerónimo was a hacienda where animals were sheared or slaughtered and was a key locale in the network of Jesuit agricultural ventures in the region. Ursula Ewald, *Estudios sobre la hacienda colonial en México: Las propiedades rurales del colegio Espíritu Santo en Puebla*, trans. Luis R Cerna (Wiesbaden: Franz Steiner Verlag, 1976), 102.

78. Ayer 1128:50v.

79. *Historia del Pueblo de Dios* (Madrid: Viuda de Manuel Fernández, 1755).

80. José Abel Ramos Soriano, *Los delincuentes de papel: Inquisición y libros en la Nueva España, 1571–1820* (Mexico City: Fondo de Cultura Económica, 2011).

81. Archivo General de la Nación/Universidad Nacional Autonoma de México, *Documentos para la historia de la cultura en México: Una biblioteca del siglo XVII—Catalogo de libros expurgados a los Jesuitas en el siglo XVIII* (Mexico City: Imprenta Universitaria, 1947), 131.

82. Eva María St. Clair Segurado, *Expulsión y exilio de la provincia jesuita mexicana (1767–1820)* (Alicante: Universidad de Alicante, 2009).

83. Van Kley, *Reform Catholicism*, 102, 94. Both Berruyer and Hardouin were specifically mentioned in Campomanes. For all on Berruyer's Bible, I am indebted to Daniel J. Watkins, *Berruyer's Bible: Public Opinion and the Politics of Enlightenment Catholicism* (Montreal: McGill-Queen's University Press, 2021).

84. Jonathan Sheehan, *The Enlightenment Bible: Translation, Scholarship, Culture* (Princeton, NJ: Princeton University Press, 2007).

85. On affective devotional imagination, see Walter Melion and Lee Palmer Wandel, *Image and Incarnation: The Early Modern Doctrine of the Pictorial Image* (Leiden: Brill, 2015).

86. Molina, *To Overcome Oneself*.

87. *Historia del Pueblo de Dios* (Madrid: Viuda de Manuel Fernández, 1755), part 1, 200–202.

88. Berruyer, *Historia* 196, 197–98. "Todo contribuía, al parecer, a justificar la resistencia de Abraham en tales circunstancias. El sacrificio de sangre

humana, ordenado por un Dios, que se ofende siempre de semejantes barbaridades: el quitar la vida á un hijo, por mano de su mismo Padre, y por mandato de un Señor, que se confiessa Padre de todos los hombres. . . . Era el camino largo, y en tres dias, quye duró la marcha, serian bien amargas las reflexiones de Abraham. No obstante, en nada se arrepintió. Su alma iba penetrada del mas vivo dolor; pero siempre muy dueño de si mismo, sin dar lugar á que en el semblante se percibiesse lo que sentía el corazon."

89. Jonathan Spence, *The Memory Palace of Matteo Ricci* (New York: Penguin Books, 1984); Ines Županov, *Disputed Mission: Jesuit Experiments and Brahmanical Knowledge in Seventeenth Century India* (Oxford: Oxford University Press, 1999); Ananya Chakravarti, *Empire of Apostles: Religion, Accommodation and the Imagination of Empire in Modern Brazil and India* (Oxford: Oxford University Press, 2018). See also Markus Friedrich on the roots of Jesuit accommodation.

90. Van Kley, *Reform Catholicism*.

91. Norman Neuerburg, "La Madre Santísima de la Luz," *Journal of San Diego History* 41, no. 2 (1995): 74–86; William B. Taylor, *Theater of a Thousand Wonders: A History of Miraculous Images and Shrines in New Spain* (Cambridge: Cambridge University Press, 2016), 277–80.

92. *Antidoto contra todo mal: La devoción a la Santísima Madre del Lumen* (Mexico City: Joseph Bernardo de Hogal, 1737).

93. "Dedicado al eterno Lumen Humanado, para que se logre la salud eterna de las almas, que con su divina Sangre Redimió."

94. Enrique Giménez López, "La devoción a la Madre Santisima de la Luz," *Revista de historia moderna* 15 (1996): 213.

95. Neuerburg, "La Madre Santísima de la Luz."

96. *Antidoto contra todo mal*.

97. Neuerburg, "La Madre Santísima de la Luz," 78.

98. In the Veracruz inventory held at the Huntington Library, the *aposento* of Pérez contains books that "correspond" to Our Lady of the Light. Aposento del Padre Thomas Perez: Libros que son del Colegio HM 15000–15003.

99. This language is amended slightly in a later inventory. A 1774 addendum refers to the adornments that belong to Nuestra Señora de la Luz and clarifies that the items do not belong to a Jesuit-sponsored confraternity. The notary still marks the items as the "alajas que pertenecen a Nuestra Señora de la Luz," but the copy is edited and written in tiny print, and tucked in between the lines is a correction that describes these items "of the College of Espíritu Santo in Puebla de Los Angeles," BHJML, Legajo 139, "Año de 1774. Nominas de division por clases de las Alajas de Oro y Plata inventariadas en los Cinco Colegios occupados en esta Ciudad [de Puebla de Los Angeles]," 1774, Fondo Jesuita, Legajo 139, Biblioteca Histórica José María Lafragua de la BUAP, f. 45, Fondo Antiguo José María Lafragua, Puebla.

100. William Taylor remarks that scholarship has looked at the issue of the religious prints largely from the vantage point of their flow as commodities, and their development as aesthetic objects. He argues that production, promotion, and consumption are not mutually exclusive: "producers and promoters were often consumers, as well as influencing consumption by others." See *Theater of a Thousand Wonders*, 453n117. The role played by confraternities as producers, promoters, and consumers is a key example (53n, 400).

101. Paul Nelles, "*Libros de Papel, Libri Bianchi, Libri Papyracel*: Note-taking Techniques and the Role of Student Notebooks in the Early Jesuit Colleges," *Archivum Historicum Societatus Iesu* 76 (January–June 2007): 106. Accordingly, the notebooks provided possibilities not only to repeat and memorize, but also to clarify what was ill understood. Reiteration was key to Jesuit education and spiritual practices.

102. Eva María St. Clair Segurado, "Difusión en América de la polémica europa en torno a la Compañía de Jesús: Literatura propagandística pro y antijesuita en Nueva España, 1754–1767," *Dimensión antropológica* 27 (2003): 24. Evidence of such literature is in remote Jesuit libraries, too. Manrique Figueroa, "Arsenals of Knowledge," 534.

103. Devotion to the Virgen del Carmen was also controversial because she descended into purgatory to liberate souls from flames. J. Carlos Vizuete Mendoza, "En las fronteras de la ortodoxia: La devoción a la Virgen de la Luz (Madre Santísima de la Luz) en Nueva España," in *Religión y heterodoxia en el mundo hispánico, siglos XIV–XVIII*, ed. Ricard Izquierdo Benito and Fernando Martínez Gil (Madrid: Sílex, 2011), 277.

104. Neuerburg, "La Madre Santísima de la Luz."

105. Postexpulsion debate about the validity of Jesuit confessional practices is noted in Eva María Mehl, "La expulsión de los Jesuitas y la represión del Jesuitismo en Nueva España," in *Espacios de saber, espacios de poder: Iglesia, universidades, y colegios en Hispanoamérica, siglos XVI–XIX*, ed. Rodolfo Aguirre Salvador (Mexico City: Universidad Nacional Autónoma de México, 2014).

106. Giménez-López notes the problem of convents—women who had images of Ignatius and Francisco Borgia, plus "corazones de Jesús, y IHS," an open book with the Jesuit motto "Ad Maijorem Dei Gloriam," plus a page from the Jesuit constitutions. Enrique Giménez López, "La devoción a la Madre Santisima de la Luz: Un aspecto de la represión del jesuitismo en la España de Carlos III," *Revista de la historia moderna* 15 (1996): 219.

107. Luisa Zahino Peñafort, *Iglesia y sociedad en México, 1765–1800: Tradición, reforma y reacciones* (Mexico City: UNAM, 1996), 168.

108. Vizuete Mendoza, "En las fronteras de la ortodoxia," 273. "Porque es devoción introducida por los jesuitas y es necesario destruir y borrar la memoria de todas sus cosas." This anxiety about continuing influence of the

Jesuits was amplified by "pretenders" who imitated Jesuit priests. Salvador Bernabéu Albert, "El vacío habitado: Jesuitas reales y simulados en México durante los años de la supresión (1767–1816)," *Historia Mexicana* 58, no. 4 (2009): 1261–303.

109. Detailed in his *Diario de peraciones del Concilio Provincial*. "los votos fueron desentonados, llenos de sangre, hízose negocio de jesuitas el que lo era de mi Señora de la Luz, y se tomó con tal arte el asunto, que le hubieran hecho causa de jesuita y fanático al que hubiera querido oponerse a aquel torrente." See Vizuete Mendoza, "En las fronteras de la ortodoxia," 273.

110. IV Council, Libro III, Titulo XXI: "de las reliquías y veneración de los santos y templos." ff.150–150v. Quoted in ibid., 256. "Con adornos del mundo, collares, gargantillas, pulseras y otros muy ajenos a la singular modestia."

111. Ibid., 258.

112. Caroline Walker Bynum, *Dissimilar Similitudes: Devotional Objects in Late Medieval Europe* (New York: Zone Books, 2020).

113. Vizuete Mendoza, "En las fronteras de la ortodoxia," 260.

114. For a typology of types of material replication in his study of how scenes from the Christian Bible have been staged in the modern United States, see especially part I, "Variations on Replication," in James S. Bielo, *Materializing the Bible: Scripture, Sensation, Place* (New York: Bloomsbury Academic, 2021).

115. Richard Kieckhefer, *The Mystical Presence of Christ: The Exceptional and the Ordinary in Late Medieval Religion* (Ithaca, NY: Cornell University Press, 2022), 179.

116. Brian R. Larkin, *The Very Nature of God: Baroque Catholicism and Religious Reform in Bourbon Mexico City* (Albuquerque: University of New Mexico Press, 2010), 54.

117. Ilona Katzew, *The Archive of the World* (Los Angeles: Los Angeles County Museum, 2022).

118. Daniel Nemser, *Infrastructures of Race: Concentration and Biopolitics in Colonial Mexico* (Austin: University of Texas Press, 2017); Hanks, *Converting Words*.

119. Larkin, *The Very Nature of God*.

120. Hughes, *Church of the Dead*; William B. Taylor, *Magistrates of the Sacred: Priests and Parishioners in Eighteenth-Century Mexico* (Palo Alto, CA: Stanford University Press, 1996).

121. Louise M. Burkhart, *Staging Christ's Passion in Eighteenth-Century Mexico* (Albany: Institute for Mesoamerican Studies, SUNY, 2023).

122. Larkin, *The Very Nature of God*, 37, 69.

123. Kieckhefer, *Mystical Presence of Christ*, 77.

124. Ibid., 33. My emphasis.

125. For decades, science studies scholars have provided useful avenues for approaching the study of inventories that are similarly dynamic, making clear how rational ordering was intertwined with affective experience, as early modern knowledge production held within it a desire to be moved by the experience of "wonder", which motivated both the act of collection and the mode display of natural and cultural objects. See Lorraine Daston, "The Factual Sensibility," *Isis* 79, no. 3 (1988): 452–67.

126. The methodology that I have in mind is in part inspired by Alessandra Russo, whose study of the gifts that Hernán Cortés sent back to Castille suggests a novel way to study inventories. Alessandra Russo argues that in gift exchange the conquerors and the conquered were engaged in episodes of creative thinking. The inventorying process (naming items gifted and received) was a set of object-oriented practices that, Russo argues, show how *inventorying* (a verb) did spatial work. That is, in the process of listing, new worlds were shaped and amplified, creating "complex dynamics where territories are redefined through the concrete presence of the travelled object." Russo, "Cortés Objects and the Idea of New Spain: Inventories as Spatial Narratives," *Journal of the History of Collections* 23, no. 2 (2011): 229–52, at 241.

127. Helen Hills, *Matter of Miracles: Neopolitan Baroque Sanctity and Architecture* (Manchester: Manchester University Press, 2016), 446–47, and ch. 10. For early sixteenth-century legislation about who could produce silver objects, the ensuing seventeenth-century silver boom that linked wealth and devotion in the material production of altarware, and some examples of Poblano artistry, see Cristina Esteras Martín, *Platería hispanoamericana, siglos XVI–XIX: Exposición diocesana badajocense* (Mexico City: Exposición Diocesana Badajocense, 1984).

128. BHJML, Legajo 139: 45v.

129. Simple corrections here include a margin note reminding scribes to please indicate the height of the silver jars (*xarras*). Another margin note indicates that the jar with Christ's shield (*el escudo de Jesus*) is on the wrong list.

130. The note explaining this difficulty is dated 1775.

131. Lee Palmer Wandel, *The Eucharist in the Reformation: Incarnation and Liturgy* (Cambridge: Cambridge University Press, 2006), 236.

132. Andrew Pickering, "The Ontological Turn: Taking Different Worlds Seriously," *Social Analysis* 61, no. 2 (2017): 136.

133. Latour, *Reassembling the Social*, 68–74.

134. Leo Cabranes-Grant, *From Scenarios to Networks: Performing the Intercultural in Colonial Mexico* (Evanston, IL: Northwestern University Press, 2016), 63.

135. Emile Durkheim, *Elementary Forms of Religious Life*, trans. Karen E. Fields (New York: Free Press, 1995); William Mazzarella, *The Mana of Mass*

Society (Chicago: University of Chicago Press, 2017); Martin Holbraad, "The Power of Powder: Multiplicity and Motion in the Divinatory Cosmology of Cuban Ifá (or Mana, Again)," in *Thinking Through Things: Theorising Artefacts Ethnographically*, ed. Amiria Henare, Martin Holbraad, and Sari Wastell (London and New York: Routledge 2007), 189–225.

136. Holbraad, "Power of Powder"; Mazzarella, *The Mana of Mass Society*.

137. FAJML, Legajo 139:21v.

138. Ibid., 23–23v.

139. Ibid., 25.

140. Ibid., 26v, 28v.

141. Ibid., 27–27v.

142. Caroline Walker Bynum, *Christian Materiality: An Essay on Religion in Late Medieval Europe* (New York: Zone Books, 2011), 35.

143. What happens when matter once considered sacred becomes national patrimony displayed in museums? See Elayne Oliphant, *The Privilege of Being Banal: Art, Secularism, and Catholicism in Paris* (Chicago: University of Chicago Press, 2021). Oliphant, however, does not deploy a notion of sacramentality to determine which objects would be considered actants in a sacred network; rather, the objects under study in her book have a Catholic history that is for some of her interlocutors connected to personal devotional meaning-making.

144. Benite, Geroulanos, and Jerr, *The Scaffolding of Sovereignty*.

145. On sacramental wealth, see Coleman, *The Spirit of French Capitalism*, 27, 29–68.

146. These would be for members of a religious congregation devoted to Santa Rosalia. There were, in fact, religious congregations on the haciendas that the *Directive* never mentions, even when describing efforts to regulate the moral and devotional worlds of slaves and servants. Ewald, *Estudios sobre la hacienda colonial*, 39. She cites the Hacienda de San Jerónimo as having three *cofradías*: Nuestra Señora de Loreto, Rosario, and Santa Rosalía. These *cofradías* had approximately six hundred pesos saved in their account at the hacienda at the time of the expulsion of the Jesuits in 1767.

147. It is technically an "instruction," but I want to disambiguate it from Aranda's instruction discussed in the first half of this Act.

148. The manuscript was not published until the twentieth century, the result of Francois Chevalier's dissertation work on the Jesuit-run hacienda. Relying upon in-text citations, Chevalier dates the the manuscript to the eighteenth century and suggests that it could not have been written prior to 1723. Francois Chevallier, ed., *Instrucción que han de guardar los hermanos administradores de haciendas del campo* (Mexico City: Centro de Investigaciones Superiores INAH, 1950), 11. In-text references include Esteyneffer's *Florilegio medicinal* which was first published in 1712. In the Asian context, a Jesuit

instruction manual pertaining to coconut production titled *Arte Palmorica* is discussed by Angela Barreto Xavier and Ines Županov in *Catholic Orientalism Portuguese Empire, Indian Knowledge (16th–18th Centuries)* (Oxford: Oxford University Press, 2014), 104–6. They give no indication that aspects of the Jesuit administrator's vocation is at stake in the production of that instruction.

149. Scholars have shown how enslaved persons utilized the legal system to bring the promises of freedom in the afterlife to a reality in their "now." Bianca Premo, *The Enlightenment on Trial: Ordinary Litigants and Colonialism in the Spanish Empire* (Oxford: Oxford University Press, 2017); Dennis N. Valdés, "The Decline of Slavery in Mexico," *The Americas* 75, no. 1 (2018): 167–94; Silva, *Urban Slavery*; Chloe Ireton, "Black Africans' Freedom Litigation Suits to Define Just War and Just Slavery in the Early Spanish Empire," *Renaissance Quarterly* 73 (2020): 1277–319. Pablo Silva makes the religious dimensions and the indigenous/black kinship networks an important part of this history. Silva, *Urban Slavery*.

150. Chevallier, *Instrucción*, 85–92.

151. William B. Taylor, *Magistrates of the Sacred: Priests and Parishioners in Eighteenth-Century Mexico* (Palo Alto, CA: Stanford University Press, 1996), 332.

152. Chevallier, *Instrucción*, 92, 86–88.

153. Ibid., 92.

154. For the patriarchal values that underwrote legal norms and shaped colonial governance in the Americas, see Bianca Premo, *Children of the Father King: Youth, Authority, and Legal Minority in Colonial Lima* (Chapel Hill: University of North Carolina Press, 2005)..

155. Ewald, *Estudios sobre la hacienda colonial*, 30–31.

156. But in Ewald's study of the haciendas affiliated with the Colegio Espíritu Santo, she finds that while higher status "servientes de razón" had initially referred to *españoles* and *criollos*, by the eighteenth century this category also included mestizos and sometimes Indians. On the mestizo as an indeterminate category, see Joan Rappaport, *The Disappearing Mestizo: Configuring Difference in the Colonial New Kingdom of Granada* (Durham, NC: Duke University Press, 2014).

157. Chevallier, *Instrucción*, paragraphs 19 and 20.

158. Juan Martínez de la Parra, *Luz de verdades católicas y explicación de la doctrina christiana que siguiendo la costumbre de la casa professa de la Compañía de México . . . se platica en su iglesia* (Mexico City: en la imprenta de Diego Fernández de Leon, 1691–1696), 198.

159. "Esso es lo que no quisieron dar a entender con este nombre nuestros mayores, que ni los senores se hagan odiosos con el entono de su dominio, ni a los esclavos se les de siempre en cara con lo abatido de su fuerte" (ibid., 198). On Seneca's qualified defense of the humanity of slaves, William Watts, "Seneca on Slavery," *The Downside Review* 90, no. 300 (1972): 189.

160. For Jesuit references to "resplendent blackness," see Larissa Brewer-Garcia, *Beyond Babel: Translations of Blackness in Colonial Peru and New Granada* (Cambridge: Cambridge University Press, 2020).

161. "Pues haced todo quanto os mandan, considerando que es el mismo Dios quien lo manda."

162. "porque al común no se le haga pesada esta devota distribución." Chevallier, *Instrucción*, Paragraph 7.

163. Chevallier, *Instrucción*, Paragraph 23.

164. Ibid., Paragraph 24, 30.

165. Ibid. He refers here to P. Bartolomé Castaño, SJ, *Catecismo breve de lo que precisamente ha de saber el Cristiano* (1644).

166. Labor mobility means that he must police the moral boundaries of his idealized community. See J. Michelle Molina, "How to Be a Country Jesuit: Continence, Care and Containment in a Racializing Religiosity," in *Jesuits and Race*, ed. Nathaniel Millet and Charles Parker (University of New Mexico Press, 2022), 133–62. The importance of penance, but especially the advocacy of frequent communion, meant that hacienda inhabitants were trained to practice a Catholicism that bore a distinctly Jesuit stamp. Since the days of Ignatius of Loyola, the Jesuits had advocated frequent communion, not only for the clergy, but "once per week" for the students at Jesuit colleges, with daily communion for the more spiritually advanced, advising his women followers that they would benefit from daily communion, if they have done the work to assure that their consciences were clear. Thus, Jesuit advocacy of frequent communion on the hacienda needs to be understood against the backdrop of a sacramental culture that demanded at minimum that all Catholics make the sacrament of penance and receive the Eucharist once per year during the Easter season. No matter how many times hacienda residents had taken communion during the year, the annual requirement took no account of how one's relationship to Christ had been mediated by Jesuits. But this is a site of theopolitical contestation as the bishop asserts his authority around the table of the Lord, ascertaining that the annual Eucharistic transaction take place under his domain, and not at the Jesuit hacienda.

167. Chevallier, *Instrucción*, Paragraph 35.

168. Ibid., Paragraph 56.

169. Ibid., Paragraph 58.

170. Delgado, *Laywomen*.

171. Chevallier, *Instrucción*, Paragraph 50.

172. Explicit racial terminology is not deployed in this document, although the author implies "blackness" in the reference to Parra's sermon.

173. Chevallier, *Instrucción*, Paragraphs 64, 65, 66.

174. David G. Sweet, "Black Robes and 'Black Destiny': Jesuit Views of African Slavery in 17th Century Latin America," *Revista de Historia de América* 86 (1978): 132.

175. Chevallier, *Instrucción*, Paragraph 63.

176. Paolo Quattrone, "Accounting for God: Accounting and Accountability Practices in the Society of Jesus (Italy, XVI–XVII)," *Accounting, Organizations and Society* 29 (2004): 647–83.

177. Hovland, "Christianity, Place/Space, and Anthropology," 331–32. Literature on Protestant evangelicals is helpful, as scholars in that field are attuned to the devotional space-making that occurs in atypical settings.

178. Newer scholarship on the Jesuit hacienda marks out hacienda aesthetics as an area of scholarship that requires greater attention with, for example, Brendan Weaver's focus on the material components of "the aesthetic-political regime" that governed hacienda life in Peru. Brendan J. M. Weaver, "Rethinking the Political Economy of Slavery: The Hacienda Aesthetic at the Jesuit Vineyards of Nasca, Peru," *Post-Medieval Archaeology* 52, no. 1 (2018): 117–33.

179. See Winchell's discussion of contemporary indigenous mobility revealing multiple spaces and places of articulation that inform their meaning-making that both centers *and* disrupts memories of forced labor on the hacienda. Mareike Winchell, "Alterable Geographies: In/Humanity, Emancipation, and the Spatial Poetics of *lo Abigarrado* in Bolivia," *Critical Times* 6, no. 2 (2023): 76.

180. J. Michelle Molina, "Fluid Indigeneity: Indians, Catholicism, and Spanish Law in the Mutable Americas," *The Immanent Frame: Secularism, Religion, and the Public Sphere* (July 12, 2017), https://tif.ssrc.org/2017/07/.

181. Florence Bernault, *Colonial Transactions: Imaginaries, Bodies, and Histories* (Durham, NC: Duke University Press, 2019). See language on "sacramental subjects" in legal cases in Premo, *The Enlightenment on Trial*.

182. These items are not sorted according to degrees of distance from the body of Christ, even though a Jesuit might have a reliquary, or a statue of Christ with Crown and *potencias*. For example, Father Vallarta has two silver vinegar vessels and our friend Aramburu had a little crown of silver for a Crucified Lord. BHJML, Legajo 139: f 32v, 33.

183. BHJML, Legajo 150, 1775, Fondo Jesuitas, Biblioteca Histórica José María Lafragua de la BUAP, 2v, Fondo Antiguo José María Lafragua, Puebla (0008).

184. For example, the Jesuit Cid is listed as prefect of the jails, and of the Congregación de los Mulatos. Zelís, *Catálogo de los sugetos de la Compañía de Jesús*. In *Memorias* Sebastián uses "de Negros."

185. Silva, *Urban Slavery*, 173.

186. BHJML, Legajo 139:42v.

187. Ibid., 34.

188. Gentry, *Power Objects*, 1. Kathryn Tanner pays attention to the relation between grace and money in Protestant theology, arguing that scholars pay attention to the material substitutions and transformations between the grace and money that mark status positions within networks of relations among Christian communities. Tanner, *Economy of Grace* (Minneapolis: Augsburg Fortress, 2005), 5, 10, 23.

189. FAJML, Legajo 139:44.

190. Silva, *Urban Slavery*. Silva's work focuses on practices of freedom-making to reshape a history that has been told largely in socioeconomic terms. For an overview of the decline of slavery in Mexico analyzed in economic terms, see Valdés, "The Decline of Slavery in Mexico." For accounts of how slaves litigated for their freedom, see Ireton, "Black Africans' Freedom"; Premo, *The Enlightenment on Trial*.

191. Silva, *Urban Slavery*, 198. For Black confraternities in Lima and Seville, see Karen Graubert, *Republics of Difference: Religious and Racial Self Governance in the Spanish Atlantic World* (Oxford: Oxford University Press, 2022), esp. 184–207.

192. On placemaking and resituating in evangelical Protestant settings, see Hovland, "Christianity, Place/Space, and Anthropology," 346.

193. Brewer-Garcia, *Beyond Babel*, 21.

194. J. Brent Crosson, "Catching Power: Problems with Possession, Sovereignty, and African Religions in Trinidad," *Ethnos* 84, no. 4 (2019): 588–614.Thus, as important as the study of rituals like Corpus Christi has been for understanding how idealized socioreligious structure is performed around the Eucharist in New Spain's urban colonial society, these celebrations are only one, albeit highly theatrical, aspect of the labor to contain or divert the flow of a shape-shifting power. William Beezley, Cheryl Martin, and William French, *Rituals of Rule, Rituals of Resistance: Public Celebrations and Popular Culture in Mexico* (Lanham, MD: Rowman & Littlefield, 1994).

195. Vizuete Mendoza, "En las fronteras de la ortodoxia."

196. Using a theopolitical frame to analyze Bourbon Crown attempts to reform confraternal devotional practices is to understand these as debates about to whom the power of the body of Christ should accrue. Rachel Johnson traces the attempt to have those lines of power move vertically, so that confraternal "charity" would have "public utility" by accruing to the body politic of the modernizing republic; see "'Burning Charity' and Love for One's Neighbor: Reformed Social Imaginaries of charity and the Common Good in Eighteenth-Century Spain and New Spain," *Eighteenth-Century Studies* 57, no. 2 (2024): 193–214.

197. Bynum, *Christian Materiality*. Such concerns were key to the way the Council of Trent defended and promoted the theology of divine presence in the Eucharist, while simultaneously bringing order to sacramental ritual practice, legislating how God's appearance would be managed and contained by a reformed priesthood.

198. Burns, "Notaries"; Kathryn Burns, *Into the Archive: Writing and Power in Colonial Peru* (Durham, NC: Duke University Press, 2010); Ann Laura Stoler, "Colonial Archives and the Arts of Governance," *Archival Science* 2 (2002): 87–109.

199. Stoler, "Colonial Archives," 87, 92–93.

200. Andrew Pickering, *The Mangle of Practice: Time, Agency, and Science* (Chicago: University of Chicago Press, 1995).

201. Recent books—with great bibliographies and adequate attention to the highly contested nature of secularization in on-the-ground forms of state formation in independent and postrevolutionary Mexico, respectively—are Voekel, *For God and Liberty*; Margaret Chowning, *Catholic Women and Mexican Politics, 1750–1940* (Princeton, NJ: Princeton University Press, 2023); Gema Kloppe-Santamaría, *In the Vortex of Violence: Lynching, Extralegal Violence and the State in Post-Revolutionary Mexico* (Berkeley: University of California Press, 2020); Laura Rojas and Susan Deeds, eds., *México a la luz de sus revoluciones, vol. 2* (Mexico City: El Colegio de México, Centro de Estudios Históricos, 2014). Especially important regarding the Mexican Revolution and sacramental ritual is Matthew Butler, "Misa a la méxicana: Los ritos de la relgión revolucionaria," in Rojas and Deeds, eds., *México a la luz de sus revoluciones*, 359–87.

Act II: Possibility?

1. Alessandro Guerra, *Il vile satellite del trono: Lorenzo Ignazio Thjúlen—Un gesuita svedese per la controrivoluzione* (Milan: Franco Angeli, 2004).

2. Lauren Berlant, *Cruel Optimism* (Durham, NC: Duke University Press, 2011). I will say more shortly about my engagement with Berlant and affect theory.

3. Scholars of religious studies have begun to look anew at relationships as key factors of religiosity. Constance Furey, "Body, Society and Subjectivity in Religious Studies," *Journal of the American Academy of Religion* 80 (2012): 7–33. This turn in the field is indebted to Robert Orsi, particularly his *Between Heaven and Earth: The Religious Worlds People Make and the Scholars Who Study Them* (Princeton, NJ: Princeton University Press, 2005), and Brenna Moore, "Friendship and the Cultivation of Religious Sensibilities," *Journal of the American Academy of Religion* 83, no. 2 (2015): 8. Notably, Brenna Moore has shown how an emphasis on spiritual friendship "shifts the attention to how the

subject comes to feel and think *religiously* not only through anonymous background discourses, but through the more personal domain of mutual bonds."

4. Thjülen wrote five versions of the conversion narrative. The first account was dictated to another Jesuit who had a better command of written Italian. Then Thjülen "finessed" the account eight years later, not only embarrassed that his poor Italian had required that he work with an editor, but also that a few details had been exaggerated. The others, whose dates are 1831 and 1833 (two were published in 1833) resemble one another. In these, he truncates the conversion narrative and narrates what had transpired after the Society of Jesus was suppressed in 1773.

5. Berlant, *Cruel Optimism*, 16.

6. Gilles Deleuze, *Spinoza: Practical Philosophy* (San Francisco: City Lights, 2001), 19.

7. Guerra emphasizes the narrative as politically and ideologically important in this turbulent era for the Jesuits as a triumphal narrative offered evidence of Jesuit perseverance and continued relevance in the years leading up to the suppression of the order. Guerra, *Il vile satellite*, 23.

8. Archivum Romanun Societatis Iesu (ARSI), *Historia Societatis 8* (hereafter Hist. Soc. 8), fol. 86, 87.

9. ARSI, *Hist. Soc.* 8, fol. 89–90. For how discourse about reason and religion posited itself as opposed to religion "founded on fables," see Helena Rosenblatt, "The Christian Enlightenment," in *The Cambridge History of Christianity*, vol. 7, *Enlightenment, Reawakening, and Revolution, 1660–1815*, ed. Steward J. Brown and Timothy Tackett (Cambridge: Cambridge University Press, 2006), 283–301.

10. Lynn Hunt, Margaret Jacob, and Wijnand Mijnhardt, *The Book That Changed Europe: Picart and Bernard's Religious Ceremonies of the World* (Cambridge, MA: Harvard University Press, 2010), 30, 129.

11. He retained this comparative world religion perspective over his lifetime. Among Thjülen's many publications later in life, he wrote a forty-eight-volume world history for school-aged boys in which he staged encounters between deceased figures from world history. Lorenzo Ignazio Thjülen, *Dialoghi nel regno de'morti* (Bologna: Nella Tipografia Arcivescovile, 1815–1819).

12. Nicholas Cronk, "Introduction," in Voltaire, *A Pocket Philosophical Dictionary* (Oxford: Oxford University Press, 2011), ix.

13. Voltaire, *Candide* (New York: W. W. Norton, 1991), 37.

14. "Cádiz, June 17. The before yesterday sailed from this bay for Corsica 1200 American Jesuits, who had been collected at Port S. Mary's. This fleet is composed of eight transports, escorted by the ship of war the Elizabeth. No others of this order now remain there, excepting a few sick persons, who will soon sent off for the same island along with 151 more, lately brought here by

the Vengeance and Good Success vessels." *The London Magazine, Or, Gentleman's Monthly Intelligencer* 37 (1768): 445.

15. Iturriaga sought to "medicate the wound" is the changed wording that Thjülen deploys when making minor edits in his second conversion narrative.

16. Iturriaga took vows as a Jesuit in 1744 and made his final vows in 1763. In Italy he wrote moral theology that he published in Venice and Assisi to escape Dominican censors. He gave "moral conferences" as the behest of the Bishop of Fano, which he later published. Iturriaga died in Fano, Italy, in 1819.

17. Aranda made a detailed list of the kinds of food to be provided on the Jesuits' ships as they crossed the Mediterranean Sea. See José Antonio Ferrer Benimeli, "La alimentación de los Jesuitas expulsos durante su viaje marítimo," in *Homenaje a Antonio de Béthencourt Massieu*, ed. Cabildo Insular de Gran Canaria (Las Palmas de Gran Canaria: Ediciones del Cabildo Insular de Gran Canaria, 1995), 581–96.

18. There is overlap in Jesuit expulsion narratives that I imagine can be explained by this kind of storytelling, but I surmise that this also points to the circulation of the expulsion narratives in manuscript form among ex-Jesuits. Sonora missionary Benito Ducrue and Mexican scholar Francisco Clavijero, for example, seem to know much of what happened in Mexico City the day the expulsion decree was announced, even though they were in Sonora and Guadalajara, respectively, and they retell stories that also conform to Och's account. Och, in turn, reports on what he had heard about the arrest in Puebla.

19. Eva María St. Clair Segurado, *Expulsión y exilio de la provincial Jesuita mexicana (1767–1820)* (Alicante: Universidad de Alicante, 2009), 107–42.

20. Rafael de Zelís, *Catálogo de los sugetos de la Compañía de Jesús que formaron la provincia de México el día del arresto, 25 de junio de 1767* (Mexico City: I. Escalante, 1871), 187.

21. Antonio López de Priego, "Carta de un religioso de los extintos Jesuitas, a una hermana suya, religiosa del convento de Santa Catarina de la Puebla de Los Angeles: Escrita en la ciudad de Bolonia, en 1 de Octubre de 1785," in *Tesoros documentales de México: Siglo XVIII*, ed. Mariano Cuevas (Mexico City: Editorial Galatea, 1944 [1785]), 25.

22. Ibid.

23. Ibid., 21. As such he draws upon the poetics of devotional literature in that the names listed of men from the Mexican Province who had died upon foreign shores take the shape of an inventory of names for heart-centered memory and prayer.

24. Ibid., 29, 32.

25. Liam M. Brockey, *Journey to the East: The Jesuit Mission to China, 1579–1724* (Cambridge, MA: Harvard University Press, 2007), 235–38.

26. Ulrike Strasser, *Missionary Men in the Early Modern World: German Jesuits and Pacific Journeys* (Amsterdam: Amsterdam University Press, 2020), 81, 103, 236, 240, and esp. ch. 2, "Braving the Waves with Saint Xavier." For details about the outbound journey as a "classroom" where one learned features of missionary life, including cleaning, teaching, praying, and of course suffering the voyage, see Brockey, *Journey to the East*, esp. ch. 6, "In the Apostle's Classroom."

27. For maintenance of their spirits through regular schedule, including prayer and reading, St. Clair Segurado, *Expulsión y exilio*, 153.

28. Och, *Missionary in Sonora*, 101.

29. Jesuit writers used precisely this language—spectacle—to indicate that they were quite conscious of being on display. The young Zelís wrote that "so innumerable were the people in the streets, the windows and balconies, who tenderly admired the beautiful order, and most of all, the cheerful and relaxed manner of these men who presently were a spectacle to the world" (Fue inumerable el gentío por las calles, ventanas y balcones, que tiernamente admiraban el bello orden y sobre todo la alegría y desenvoltura de unos hombres que presentemente eran el espectáculo del mundo; con esta graciosa ordenanza dimos fin al primer viaje de nuestra larga peregrinación, y nunca imaginada fortuna). Zelís, *Catálogo de los sugetos de la Compañía de Jesús*, 185–86. At Jalapa, one of the various "collection points" designated as a stopping place for a day or two rest before pushing on to Veracruz, the Jesuits road into town on horseback, soaking wet from torrential rain. "Such a novelty," wrote López de Priego, "that there was not a door, window, or rooftop that was not crowned with people, making it necessary for the soldiers to open a breech through the streets so that those in litters could pass through." López de Priego, "Carta de un religioso," 24.

30. Ibid., 37, 38.

31. Och, *Missionary in Sonora*, 106.

32. Instrucción, "Instructions for the Captains of the Ships," 1767, Cuba, 1123, 459–62: AGI.

33. Even Hidalgo, leader of independence movement in the early nineteenth century, had to defend his Catholicism in Reformation terms, expressly denying that he "followed the perverse dogmas of Luther." Alicia Mayer, *Lutero en el paraíso: La Nueva España en el espejo del reformador alemán* (Mexico City: Universidad Nacional Autónoma de México/Fondo de Cultura Económica/Instituto de Investigaciones Históricas, 2008).

34. López de Priego, "Carta de un religioso," 39–40.

35. Lauren Berlant, *On the Inconvenience of Other People (Writing Matters!)* (Durham, NC: Duke University Press, 2022).

36. Berlant, *Cruel Optimism*, 25.

37. See Markus Friedrich, *The Jesuits*, trans. John Noel Dillon (Princeton, NJ: Princeton University Press, 2022), on accommodation.

38. Och never states what was so urgent about destroying said materials, and he differentiates his own books from those owned by the college. *Missionary in Sonora*, 58, 59, 62, 66.

39. Ibid., 57–58.

40. St. Clair Segurado, *Expulsión y exilio*, 67. Och's narrative gives details about recalcitrant carriage owners.

41. Rafael Zelís, "Viajes en su destierro," in *Tesoros documentales de México: Siglo XVIII*, ed. Mariano Cuevas (Mexico City: Editorial Galatea, 1944 [1785]), 188. Zelís says goodbye to his mother on November 20, 1767, and boards the small frigate of don Francisco Echave among seventy other passengers and sailors who didn't know what they were doing. Te Deums were sung in common on board, although after all the family love, his stay in Cuba was described as a solitary two months. Zelís, "Carta de un religioso de los extintos Jesuita," 194. Zelís does not mention Thjülen, but he was aboard the Ragusa ship that broke down. He was transferred to an English ship called "El Nerón." All chapters discuss journeys, so once he settles down in Bologna, he does not write about ordinary details until he makes a trip to Ciudad de Bertinoro to be ordained a priest in 1775. No mention of the suppression of the Order, but he does describe a trip to the Sanctuary of Our Lady of Loreto, where he notes that he encountered the cardinal of York on the same road. Zelís, "Carta de un religioso de los extintos Jesuita," 223. His final trip is in 1777, when he moves from Bologna to Rome. His travel account ends there. He is among the Jesuits who "secularized" after arriving in Italy. Zelís is the author of a *Catalogue of the Province of Mexico*, which includes important data about who had died in exile, including those who secularized. Following his own death in 1798, the ex-Jesuit P. Pedro Márquez continued the task.

42. Och, *Missionary in Sonora*, 80–81.

43. St. Clair Segurado, *Expulsión y exilio*, 142–45.

44. Archivo Geneal de Indias (AGI) Cuba, 222B, Libro de asientos de entradas y salidas en la Casa de Depósito de las regulares de la Compañía que llegan a la Habana y con destino a España, 1767, 611–724.

45. St. Clair Segurado, *Expulsión y exilio*, 143–44, 53, 211–15.

46. Benno Franciscus Ducrue and Ernest J Burrus, *Ducrue's Account of the Expulsion of the Jesuits from Lower California (1767–1769): An Annotated English Translation of Benno Ducrue's Relatio Expulsionis* (Rome: Jesuit Historical Institute, 1967), 98

47. "Hay también en la oración otra cosa que es de Dios y el puramente lo da; que es una consolación, una alegría interior, una quietación del entendimiento, un gusto, una luz, un pasar adelante mejor, un entender mejor las

cosas: todo esto es particular gracia de la oración y que anima a ir por delante, y da reliquias para ayudarse en el camino." Jeronimo Nadal, *Pláticas espirituales del P. Jerónimo Nadal, SJ, en Coimbra* (Granada: Facultad Teológicas de la Compañía de Jesus, 1945 [1561]), 191. Jean Leclercq described consolation for the twelfth-century Cistercians as "an inner song, a slight murmur, a silent word" and insisted that this momentary "adhesion of the spirit [was] not the result of striving: it is a taste, a relish, a wisdom, and not a science." Jean Leclercq, *The Love of Learning and the Desire for God: A Study of Monastic Culture*, trans. Catherine Misrahi (New York: Fordham University Press, 1974), 39, 42.

48. The 1945 published book (Nadal, *Pláticas espirituales*) indicates that in the manuscript, the word *reliquias* was written as *arreliquias*, which seems to imply "making a relic of," in other words, to offer tangible access to the sacred, as would a saint's relics.

49. For a discussion of Ignatius as a sixteenth-century model for an emotionally sustaining father-son relationship that is both companionate and hierarchical, see Ulrike Strasser, "The First Form and Grace: Ignatius of Loyola and the Reformation of Masculinity," in *Masculinity in the Reformation Era*, ed. Scott H. Hendrix and Susan C. Karant-Nunn (Kirksville, MO: Truman State University Press, 2008), 450–70.

50. Brenna Moore, "Friendship and the Cultivation of Religious Sensibilities," *Journal of the American Academy of Religion* 83, no. 2 (2015): 3; Brenna Moore, *Kindred Spirits: Friendship and Resistance at the Edge of Modern Catholicism* (Chicago: University of Chicago Press, 2021).

51. Most famous is Miguel Sánchez's *Imagen de la Virgen María Madre de Dios de Guadalupe* (1648).

52. Mayer, *Lutero en el paraíso*, 320, 326.

53. See Francisco Javier Rodríguez, SJ, *Sermón de Nuestra Señora de Guadalupe* (Mexico City: Joseph Antonio de Hogal, 1766), as referenced in ibid., 332.

54. Miguel Nuñez de Godoy, canon of Guadalajara, *Desagravios de Cristo sacramentado* (Mexico City: Francisco Ribera, 1712), as referenced in ibid., 322.

55. In second version, he edits to make clear his words: "Listen to me, Father, I am with you. I am never returning to the ship."

56. Christopher Wild, "Techne tes periagogeis: Conversion and the Art of Spiritual Navigation," in *Konversion als Medium der Selbstbeschreibung in Spätantike, Mittelalter und Früher Neuzeit*, ed. Werner Röcke, Ruth von Bernuth, and Julia Weitbrecht (Berlin: De Gruyter, 2015), 61–83; and Christopher Wild, *Descartes' Meditative Turn: Cartesian Thought as Spiritual Practice* (Stanford, CA: Stanford University Press, 2024).

57. Guerra, *Il vile satellite del trono*, 24.

58. Inmaculada Fernández Arrillaga, "Los novicios del la Compañía de Jesús: La disyuntiva ante el autoexilio y su estancia en Italia," *Hispania Sacra*, 109: 169–96.

59. Thomas Keenan, "Paradoxes of Recognition: How to Make a Refugee" (Borders and Borders and Crossings: Contemporary Arts and Techniques of Migration, UC Berkeley CICI, 2023).

Act III. Ruination

1. Sebastián was born in Barrameda, Spain, in 1736 and entered the Society of Jesus in Seville in 1754. He came to Mexico City to study theology at the Colegio Máximo in 1761. He was ordained a priest in Oaxaca in 1765. At the time of the arrest he was working at the Mission of Tubares in Chínipas. He was a *coadjutor espiritual*, indicating that he was a priest but never took the fourth vows. He died in Bologna, Italy, in 1815.

2. José Felix de Sebastián, *Memorias de los Padres y Hermanos de la Compañía de Jesus de la Provincia de Nueva España difuntos despues del arresto acaecido en la Capital de Mexico el día 25 de Junio del año 1767*, 1767–1796, A.531, 1, Archiginnasio.

3. Ibid., I, preface.

4. David Kennedy, *Elegy* (London: Routledge, 2008), 11.

5. Ibid., 13.

6. Sebastián, *Memorias*, I:1.

7. For suicide as offering some possibilities for preparation for death, see Riika Miettinen, " 'Lord Have Mercy on Me': Spiritual Preparations for Suicide in Early Modern Sweden," in *Preparing for a Good Death in Medieval and Early Modern Northern Europe*, ed. Anu Lahtinen and Mia Korpiola (Leiden: Brill, 2018): 160–86.

8. David Brading, *The First America: The Spanish Monarchy, Creole Patriots, and the Liberal State, 1492–1867* (Cambridge: Cambridge University Press, 1991); Jorge Cañizares-Esguerra, *How to Write the History of the New World: Histories, Epistemologies, and Identities in the Eighteenth-Century Atlantic World* (Stanford, CA: Stanford University Press, 2001); Charles E. Ronan, *Francisco Javier Clavigero, S.J., (1731–1787), Figure of the Mexican Enlightenment: His Life and Works* (Chicago: Loyola University Press, 1977).

9. For a detailed bibliography of these "singular" authors, with pertinent bibliography, see Silvia Vargas Alquicira, *La singularidad novohispana en los jesuitas del siglo XVIII* (Mexico City: UNAM, 1989), 11–167.

10. For an updated analysis of the range of possibilities writing on the New World could take, see Niccoló Guasti, "Catholic Civilization and the Evil Savage: Juan Nuix Facing the Spanish *Conquista* of the New World," in

Encountering Otherness: Diversities and Transcultural Experiences in Early Modern European Culture, ed. Guido Abbattista (Trieste: EUT, 2011), 285–302.

11. Sebastián, *Memorias*, I:2.

12. "Las Religiosos de aquel Convento, expusieron su cadaver sin ninguno de los honores, que se acostombran en aquella tierra a los Sacerdotes, por lo que un Oficial que vio estas sordidez pago a los Frayles la cera [wax] y quanto fue necessario para el entierro."

13. Sebastián, *Memorias*, I:15, 24, 63–64. Sebastián does not have his birthdate nor the date he entered the Society.

14. Ibid., I:3–4. Zelís has his death date as August 1, but Sebastián de Félix preferred to mark his death as taking place on July 31, the feast day of San Ignacio.

15. J. R. McNeill, "Yellow Jack and Geopolitics: Environment, Epidemics, and the Struggles for Empire in the American Tropics, 1640–1830," *Review (Fernand Braudel Center)* 27, no. 4 (2004): 343–64.

16. Robert W. Patch, "Sacraments and Disease in Mérida, Yucatan, Mexico, 1648–1727," *The Historian* 58, no. 4 (1996): 731–43. For public health efforts to eradicate yellow fever in Veracruz in the late eighteenth century, see Andrew L. Knaut, "Yellow Fever and the Late Colonial Public Health Response in the Port of Veracruz," *Hispanic American Historical Review* 77, no. 4 (1997): 619–44.

17. Sebastián, *Memorias*, I:22–23, 25–26, 30–31, 67–68.

18. Ibid., I:86–89. On the expulsion of the missionaries from northern New Spain, see Brandon Bayne, *Missions Begin with Blood: Suffering and Salvation in the Borderlands of New Spain* (New York: Fordham University Press, 2021), especially the chapter "Uprooted." Bayne points out that "exile" was already a trope well used by Jesuits as missionaries on the northern frontier used the term to capture how they experienced the distance from beloved family members overseas.

19. P. Henrique Kirtzel (German) (#77) died in Aguacatlán on August 31, 1768; P. Francisco Villarroya (Spanish) (#78) died in Pueblo de Ystlán on September 1, 1768; P. Nicolas Perera (#79) died in Pueblo de Ystlán, also on September 1, 1768; P. Miguel Fernández Somero (#80) died in Pueblo de Ystlán, also on September 1, 1768. P. Lucas Merino, (Spanish) (#81) died in Pueblo de Ystlán on September 2, 1768; P. Maximiliano le Roy (French) (#82), who left New Orleans when the Society was expelled from France in 1763, died on September 2, 1768; P. Alexandro Rapicani (#83) born in Bremen, died September 3, 1768; P. Joseph Ronderos (#84), born in Puebla, died on September 4, 1768, in Pueblo de Ystlán; P. Pio Laguna (#85) died in Pueblo de Ystlán on September 4, 1768; P. Francisco Pascua (#86) died in Pueblo de Ystlán on September 4, 1768; P. Francisco Hlava (born in Prague), "una verdadero

misionero Jesuita," died in Pueblo de Ystlán on September 7, 1768; P. Juan Nentvig (#88), (b. in Glatz in Bohemia), died September 11, 1768, in Pueblo de Ystlán; Padre Pedro Diez (#89) died in Pueblo de Ystlán on September 14, 1768.

20. Padre Fernando Borra (#90) died September 28, 1768, in Pueblo de Magdalena; Padre Manuel Aguirre (#91) died September 25, 1768, in Pueblo de Magdalena; Padre Joseph Liebana (#92) died October 7, 1768; Padre Ramon Sánchez, b. 1736, died on November 9, 1768; P. Joseph Watzetk (Moravia) (#96) died November 10, 1768, in Pueblo de Aguacatlán; P. Bartholome Saens (#97) died in the Pueblo de Tequila on November 18, 1768.

21. Padre Francisco Xavier Paver (#103), born in Germany, died in Puerto Santa María on January 6, 1770; P. Joseph Cabrera Roldan (#116) survived the trek from Guaymas and made it to Spain. When he died on September 21, 1770, in Santa María, Sebastián does not yet mention that these men were imprisoned.

22. St. Clair Segurado, *Expulsión y exilio*, 129–38.

23. Sebastián, *Memorias*, I:31–33.

24. Padre José Ignacio Calderón is noted in Act I as the Jesuit who had an English-language book on his desk that was the property of the surgeon in the city, Don Juan Mantagas. He also had a papal marriage dispensation conferred belonging to Don Manuel Francisco Trujillo Labrador, which had been given to Calderón for safekeeping. Ayer 1128: f. 27v.

25. Sebastián, *Memorias*, I:33–34 (also spelled Hurtasun); I:37.

26. Ibid., I:71–72.

27. This comes from his description of P. Juan Zepeda (#45), who became gravely ill in Havana and was taken to a hospital, "where *santamente* he gave his spirit to the Lord on November 27, 1767." Ibid., I:47–49.

28. This is unlike a notable Jesuit who committed suicide in the seventeenth century. When Nicolas Trigault hanged himself in China in 1628, his local brethren kept a tight lid on the nature of his death, and the order appears to have suppressed that information. Anne-Marie Logan and Liam M. Brockey, "Nicolas Trigault, SJ: A Portrait by Peter Paul Rubens," *Metropolitan Museum Journal* 38 (2003): 161–67.

29. Susan Stewart, *The Ruins Lesson: Meaning and Material in Western Culture* (Chicago: University of Chicago Press, 2020), 2.

30. John W. O'Malley, "To Travel to Any Part of the World: Jerónimo Nadal and the Jesuit Vocation," in *Saints or Devils Incarnate?: Studies in Jesuit History* (Leiden: Brill, 2013), 147–64.

31. Thank you, Madison Brown, for introducing me to Hollis Frampton's experimental film wherein he burns individual photos on a hot plate while commenting on the past and present of the disappearing subjects. Hollis Frampton, *Nostalgia* (1971).

32. Sebastián, *Memorias*, I:55–56.
33. Ibid., I:200–201.
34. Ibid., I:50–51.
35. He also maintained a steady correspondence with women who had made the Spiritual Exercises with him. J. Michelle Molina, "Technologies of the Self: The Letters of 18th Century Mexican Jesuit Spiritual Daughters," *History of Religions* (2008): 282–303.
36. Sebastián, *Memorias*, I:129–35.
37. Ibid., I:135–39.
38. On Xavier as a model for mobility, metamorphosis, and emotional self-governance in the face of dangers at sea, see Ulrike Strasser, "Copies with Souls: The Late Seventeenth Century Marianas Martyrs and the Question of Clerical Reproduction," *Journal of Jesuit Studies* 2 (2015): 558–85; Ulrike Strasser, *Missionary Men in the Early Modern World: German Jesuits and Pacific Journeys* (Amsterdam: Amsterdam University Press, 2020). See also J. Michelle Molina, *To Overcome Oneself: The Jesuit Ethic and the Spirit of Global Expansion* (Berkeley: University of California Press, 2013), chs. 2, 3, 5.
39. For linguistic transformation as cultural transformation, see William Hanks, *Converting Words: Maya in the Age of the Cross* (Berkeley: University of California Press, 2010). See also Daniel Nemser, *Infrastructures of Race: Concentration and Biopolitics in Colonial Mexico* (Austin: University of Texas Press, 2017).
40. Sebastián, *Memorias*, I:52–54.
41. Ibid., I:57–60.
42. Ibid., I:61–63.
43. Ibid., I:110–12.
44. Another of Sebastián's companions, Ramón Sánchez, died on November 9, 1768. While Sebastián did not claim to know him personally, he and Sánchez studied theology together at the Colegio Máximo in 1761, and both men were ordained as priests on the same day in 1765. See Francisco Zambrano and José Gutiérrez Casillas, *Diccionario Bio-bibliográfico de la Compañía de Jesús en México* (Mexico City: Editorial Jus, 1961), vol. 15/16.
45. Sebastián, *Memorias*, I:51–52, 56–57, 119–20. Laudner died with all the signs of predestination on December 1, 1767. Villar died on December 3, 1767, the feast day of San Francisco Xavier, which would have been read as a sign that he is also a *"verdadero"* missionary. Urroz died on November 1, 1768, in a Havana hospital.
46. Ibid., I:168–69. Here he makes a comment about the century ("aviendo passado al Reyno de Nueva España siendo joven de gran delicadeza de espíritu facilmente le fastidiaron las esperanzas del Siglo [a youth with great delicacy of spirit that was easily bothered by the hopes of the Century] y todo deseoso de

caminar seguramente por el verdadero camino de la gloria immortal, pretendio y fue admitido en la Compañía el dia 27 de Abril de 1765."

47. Ibid., I:140–42.

48. Ibid., I:176–77, 202.

49. Ibid., I:206–8.

50. He makes no mention of the rebellion in Guanajuato at the time of the arrest.

51. Sebastián, Memorias, I:165–66, 180–82.

52. Ibid., I:208–10.

53. El Padre Bernardino Ortíz (#147) was admitted to the Philippine province, but he was dismissed. To be readmitted he went from the Philippines to Rome and presented himself to the Padre General. He was readmitted, sent to Seville, and then eventually sent on mission to Nueva España as Coadjutor Espiritual formado. He went to Sinaloa, then to Colegio del Espíritu Santo in Puebla. After the arrest, he made it to Havana, was then sent to hospital to recover. He lived in a palace in the country about a league outside of Bologna. "Here he became sick and was sent to Nuestro Hospital, giving thanks to die a Jesuit . . . on February 9, 1773." He is among the last to die as a Jesuit.

54. Sebastián, Memorias, I:220–21.

55. Ibid., I:222–32. Buried at San Martin, convento de los Religiosos Carmelitanos Calzados de la Congregación de Mantua. Appropriately, his is the final death of 1773.

56. Luengo, Diario, April 14, 1769, quoted in Inmaculada Fernández Arrillaga and Elisabetta Marchetti, La Bolonia que habitaron los Jesuitas hispánicos (1768–1773) (Bologna: Dupress, 2012).

57. Some peninsular Jesuits forged close bonds with men from the Mexican Province, but Astorgano notes that this became a possibility after the Suppression in 1773. For Hervás de Panduro's "filomexicanismo" and his discussions about Nahuatl culture and the study of indigenous Mexican languages with Francisco Javier Clavigero and Miguel del Barco, see Antonio Astorgano Abajo, "Hervás y Panduro y sus amigos ante la mexicanidad," in Ilustración en el mundo hispánico: Preámbulo de las independencias (Tlaxcala: Gobierno del Estado de Tlaxcala, Universidad Iberoamericana, 2009).

58. For travel writing and some attention to the quotidian, one must turn to López de Priego or Zelís. Both describe something of Italy, but especially the uniqueness of Bologna, with its miles of porticos, including one that traces a path up into the hills to the shrine of Our Lady of San Lucas. Luengo describes Jesuits passing the afternoons visiting each other in their scattered houses. Fernández Arrillaga and Marchetti, La Bolonia que habitaron los Jesuitas, 12. There are hints of this in Sebastián's accounts, but he describes socializing, perhaps rightly so, as "ministry."

59. St. Clair Segurado, *Expulsión y exilio*, 323–24; Fernández Arrillaga and Marchetti, *La Bolonia que habitaron los Jesuitas*, 21, 39.

60. Thomas W. Laqueur, *The Work of the Dead: A Cultural History of Mortal Remains* (Princeton, NJ: Princeton University Press, 2015), 372, 73.

61. Zelís includes everyone, but he left the Order. The in-house census also includes the secularized. The Spanish Crown counts them as victories. So their absence must be a registration of sense of defeat? Sarmiento, mentioned in Act I as one of the stragglers, is among those who left the order. After traveling to Spain with the rest of the Jesuits, he made the decision to be secularized while housed at Puerto Santa María and is listed as having died in Zacatecas, Mexico, in 1813, which means he returned before the Society was reestablished. For the names of the men who secularized and also those who married, see José Antonio Ferrer Benimeli, "Los 'otros' jesuitas de Bolonia," in *Un hombre de bien: Saggi di lingue e letterature iberiche in onore di Rinaldo Froldi*, ed. Patrizia Garelli and Giovanni Marchetti (Alessandria: Edizioni dell'Orso, 2004), 483–503; Antonio Astorgano Abajo, "Pinceladas sobre la literatura silenciada de los jesuitas expulsos a través de la Biblioteca jesuítico-española de Hervás y Panduro," in *Escrituras silenciadas: El paisaje como historiografía*, ed. José F. Forniés Casals and Paulina Numhauser (Alcalá de Henares: Universidad de Alcalá, 2013), 411–30.

62. Sebastián, *Memorias*, I:418.

63. Miguel Venegas, *Vida y virtudes de Juan Bautista Zappa de la Compañía de Jesús* (Barcelona: Pablo Nadal, 1754), 30.

64. Following the extinction of the order, representatives of the Crown have the infirm evaluated: When will they be well enough to travel to Italy? Viceregal authorities keep an eye on these Jesuits as well as "imaginary" Jesuits, that is, some picaresque figures who pretended to be Jesuits. See Salvador Bernabéu Albert, "El vacío habitado: Jesuitas reales y simulados en México durante los años de la Supresión (1767–1816)," *Historia mexicana* 58, no. 4 (2009): 1261–303.

65. The various provinces had the same goal: The Paraguay Jesuits were concentrated in Faenza, the Chileans in Imola.

66. Luengo refers to scarcity of books and tables, etc., to continue studies. The Jesuit Idiáquez makes efforts to raise funds to set up a college near the (Italian) College of Santa Lucia. Fernández Arrillaga and Marchetti, *La Bolonia que habitaron los Jesuitas*, 15.

67. Sebastián mentions that Ignacio Maldonado traveled around Europe after the expulsion. He died in Frascati on September 1, 1777.

68. Rodríguez visited different parts of Italy to study science in order "to soothe his soul" and wrote letters to his benefactors in America, requesting support for the exiled Jesuits.

69. Sebastián, *Memorias*, II:238–42.

70. Fernández Arrillaga and Marchetti, *La Bolonia que habitaron los Jesuitas*, 36–37.

71. Astorgano Abajo, "Hervás y Panduro y sus amigos."

72. Sebastián, *Memorias*, I:75.

73. See also J. Michelle Molina, "How to Be a Country Jesuit: Continence, Care and Containment in a Racializing Religiosity," in *Jesuits and Race*, ed. Nathaniel Millet and Charles Parker (Albuquerque: University of New Mexico Press, 2022), 133–62.

74. Chevallier, *Instrucción*, Paragraph 1.

75. Sebastián, *Memorias*, I:78–29.

76. Ibid., I:238–41.

77. Chevallier, *Instrucción*.

78. He died on September 5, 1774, and was buried in the parish church of Santa Maria Invado de Canonigos Reglares del Salvador.

79. Other hacienda administrators mentioned in Sebastián's manuscript include Hermano Sebastián Vargara (#108), Hermano Francisco Pardo (#35) Hermano Joseph Jordan (#9), Hermano Gines Martínez (#27).

80. Sebastián, *Memorias*, I:291–93.

81. Ibid., I:445.

82. P. Joseph Piedra, #324, ibid., II:143. There are many other examples: see P. Francisco Xavier Evangelista Contreras, ibid., II:140–42.

83. "Prenationalist" arguments are best represented by Miguel Battlori, *La cultura hispano-italiana de los jesuitas expulsos: Españoles, hispano-americanos, filipinos, 1767–1814* (Madrid: Editorial Gredos, 1966). See also Brading, *The First America*. Karen Stolley complicates this narrative of nostalgia as a desire for lost homeland. Stolley, "East from Eden: Domesticating Exile in Jesuit Accounts of Their 1767 Expulsion from Spanish America," in *Jesuit Accounts of the Colonial Americas: Intercultural Transfers, Intellectual Disputes, and Textualities*, ed. Marc André Bernier, Clorinda Donato, and Hans-Jürgen Lüsebrink (Toronto: University of Toronto Press, 2014), 256–57. As far as Sebastián is concerned, the important homeland—the "place-that-was" is the Jesuit Mexican Province, and there is no indication that there will be a "place-to-come."

84. Sebastián, *Memorias*, II:571. P. Francisco Xavier Gonzales, b. 1718 in Asturias.

85. Ibid., I:529.

86. Ibid., II:134. "Seedbed" (almácigo) of virtues, where devotion and piety are rooted." Ibid., II:150. For Tepotzotlán as "a center of all his pleasures," see I:556. On Vallejo as author of a book on the history of Saint Joseph published in 1774 see Astorgano Abajo, "Hervás y Panduro y sus amigos"; Antonio Astorgano Abajo, "La difícil circulación de los libros devocionales del Jesuita mexicano

José Ignacio Vallejo (1772–1788)," *Clio: Revísta de pesquisa histórica* 32, no. 1 (2014): 102–55.

87. Laqueur, *The Work of the Dead*, xiv.

88. Ibid., d, 10. Drew Faust's *Republic of Suffering* draws attention to the importance of the deathbed scene, and in her book anxious bed-side listeners document the last words of the dying.

89. See Verónica Zárate Toscano, *Los nobles ante la muerte en México: Actitudes, ceremonias, y memoria, 1750–1850* (Mexico City: El Colegio de México, 2005). For a good example of the care generally taken to describe the good death of a family member who died at a distance, see María Cristina Torales Pacheco, "Del nacimiento a la muerte en las familias de la élite novohispana del siglo XVIII," in *Familia y vida privada en la historia de Iberoamérica*, ed. Pilar Gonzalbo Aizpuru and Cecilia Rabell Romero (Mexico City: El Colegio de México/Instituto de Investigaciones Sociales de la Universidad Nacional Autónoma de México, 1996).

90. After the Restoration in 1814, Jesuit deaths that took place during the "suppression" are commemorated as martyrdoms suffered for the continuation, not of the Society of Jesus, but of the embattled Catholic Church. Franco Motta and Eleonora Rai, "Martyrs and Missionaries: Strategies of Jesuit Sainthood between the Suppression and the Restoration," *Journal of Jesuit Studies* 9 (2022): 95–124.

91. This is striking, given Zárate Toscano's difficulties finding evidence for the cause of death from across a range of different sources. Zárate Toscano, *Los nobles ante la muerte*, 206.

92. Sebastián, *Memorias*, I:408.

93. Ibid., II:349.

94. Ibid.

95. Aposento del Padre Thomas Perez: Libros que son del Colegio HM15000–15003: ff.20–25.

96. Sebastián, *Memorias*, II:350.

97. Ibid., II:351.

98. Ibid., I:244–45.

99. Ibid., I:385–88. Dávila suffers an ugly death, but see Zambrano for tidbits on how he burned his papers prior to death. He was a companion to the heavy hitters Clavigero, Abad, Allegre, Campoy. A forgotten monumental monument?

100. Jordan N. Burns, Rodolfo Acuna-Soto, and David W. Stahle, "Drought and epidemic typhus, Mexico, 1655–1918," *Emerging Infectious Diseases* 20, no. 3 (2014): 442. See also P. Victor Proton (#280), a former hacienda administrator at San Antonio de Oculmán, who "lived alone" but died of a "furioso tabardillo." Sebastián, *Memorias*, I:539–41.

101. Sebastián, *Memorias*, I:516–17.

102. Ibid., I:296–300.

103. Ibid., I:392–93.

104. Ibid., I:246.

105. Not every use of "fuera de sí" is so dire. [Lándivar]; a sad man is Hilario Ugarte. Ibid., II:359. H. Joseph Castañeda (#250) is "casi fuera de sí . . . agravose del todo en su demencia." But another suicide is H. Rafael Buitrón (#275). He had been "struck" by a great melancholy in 1784, engulfed in great scruples that degenerated his mind into deliriums. "Seguía con más frequencia en sus devociones, per de continue se conocia asaltado de una grande descomposición en sus fantasia, originada de predominante humor melancólico. Todos lo compadecían mas no le podian dar Socorro en las terribles, y miserables circunstancias en que se hallan. Poner el en el Hospital de los dementes parecía crueldad, pues no daba en furias." He threw himself out the window. He was taken to the Hospital Santa Maria de la Vida, where they administered the last rites, and he died the next morning. "Sugeto de grande Inocencia de costumbres, y de via immaculada. Su cadáver fue sepultado en la Yglesia de dicho Hospital" (ibid., I:521–24).

106. Muñoz mentions Madre Santísima de la Luz in a dedication he wrote on a slip of paper at the time of his vows in 1749, which he carried all his life. Sebastián quotes from it in his entry written at Muñoz's death in 1792. The key date here is 1749, demonstrating that she was popular among Jesuits prior to her becoming "notorious" for being a Jesuit devotion. P. Juan Joseph Muñoz (#360) was born in Guatemala on November 18, 1726, another devotee of La Luz. The Dolorosa is most common, and la Luz gets a fair share of mentions, although most mention only "the blessed Virgin." Muñoz held the missing key at Colegio Espíritu Santo because he was at Colegio Máximo the time of the arrest when he was "sentenced to a perpetual exile." The latter is Sebastián's new phrasing in the 1790s.

107. Sebastián, *Memorias*, II:237–38. He died on October 24, 1792.

108. Ibid., II:162, 237–38. Vallarta died on October 24, 1792.

109. I borrow this tidy phrase from Ryan Dohoney, who captures the way in which mourning draws small groups together to creative purpose. Ryan Dohoney, *Morton Feldman: Friendship and Mourning in the New York Avant-Garde* (New York: Bloomsbury Academic, 2022).

110. Sebastián, *Memorias*, I:413–15.

111. Ibid., I:580.

112. Ibid., I:253–54. Salazar died on March 21, 1775.

113. The term is Laqueur's, and it refers to the work of community building that collecting the dead performs. Laqueur, *The Work of the Dead*, 41.

114. Padre Joseph Sánchez (#315); Sebastián, *Memorias*, II:108–11.

115. Francisco "Pancho" Alegría, d. 1791. Sebastián later writes him up in *Memorias*, II:201. Hilario Ugarte died in 1796. Felix de Sebastián to Eligio Fernández August 16, 1788. Vitae 1006, ARSI. Unnumbered.

116. For mimesis as a motor for Jesuit replication, see Strasser, "Copies with Souls."

117. Battlori, *La cultura hispano-italiana*.

118. He was buried at the parish of San Martín and "was mourned by all." (Sebastián does not say this about everyone.) Sebastián, *Memorias*, I:398.

119. He does not say what he wrote.

120. Sebastián, *Memorias*, II:237, 301, 571.

121. Stewart, *The Ruins Lesson*, 8.

122. Keeping prophecies alive among the reading public was something of a campaign for some Jesuits. See Emanuele Colombo, "Jesuit at Heart: Luigi Mozzi de'Capitani (1746–1813) between Suppression and Restoration," in *Jesuit Survival and Restoration: A Global History, 1773–1900*, ed. Robert Maryks and Jonathan Wright (Leiden: Brill, 2014), 213–16; and especially Inmaculada Fernández Arrillaga, "Profecías, coplas, creencias y devociones de los Jesuitas expulsos durante su exilio en Italia," *Revista de historia moderna* 16 (1997): 83–98.

123. Laqueur, *The Work of the Dead*, 398.

124. O'Malley, "To Travel to Any Part of the World," 163.

Concluded: The Mexican Province

1. I am perpetually inspired by Merleau-Ponty's conceptualization of freedom as an action of gearing into the future. Maurice Merleau-Ponty, *Phenomenology of Perception* (Englewood Cliffs, NJ: Routledge, 2012). I am also deeply appreciative of Matthew O'Hara's attention to innovative future-making grounded in "traditional" practices taken up by early modern New Spaniards. Matthew O'Hara, *The History of the Future in Colonial Mexico* (New Haven, CT: Yale University Press, 2018), 8.

2. It remains unclear to me why Sebastián did not continue his project. Illness? Napoleon's invasion of Italy?

3. Rebecca Schneider, "Performance Remains," *Performance Research* 6, no. 2 (2001): 100–108.

4. Wendy Bellion and Kristel Smentek, "Things Change," in *Material Cultures of the Global Eighteenth Century: Art, Mobility, and Change*, ed. Wendy Bellion and Kristel Smentek (New York: Bloomsbury Visual Arts, 2023), 2–3. For a reflection on the bundles of affordances possible in an object, see Webb Keane, "Rotting Bodies: The Clash of Stances toward Materiality and Its Ethical Affordances," *Current Anthropology* 55 (2014): 312–21. Tracing the

continued use of popular catechisms is a promising avenue for thinking about how continuities in Ignatian devotional ideals might have remained in use.

5. For an essay that offers multiple examples of contested engagement with Catholic objects, O'Sullivan notes that one twentieth-century "'engagement' was to dynamite" a monument to the Sacred Heart of Jesus in Guanajuato in 1928. See Lucy O'Sullivan, "Martyrdom in the Age of Mechanical Reproduction: The Photograph as Testimony and Trace in Mexico's Cristero War (1926–29)," *Latin American and Latinx Visual Culture* 6, no. 1 (2024): 1–19. In the U.S. context, see Katherine Dugan and Karen E. Park, *American Patroness: Marian Shrines and the Making of U.S. Catholicism* (New York: Fordham University Press, 2024).

6. Philip Endean, "The Spiritual Exercises," in *Cambridge Companion to the Jesuits*, ed. Thomas Worcester (Cambridge: Cambridge University Press, 2008), 52–67.

7. J. Michelle Molina, *To Overcome Oneself: The Jesuit Ethic and the Spirit of Global Expansion* (Berkeley: University of California Press, 2013).

8. Niccoló Guasti, "Rasgos del exilio Italiano de los Jesuitas Españoles," *Hispania Sacra* 61, no. 123 (January–June 2009): 257–78.

9. Salvador Bernabéu Albert poses a query about continuity through non-Jesuit mediators, asking scholars to pay attention to "what happened to the numerous administrators and employees of the Jesuits and how they maintained in their devotions the flame of Jesuitism in a hostile environment" (1299). I do think devotions begun by the Jesuits do not disappear, but they become incorporated into Catholicism writ large, much in the same way that the rosary, once strongly associated with the Dominicans, no longer reads as particular to that religious order of men. Albert, "El vacío habitado: Jesuitas reales y simulados en México durante los años de la supresión (1767–1816)." *Historia mexicana* 58, no. 4 (2009): 1261–1303.

10. Jorge Cañizares-Esguerra, *How to Write the History of the New World: Histories, Epistemologies, and Identities in the Eighteenth-Century Atlantic World* (Stanford, CA: Stanford University Press, 2001).

11. Armand Petrucci, *Writing the Dead: Death and Writing Strategies in the Western Tradition*. Stanford, CA: Stanford University Press, 1998.

12. Elin Diamond, *Unmaking Mimesis: Essays on Feminism and Theatre* (Englewood Cliffs, NJ: Routledge, 1997), 85.

13. Schneider, "Performance Remains," 103.

14. Laurent Olivier, *Dark Abyss of Time: Archaeology and Memory*, trans. Arthur Greenspan (Lanham, MD: Rowman & Littlefield, 2015), 186.

15. The classic example is a juxtaposition of "Hitchcock-baby-Hitchcock vs. Hitchcock-bathing beauty-Hitchcock." In both setups, the first and third frame depicts Hitchcock standing, looking into the distance, with the same small

smile on his face, but his "intention" or the mood of the scene is dramatically different whether one cuts to the cute baby in the pram or to the woman on the sand.

16. Alfred Gell, *Art and Agency: An Anthropological Theory* (Oxford: Oxford University Press, 1998), 98.

17. Massimo Leone and Richard Parmentier, "Representing Transcendence: The Semiosis of Real Presence," *Signs and Society* 2, no. Supplement 1 (2014): 52. This is why I scratch my head when reading debates about how "Christianity" is defined in the anthropology of Christianity. Call me nominalist if you must, but just dig in: How are people using and reusing available discourses and practices, how are those anchored in material and spatiotemporal networks, how are these seemingly local practices tied to global forces? Experiences of transcendence are anchored in all of these, but everything is always in flux, even when it feels static. For an assessment that sees the definitional problem as more urgent than I do, see Jon Bialecki, "Virtual Christianity in an Age of Nominalist Anthropology," *Anthropological Theory* 12, no. 3 (2012): 295–319. I appreciate Jean Comaroff's broad take on the field and why these questions about the autonomy of the virtual are coming up now. Comaroff, "Anthropology, Theology, Critical Pedagogy: A Conversation with Jean Comaroff and David Kyuman Kim," *Cultural Anthropology* 26, no. 2 (2011): 158–78. While not directly related to Christianity, Ryan Dohoney offers an important methodological correction to affect theory using Whitehead to level critique at "the autonomy of affect." Dohoney, "A. N. Whitehead, Feeling, & Music: On Some Potential Modifications for Affect Theory, in *Sound and Affect*, ed. J. Lochhead, E. Mendieta, and D. S. Steven (Chicago: University of Chicago Press, 2002), 268–85.

18. J. Michelle Molina, "Making a Home in an Unfortunate Place: Phenomenology and Religion," in *Anthropology of Catholicism: A Reader*, ed. Kristin Norget, Valentina Napolitano, and Maya Mayblin (Berkeley: University of California Press, 2017), 256–70.

19. For a brief account of the uncertainties that that plagued the Spanish Crown's accounting efforts, see Luisa Zahino Peñafort, *Iglesia y sociedad en México, 1765–1800: Tradición, reforma y reacciones* (Mexico City: UNAM, 1996), 167–206.

Bibliography

Archives and Libraries

Italy
Archivum Romanum Societatus Iesu (ARSI), Rome, Italy.
Biblioteca Nazionale Centrale "Vittorio Emanuele II" (BNC), Rome, Italy.
Biblioteca Nazionale Marciana, Venice, Italy.
Biblioteca Comunale dell'Archiginnasio (BA), Bologna, Italy.

Mexico
Archivo General de la Nación (AGN), Mexico City, Mexico.
Biblioteca Histórica José María Lafragua (BUAP), Puebla, Mexico.
Biblioteca del Museo Franz Mayer, Mexico City, Mexico.

Spain
Archivo General de Indias (AGI), Sevilla, Spain.
Archivo Histórico de la Nación (AHN), Madrid, Spain.
Archivo Histórico de Loyola (AHL), Azpieta, Spain.

United States
Huntington Library, San Marino, California, USA.
Newberry Library, Chicago, Illinois, USA.

Works Cited

Alarcón, Alma Montero. "Platería en el antiguo colegio jesuita noviciado de Tepotzotlán, año de 1767." In *El tesoro del lugar florido: Estudios sobre la plata iberoamericana, siglos XVI–XIX*, ed. Juan Haroldo Rodas Estrada, Nuria Salazar Simarro, and Jesús Paniagua Pérez, 487–518. Mexico City: El Forastero, 2017.

Albert, Salvador Bernabéu. "El vacío habitado: Jesuitas reales y simulados en México durante los años de la supresión (1767–1816)." *Historia mexicana* 58, no. 4 (2009): 1261–1303.

Antidoto contra todo mal: La devoción a la Santísima Madre del Lumen. Mexico City: Joseph Bernardo de Hogal, 1737.

Aposento del Padre Thomas Perez: Libros que son del colegio HM 15000–15003, Veracruz, 1771. Huntington Library, San Marino, CA.

Astorgano Abajo, Antonio. "Hervás y Panduro y sus amigos ante la mexicanidad." In *Ilustración en el mundo hispánico: Preámbulo de las independencias*, 201–54. Tlaxcala: Gobierno del Estado de Tlaxcala, Universidad Iberoamericana, 2009.

———. "La difícil circulación de los libros devocionales del Jesuita mexicano José Ignacio Vallejo (1772–1788)." *Clio: Revísta de pesquisa histórica* 32, no. 1 (2014): 102–55.

———. "Pinceladas sobre la literatura silenciada de los jesuitas expulsos a través de la Biblioteca Jesuítico-Española de Hervás Y Panduro." In *Escrituras silenciadas: El paisaje como historiografía*, ed. José F. Forniés Casals and Paulina Numhauser, 411–30. Alcalá de Henares: Universidad de Alcalá, 2013.

Auslander, Leora. "Beyond Words." *American Historical Review* 110, no. 4 (2005): 1015–45.

Ayer 1128. Documents concerning the expulsion of the Jesuits from Mexico in 1767 [manuscript], 1767–1781. Newberry Library, Chicago.

Bargellini, Clara. "El arte de las misiones del norte de la Nueva España." *História, histórias* 1, no. 2 (2013): 123–66.

Battlori, Miguel. *La cultura hispano-italiana de los jesuitas expulsos: Españoles, hispano-americanos, filipinos, 1767–1814*. Madrid: Editorial Gredos, 1966.

Bayne, Brandon. *Missions Begin with Blood: Suffering and Salvation in the Borderlands of New Spain*. New York: Fordham University Press, 2021.

Beezley, William, Cheryl Martin, and William French. *Rituals of Rule, Rituals of Resistance: Public Celebrations and Popular Culture in Mexico*. Lanham, MD: Rowman & Littlefield, 1994.

Bellion, Wendy, and Kristel Smentek. "Things Change." In *Material Cultures of the Global Eighteenth Century: Art, Mobility, and Change*, ed. Wendy Bellion and Kristel Smentek, 1–13. New York: Bloomsbury Visual Arts, 2023.

Benedict, Harold Bradley. "The Sale of the Hacienda of Tobaloapa: Jesuit Property Redistribution." *The Americas* 32 (October 1975): 177–95.

Benimeli, José Antonio Ferrer. "La alimentación de los jesuitas expulsos durante su viaje marítimo." In *Homenaje a Antonio de Béthencourt Massieu*, ed. Cabildo Insular de Gran Canaria, 581–96. Las Palmas de Gran Canaria: Ediciones del Cabildo Insular de Gran Canaria, 1995.

———. "Los 'otros' jesuitas de Bolonia." In *Un hombre de bien: Saggi di lingue e letterature iberiche in onore di Rinaldo Froldi*, ed. Patrizia Garelli and Giovanni Marchetti, 483–503. Alessandria: Edizioni dell'Orso, 2004.

Benite, Zvi Ben-Dor, Stefanos Geroulanos, and Nicole Jerr. *The Scaffolding of Sovereignty: Global and Aesthetic Perspectives on the History of a Concept*. New York: Columbia University Press, 2018.

Benton, Lauren. *A Search for Sovereignty*. Cambridge: Cambridge University Press, 2009.

Berlant, Lauren. *Cruel Optimism*. Durham, NC: Duke University Press, 2011.
———. *On the Inconvenience of Other People (Writing Matters!)*. Durham, NC: Duke University Press, 2022.
Bernabéu Albert, Salvador. "El vacío habitado: Jesuitas reales y simulados en México durante los años de la supresión (1767–1816)." *Historia mexicana* 58, no. 4 (2009): 1261–303.
Bernault, Florence. *Colonial Transactions: Imaginaries, Bodies, and Histories*. Durham, NC: Duke University Press, 2019.
Bialecki, Jon. "Virtual Christianity in an Age of Nominalist Anthropology." *Anthropological Theory* 12, no. 3 (2012). 295–319.
Bielo, James S. *Materializing the Bible: Scripture, Sensation, Place*. New York: Bloomsbury Academic, 2021.
Brading, David. *The First America: The Spanish Monarchy, Creole Patriots, and the Liberal State, 1492–1867*. Cambridge: Cambridge University Press, 1991.
Brewer-Garcia, Larissa. *Beyond Babel: Translations of Blackness in Colonial Peru and New Granada*. Cambridge: Cambridge University Press, 2020.
Brockey, Liam M. *Journey to the East: The Jesuit Mission to China, 1579–1724*. Cambridge, MA: Harvard University Press, 2007.
Burke, Juan Luis. *Architecture and Urbanism in Viceregal Mexico: Puebla de los Ángeles, Sixteenth to Eighteenth Centuries*. New York: Routledge, 2021.
Burkhart, Louise M. *Staging Christ's Passion in Eighteenth-Century Mexico*. Albany: Institute for Mesoamerican Studies, SUNY, 2023.
Burns, Jordan N., Rodolfo Acuña-Soto, and David W. Stahle. "Drought and Epidemic Typhus, Mexico, 1655–1918." *Emerging Infectious Diseases* 20, no. 3 (2014): 4420447.
Burns, Kathryn. *Into the Archive: Writing and Power in Colonial Peru*. Durham, NC: Duke University Press, 2010.
———. "Notaries, Truth, Consequences." *American Historical Review* 110, no. 2 (April 2005): 350–79.
Burton, Antoinette M. *Archive Stories : Facts, Fictions, and the Writing of History*. Durham, NC: Duke University Press, 2005.
Butler, Matthew. "Misa a la méxicana: Los ritos de la religión revolucionaria." In *México a la luz de sus revoluciones*, ed. Laura Rojas and Susan Deeds, 359–87. Mexico City: El Colegio de México, 2014.
Bynum, Caroline Walker. *Christian Materiality: An Essay on Religion in Late Medieval Europe*. New York: Zone Books, 2011.
———. *Dissimilar Similitudes: Devotional Objects in Late Medieval Europe*. New York: Zone Books, 2020.
Cabranes-Grant, Leo. *From Scenarios to Networks: Performing the Intercultural in Colonial Mexico*. Evanston, IL: Northwestern University Press, 2016.

Cañizares-Esguerra, Jorge. *How to Write the History of the New World: Histories, Epistemologies, and Identities in the Eighteenth-Century Atlantic World.* Stanford, CA: Stanford University Press, 2001.

Carruthers, Mary. *The Craft of Thought: Meditation, Rhetoric, and the Making of Images.* Cambridge: Cambridge University Press, 1998.

Casanova, José, and Thomas Banchoff, eds. *The Jesuits and Globalization: Historical Legacies and Contemporary Challenges.* Washington, DC: Georgetown University Press, 2016.

Castro Gutiérrez, Felipe. *Nueva ley y nuevo rey: Reformas borbónicas y rebelión popular en Nueva España.* Mexico City: Colegio de Michoacan/UNAM, 1986.

Chakravarti, Ananya. *Empire of Apostles: Religion, Accommodation, and the Imagination of Empire in Modern Brazil and India.* Oxford: Oxford University Press, 2018.

Chevallier, Francois, ed. *Instrucción que han de guardar los hermanos administradores de haciendas del campo.* Mexico City: Centro de Investigaciones Superiores INAH, 1950.

Chowning, Margaret. *Catholic Women and Mexican Politics, 1750–1940.* Princeton, NJ: Princeton University Press, 2023.

Clossey, Luke. *Salvation and Globalization in the Early Jesuit Missions.* Cambridge: Cambridge University Press, 2008.

Colección General de las providencias hasta aquí tomadas por el gobierno sobre el estrañamiento y ccupación de temporalidades de los regulares de la compañía que existian en los dominios de S. M. de España, Indias, e Islas Filipinas. Madrid: Imprenta Real de la Gazeta, 1767.

Coleman, Charly. *The Spirit of French Capitalism: Economic Theology in the Age of Enlightenment.* Palo Alto, CA: Stanford University Press, 2022.

———. "Vagaries of Disenchantment: God, Matter, and Mammon in the Eighteenth Century." *Modern Intellectual History* 14, no. 3 (2017): 869–81.

Colombo, Emanuele. "Jesuit at Heart: Luigi Mozzi De'capitani (1746–1813) between Suppression and Restoration." In *Jesuit Survival and Restoration. A Global History, 1773–1900,* ed. Robert Maryks and Jonathan Wright, 212–28. Leiden: Brill, 2014.

Comaroff, Jean. "Anthropology, Theology, Critical Pedagogy: A Conversation with Jean Comaroff and David Kyuman Kim." *Cultural Anthropology* 26, no. 2 (2011): 158–78.

Crosson, J. Brent. "Catching Power: Problems with Possession, Sovereignty, and African Religions in Trinidad." *Ethnos* 84, no. 4 (2019): 588–614.

Daston, Lorraine. "The Factual Sensibility." *Isis* 79, no. 3 (1988): 452–67.

Decorme, Gerard, SJ. *La obra de los Jesuitas mexicanos durante la época colonial, 1572–1767.* Mexico City: Antigua Librería Robredo de José Porrúa é Hijos, 1941.

Deleuze, Gilles. *Spinoza: Practical Philosophy*. San Francisco: City Lights, 2001.

Delgado, Jessica L. *Laywomen and the Making of Colonial Catholicism in New Spain, 1630–1790*. Cambridge: Cambridge University Press, 2018.

Diamond, Elin. *Unmaking Mimesis: Essays on Feminism and Theatre*. Englewood Cliffs, NJ: Routledge, 1997.

Díaz, Mónica. "The Education of Natives, Creole Clerics, and the Mexican Enlightenment." *Colonial Latin American Review* 24, no. 1 (2015): 60–83.

Dohoney, Ryan. "A. N. Whitehead, Feeling, & Music: On Some Potential Modifications for Affect Theory." In *Sound and Affect*, ed. J. Lochhead, E. Mendieta, and D. S. Steven, 265–85. Chicago: University of Chicago Press, 2022.

———. *Morton Feldman: Friendship and Mourning in the New York Avant-Garde*. New York: Bloomsbury Academic, 2022.

———. *Saving Abstraction: Morton Feldman, the De Menils, and the Rothko Chapel*. Oxford: Oxford University Press, 2019.

Ducrue, Benno Franciscus, and Ernest J. Burrus. *Ducrue's Account of the Expulsion of the Jesuits from Lower California (1767–1769): An Annotated English Translation of Benno Ducrue's Relatio Expulsionis*. Rome: Jesuit Historical Institute, 1967.

Dugan, Katherine and Karen E. Park, *American Patroness: Marian Shrines and the Making of U.S. Catholicism*. New York: Fordham University Press, 2024.

Durkheim, Emile. *Elementary Forms of Religious Life*. Trans. Karen E. Fields. New York: Free Press, 1995.

Endean, Philip. "The Spiritual Exercises." In *Cambridge Companion to the Jesuits*, ed. Thomas Worcester, 52–67. Cambridge: Cambridge University Press, 2008.

Esteras Martín, Cristina. *Platería hispanoamericana, siglos XVI–XIX: Exposición diocesana badajocense*. Mexico City: Exposición Diocesana Badajocense, 1984.

Ewald, Ursula. *Estudios sobre la hacienda colonial en México: Las propiedades rurales del Colegio Espíritu Santo en Puebla*. Trans. Luis R. Cerna. Wiesbaden: Franz Steiner Verlag, 1976.

Fabbri, Maurizio. "Utopías posibles al acabar un siglo: Montengón y Thjulén." In *Homenaje a José Maravall*, ed. María del Carmen Iglesias Cano, Carlos Vicente Moya Valgañón, and Luis Rodríguez Zúñiga, 2:65–78. Madrid: Centro Investigaciones Sociológicas, 1985.

Farge, Arlette, Thomas Scott-Railton, and Natalie Zemon Davis. *The Allure of the Archives*. New Haven, CT: Yale University Press, 2013.

Fernández Arrillaga, Inmaculada. "Los novicios del la Compañía de Jesús: La disyuntiva ante el autoexilio y su estancia en Italia." In *Y en el tercero pereserán: Gloria, caida, y exilio de los jesuitas españoles en el siglo XVIII*, ed. Enrique Giménez López, 169–96. Alicante: Universidad de Alicante.

———. "Profecías, coplas, creencias y devociones de los jesuitas expulsos durante su exilio en Italia." *Revista de historia moderna* 16 (1997): 83–98.
Fernández Arrillaga, Inmaculada, and Elisabetta Marchetti. *La Bolonia que habitaron los jesuitas hispánicos (1768–1773)*. Bologna: Dupress, 2012.
Frampton, Hollis. "(nostalgia)." Film. 36 minutes. 16 millimeter. 1971.
Friedrich, Markus. *The Jesuits*. Trans. John Noel Dillon. Princeton, NJ: Princeton University Press, 2022.
García-Monge Carretero, M. Isabel. "Inventarios de las bibliotecas de jesuitas en la colección biblioteca de cortes de la Real Academia de la Historia." In *La memoria de los libros: Estudios sobre la historia del escrito y de la lectura en Europa y America*, 207–27. Salamanca: Cilengua, 2004.
Gell, Alfred. *Art and Agency: An Anthropological Theory*. Oxford: Oxford University Press, 1998.
Gentry, James Duncan. *Power Objects in Tibetan Buddhism: The Life, Writings, and Legacy of Sokdokpa Lodrö Gyeltsen*. Leiden: Brill, 2017.
Giménez López, Enrique. "La devoción a la Madre Santisima de la Luz: Un aspecto de la represión del jesuitismo en la España de Carlos III." *Revista de la historia moderna* 15 (1996): 213–31.
Göktürk, Deniz. *Tracing Complicity through Personal Archives and Machine Learning: On the Art of Border Trouble*. Berkeley: Center for Interdisciplinary Critical Inquiry, UC Berkeley, 2023.
Gonzalbo Aizpuru, Pilar. *La educación popular de los Jesuitas*. Mexico City: Universidad Iberoamericana, 1989.
Grafe, Regina. "An Empire of Debt?" In *A World of Public Debts: A Political History*, ed. Nicolas Barreyre and Nicolas Delalande, 5–35. Cham, Switzerland: Palgrave Macmillan, 2020.
Graubert, Karen B. *Republics of Difference: Religious and Racial Self Governance in the Spanish Atlantic World*. Oxford: Oxford University Press, 2022.
Greenblatt, Stephen. "A Mobility Studies Manifesto." In *Cultural Mobility: A Manifesto*, ed. Stephen Greenblatt, 250–53. Cambridge: Cambridge University Press, 2010.
Guasti, Niccolò. "The Age of Suppression: From the Expulsions to the Restoration of the Society of Jesus (1759–1820)." In *The Oxford Handbook of the Jesuits*, ed. Ines Županov, 918–49. Oxford: Oxford University Press, 2017.
———. "Catholic Civilization and the Evil Savage: Juan Nuix Facing the Spanish *Conquista* of the New World." In *Encountering Otherness: Diversities and Transcultural Experiences in Early Modern European Culture*, ed. Guido Abbattista, 285–302. Trieste: EUT, 2011.
———. "Rasgos del exilio Italiano de los Jesuitas Españoles." *Hispania Sacra* 61, no. 123 (January–June 2009): 257–78.

Guerra, Alessandro. *Il vile satellite del trono: Lorenzo Ignazio Thjúlen—Un gesuita svedese per la controrivoluzione*. Milan: Franco Angeli, 2004.
Hadot, Pierre. *Philosophy as a Way of Life: Spiritual Exercises from Socrates to Foucault*. Malden, MA: Wiley-Blackfield, 1995.
Hanks, William. *Converting Words: Maya in the Age of the Cross*. Berkeley: University of California Press, 2010.
Hartman, Saidiya. *Wayward Lives, Beautiful Experiments: Intimate Histories of Social Upheaval*. New York: W. W. Norton, 2019.
Herzog, Tamar. *Defining Nations: Immigrants and Citizens in Early Modern Spain and Spanish America*. New Haven, CT: Yale University Press, 2003.
———. *Mediación, archivos y ejercicio: Los escribanos de Quito (siglo XVII)*. Frankfurt: V. Klostermann, 1996.
Hills, Helen. *Matter of Miracles: Neapolitan Baroque Sanctity and Architecture*. Manchester: Manchester University Press, 2016.
Holbraad, Martin. "The Power of Powder: Multiplicity and Motion in the Divinatory Cosmology of Cuban Ifá (or Mana, Again)." In *Thinking Through Things: Theorising Artefacts Ethnographically*, ed. Amiria Henare, Martin Holbraad, and Sari Wastell, 189–225. London: Routledge, 2007.
Hovland, Ingie. "Christianity, Place/Space, and Anthropology: Thinking across Recent Research on Evangelical Place-Making." *Religion* 46, no. 3 (2016): 331–58.
Hughes, Jennifer Scheper. *The Church of the Dead: The Epidemic of 1576 and the Birth of Christianity in the Americas*. New York: New York University Press, 2021.
Hunt, Lynn, Margaret Jacob, and Wijnand Mijnhardt. *The Book That Changed Europe: Picart and Bernard's Religious Ceremonies of the World*. Cambridge, MA: Harvard University Press, 2010.
Instrucción. Cuba, 1123, 459–62. Archivo General de las Indias, 1767.
"Inventario de la expurgación de libros en los colegios Jesuíticos del Espíritu Santo y de San Javier en Puebla." *Documentos para la historia de la cultura en México, una biblioteca del siglo XVII: Catálogo de libros expurgados a los jesuitas en el siglo XVIII*. Mexico City: Imprenta Universitaria, UNAM, 1947.
Ireton, Chloe. "Black Africans' Freedom Litigation Suits to Define Just War and Just Slavery in the Early Spanish Empire." *Renaissance Quarterly* 73 (2020): 1277–319.
Johnson, Paul, Pamela E. Klassen, and Winnifred Fallers Sullivan. *Ekklesia: Three Inquiries in Church and State*. Chicago: University of Chicago Press, 2018.
Jones, Lindsay. *The Hermeneutics of Sacred Architecture: Experience, Interpretation, Comparison, Vol. 1*. Cambridge, MA: Harvard University Press, 2000.
Kantorowicz, Ernst. *The King's Two Bodies: A Study in Medieval Political Theology*. Princeton, NJ: Princeton University Press, 1957.

Katzew, Ilona. *The Archive of the World*. Los Angeles: Los Angeles County Museum, 2022.

Keane, Webb. "On Semiotic Ideology." *Signs and Society* 6, no. 1 (2018): 64–87.

———. "Rotting Bodies: The Clash of Stances toward Materiality and Its Ethical Affordances." *Current Anthropology* 55 (2014): 312–21.

Keating, Jessica, and Lia Markey. "'Indian' Objects in Medici and Austrian-Habsburg Inventories: A Case Study of the Sixteenth-Century Term." *Journal of the History of Collections* 23, no. 2 (2011): 283–300.

Keenan, Thomas. "Paradoxes of Recognition: How to Make a Refugee." Borders and Borders and Crossings: Contemporary Arts and Techniques of Migration, UC Berkeley CICI, 2023.

Kennedy, David. *Elegy*. London: Routledge, 2008.

Kieckhefer, Richard. *The Mystical Presence of Christ: The Exceptional and the Ordinary in Late Medieval Religion*. Ithaca, NY: Cornell University Press, 2022.

Kloppe-Santamaría, Gema. *In the Vortex of Violence: Lynching, Extralegal Violence and the State in Post-Revolutionary Mexico*. Berkeley: University of California Press, 2020.

Knaut, Andrew L. "Yellow Fever and the Late Colonial Public Health Response in the Port of Veracruz." *Hispanic American Historical Review* 77, no. 4 (1997): 619–44.

Laqueur, Thomas W. *The Work of the Dead: A Cultural History of Mortal Remains*. Princeton, NJ: Princeton University Press, 2015.

Larkin, Brian R. *The Very Nature of God: Baroque Catholicism and Religious Reform in Bourbon Mexico City*. Albuquerque: University of New Mexico Press, 2010.

Latour, Bruno. *Reassembling the Social: An Introduction to Actor-Network Theory*. Oxford: Oxford University Press, 2005.

Leclercq, Jean. *The Love of Learning and the Desire for God: A Study of Monastic Culture*. Trans. Catherine Misrahi. New York: Fordham University Press, 1974.

Lehner, Ulrich L. *The Catholic Enlightenment: The Forgotten History of a Global Movement*. Oxford: Oxford University Press, 2016.

Lehner, Ulrich L., and Michael O'Neill Printy. *A Companion to the Catholic Enlightenment in Europe*. Leiden: Brill, 2010.

Leone, Massimo, and Richard Parmentier. "Representing Transcendence: The Semiosis of Real Presence." *Signs and Society* 2, Supplement 1 (2014): 1–22.

Libro de asientos de entradas y salidas en la casa de depósito de las regulares de la compañía que llegan a la habana y con destino a España. Cuba 1099, Partes de la Casa de Depósito Archivo General de las Indias.

"List of the Gold and Silver Adornments, divided by class, belonging to the Five Colleges occupied in this City, 1774." Legajo 139. Fondo jesuita. Fondo Antiguo, Biblioteca Histórica José María Lafragua de la BUAP.

Logan, Anne-Marie, and Liam M. Brockey. "Nicolas Trigault, SJ: A Portrait by Peter Paul Rubens." *Metropolitan Museum Journal* 38 (2003): 157–67.
López de Priego, Antonio. "Carta de un religioso de los extintos jesuitas, a una hermana suya, religiosa del convento de Santa Catarina de la puebla de Los Angeles: Escrita en la ciudad de Bolonia, En 1 de octubre de 1785." In *Tesoros documentales de México: Siglo XVIII*, ed. Mariano Cuevas, 9–405. Mexico City: Editorial Galatea, 1944.
Lynch, John. "The Expulsion of the Jesuits and the Late Colonial Period." In *The Cambridge History of Religions in Latin America*, ed. Virgina Garrard Burnett, Paul Preson, and Stephen C. Dove, 220–30. Cambridge: Cambridge University Press, 2016.
Manrique, Carlos. "Spiritual Memory, Spatial Affects, and Churchstateness in Popular Uprising in Afro-Columbia's Pacific Littoral." *Political Theology* 25, no. 3 (2024): 258–77.
Manrique Figueroa, César. "Arsenals of Knowledge: Reconstructing the Contents and Purpose of the Lost Jesuit Libraries of Northern Mexico." *Journal of Jesuit Studies* 10 (2023): 520–36.
Marder, Michael. *Dust*. New York: Bloomsbury, 2016.
Marocci, Giuseppe. "Saltwater Conversion: Trans-Oceanic Sailing and Religious Transformation in the Iberian World." In *Space and Conversion in Global Perspective*, ed. Giuseppe Marcocci, Aliocha Maldavsky, Wietse de Boer, and Ilaria Pavan, 235–59. Leiden: Brill, 2014.
Martínez-Serna, J. Gabriel. "Procurators and the Making of the Jesuits' Atlantic World." In *Soundings in Atlantic History: Latent Structures and Intellectual Currents, 1500–1830*, ed. Bernard Bailyn and Patricia E. Denault, 181–209. Cambridge: Cambridge University Press, 2009.
Martins Torres, Andreia. "El quimono en la Nueva España: Una manifestación local de una moda global en los siglos XVII y XVIII." *Conservar património* 31 (2019): 79–95.
Maryks, Robert, and Jonathan Wright, eds. *Jesuit Survival and Restoration: A Global History, 1773–1900*. Leiden: Brill, 2015.
Mayer, Alicia. *Lutero en el paraíso: La Nueva España en el espejo del reformador alemán*. Mexico City: Universidad Nacional Autónoma de México/Fondo de Cultura Económica/Instituto de Investigaciones Históricas, 2008.
Mazzarella, William. *The Mana of Mass Society*. Chicago: University of Chicago Press, 2017.
McAllister, Carlota, and Valentina Napolitano. "Introduction: Incarnate Politics Beyond the Cross and the Sword." *Social Analysis* 64, no. 4 (2020): 1–20.
McGreevy, John. *American Jesuits and the World: How an Embattled Religious Order Made Modern Catholicism Global*. Princeton, NJ: Princeton University Press, 2016.

McManus, Stuart M. "The Art of Being a Colonial *Letrado*: Late Humanism, Learned Sociability and Urban Life in Eighteenth-Century Mexico City." *Estudios de historia novohispana* 56 (2017): 40–64.
McNeill, J. R. "Yellow Jack and Geopolitics: Environment, Epidemics, and the Struggles for Empire in the American Tropics, 1640–1830." *Review (Fernand Braudel Center)* 27, no. 4 (2004): 343–64.
Mehl, Eva María. "La expulsión de los jesuitas y la represión del jesuitismo en Nueva España." In *Espacios de saber, espacios de poder: Iglesia, universidades, y colegios en Hispanoamérica, siglos XVI–XIX*, ed. Rodolfo Aguirre Salvador, 317–45. Mexico City: Universidad Nacional Autónoma de México, 2014.
Melion, Walter, and Lee Palmer Wandel. *Image and Incarnation: The Early Modern Doctrine of the Pictorial Image*. Leiden: Brill, 2015.
Melvin, Karen. *Building Colonial Cities of God: Mendicant Orders and Urban Cultures in New Spain, 1570–1800*. Palo Alto, CA: Stanford University Press, 2012.
Merleau-Ponty, Maurice. *Phenomenology of Perception*. Trans. Donald Landes. Englewood Cliffs, NJ: Routledge, 2012.
Miettinen, Riika. "'Lord Have Mercy on Me': Spiritual Preparations for Suicide in Early Modern Sweden." In *Preparing for a Good Death in Medieval and Early Modern Northern Europe*, ed. Anu Lahtinen and Mia Korpiola, 160–86. Leiden: Brill, 2018.
Mittermaier, Amira. "Beyond the Human Horizon." *Religion and Society: Advances in Research* 12 (2021): 21–38.
Molina, J. Michelle. "Fluid Indigeneity: Indians, Catholicism, and Spanish Law in the Mutable Americas." *The Immanent Frame: Secularism, Religion, and the Public Sphere* (July 12, 2017). https://tif.ssrc.org/2017/07/.
———. "How to Be a Country Jesuit: Continence, Care and Containment in a Racializing Religiosity." In *Jesuits and Race*, ed. Nathaniel Millet and Charles Parker, 133–62. Albuquerque: University of New Mexico Press, 2022.
———. "Making a Home in an Unfortunate Place: Phenomenology and Religion." In *Anthropology of Catholicism: A Reader*, ed. Kristin Norget, Valentina Napolitano, and Maya Mayblin. Berkeley: University of California Press, 2017.
———. "Technologies of the Self: The Letters of 18th Century Mexican Jesuit Spiritual Daughters." *History of Religions* (2008). https://www.journals.uchicago.edu/doi/10.1086/589782.
———. *To Overcome Oneself: The Jesuit Ethic and the Spirit of Global Expansion*. Berkeley: University of California Press, 2013.
Moore, Brenna. "Friendship and the Cultivation of Religious Sensibilities." *Journal of the American Academy of Religion* 83, no. 2 (2015): 437–63.
———. *Kindred Spirits: Friendship and Resistance at the Edge of Modern Catholicism*. Chicago: University of Chicago Press, 2021.

Mörner, Magnus. "Los motivos de la expulsión de los jesuitas del imperio español." *Historia mexicana* 16, no. 1 (1966): 1–14.

Motta, Franco, and Eleonora Rai. "Martyrs and Missionaries: Strategies of Jesuit Sainthood between the Suppression and the Restoration." *Journal of Jesuit Studies* 9 (2022): 95–124.

Nadal, Jeronimo. *Pláticas espirituales del P. Jerónimo Nadal, SJ, en Coimbra*. Granada: Facultad Teológicas de la Compañía de Jesus, 1945 [1561].

Nelles, Paul. "*Libros De Papel, Libri Bianchi, Libri Papyracel*: Note-Taking Techniques and the Role of Student Notebooks in the Early Jesuit Colleges." *Archivum Historicum Societatus Iesu* 76 (January–June 2007): 75–112.

Nemser, Daniel. *Infrastructures of Race: Concentration and Biopolitics in Colonial Mexico*. Austin: University of Texas Press, 2017.

Neuerburg, Norman. "La Madre Santísima de la Luz." *Journal of San Diego History* 41, no. 2 (1995): 74–76.

Och, Joseph, S.J. *Missionary in Sonora: The Travel Reports of Joseph Och, S.J., 1755–1767*. Trans. Theodore E. Treutlein. San Francisco: California Historical Society, 1965.

O'Hara, Matthew. *The History of the Future in Colonial Mexico*. New Haven, CT: Yale University Press, 2018.

Oliphant, Elayne. *The Privilege of Being Banal: Art, Secularism, and Catholicism in Paris*. Chicago: University of Chicago Press, 2021.

O'Malley, John W. "To Travel to Any Part of the World: Jerónimo Nadal and the Jesuit Vocation." In *Saints or Devils Incarnate?: Studies in Jesuit History*, 147–64. Leiden: Brill, 2013.

O'Sullivan, Lucy. "Martyrdom in the Age of Mechanical Reproduction: The Photograph as Testimony and Trace in Mexico's Cristero War (1926–29)." *Latin American and Latinx Visual Culture* 6, no. 1 (2024): 1–19.

Olivier, Laurent. *The Dark Abyss of Time: Archaeology and Memory*. Trans. Arthur Greenspan. Lanham, MD: Rowman & Littlefield, 2015.

Orsi, Robert. *Between Heaven and Earth: The Religious Worlds People Make and the Scholars Who Study Them*. Princeton, NJ: Princeton University Press, 2005.

———. *History and Presence*. Cambridge, MA: Harvard University Press, 2016.

Osorio Romero, Ignacio. *Historia de las bibliotecas en Puebla*. Mexico City: SEP, Dirección General de Bibliotecas, 1988.

———. *Historia de las bibliotecas novohispanos*. Mexico City: SEP, 1986.

Palacios, Joy. *Ceremonial Splendor: Performing Priesthood in Early Modern France*. Philadelphia: University of Pennsylvania Press, 2022.

Parra, Juan Martínez de la. *Luz de verdades católicas y explicación de la doctrina christiana que siguiendo la costumbre de la casa professa de la compañía de México . . . se platica en su iglesia*. Mexico City: En la imprenta de Diego Fernández de Leon, 1691–1696.

Patch, Robert W. "Sacraments and Disease in Mérida, Yucatan, Mexico, 1648–1727." *The Historian* 58, no. 4 (1996): 731–43.
Petrucci, Armand. *Writing the Dead: Death and Writing Strategies in the Western Tradition*. Stanford, CA: Stanford University Press, 1998.
Pickering, Andrew. *The Mangle of Practice: Time, Agency, and Science*. Chicago: University of Chicago Press, 1995.
———. "The Ontological Turn: Taking Different Worlds Seriously." *Social Analysis* 61, no. 2 (2017): 134–50.
Premo, Bianca. *Children of the Father King: Youth, Authority, and Legal Minority in Colonial Lima*. Chapel Hill: University of North Carolina Press, 2005.
———. *The Enlightenment on Trial: Ordinary Litigants and Colonialism in the Spanish Empire*. Oxford: Oxford University Press, 2017.
Quattrone, Paolo. "Accounting for God: Accounting and Accountability Practices in the Society of Jesus (Italy, XVI–XVII)." *Accounting, Organizations and Society* 29 (2004): 647–83.
Ramos Soriano, José Abel. *Los delincuentes de papel: Inquisición y libros en la Nueva España, 1571–1820*. Mexico City: Fondo de Cultura Económica, 2011.
Rappaport, Joan. *The Disappearing Mestizo: Configuring Difference in the Colonial New Kingdom of Granada*. Durham, NC: Duke University Press, 2014.
Reinhardt, Richard. "Francis of Assisi's Perfect Jouissance: Theorizing Conversion through Objects and Affects in Early Franciscan Fragments." *Material Religions* 18, no. 2 (2022): 228–49.
Riley, James D. "The Wealth of the Jesuits in Mexico, 1670–1767." *The Americas* 33, no. 2 (1976): 226–66.
Rojas, Laura, and Susan Deeds, eds. *México a la luz de sus revoluciones*, vol. 2. Mexico City: El Colegio de México, Centro de Estudios Históricos, 2014.
Ronan, Charles E. *Francisco Javier Clavigero, S.J., (1731–1787), Figure of the Mexican Enlightenment: His Life and Works*. Chicago: Loyola University Press, 1977.
Ruiu, Adina. "French and Canadian Jesuit History Writing: A Bridge between the 'Old' and the 'New' Society. In *The Oxford Handbook of the Jesuits*, ed. Ines G. Županov, 974–1003. Oxford: Oxford University Press, 2019.
Russell, Camilla. *Being a Jesuit in Renaissance Italy: Biographical Writing in the Early Global Age*. Cambridge, MA: Harvard University Press, 2022.
Russo, Alessandra. "Cortés Objects and the Idea of New Spain: Inventories as Spatial Narratives." *Journal of the History of Collections* 23, no. 2 (2011): 229–52.
Saramago, Jose. *All the Names*. New York: Mariner Books, 2001.
Schneider, Rebecca. "Performance Remains." *Performance Research* 6, no. 2 (2001): 100–108.
———. *Theatre & History*. London: Bloomsbury, 2014.

Schroeder, Susan. "Jesuits, Nahuas and the Good Death Society in Mexico City, 1710–1767." *Hispanic American Historical Review* 80, no. 1 (2000): 43–76.

Sebastián, José Felix de. *Memorias de los padres y hermanos de la Compañía De Jesus de la provincia de Nueva España difuntos despues del arresto acaecido en la capital de Mexico el día 25 de junio del año 1767.* Archiginnasio, 1767–1783.

Shapton, Leanne. *Important Artifacts and Personal Property from the Collection of Lenore Dooland Harold Morris, Including Books, Street Fashion, and Jewelry.* New York: Strachan & Quinn Auctioneers, 2009.

Sheehan, Jonathan. *The Enlightenment Bible: Translation, Scholarship, Culture.* Princeton, NJ: Princeton University Press, 2007.

Silva, Pablo Sierra. *Urban Slavery in Colonial Mexico: Puebla de Los Ángeles, 1531–1706.* Cambridge: Cambridge University Press, 2018.

Spence, Jonathan. *The Memory Palace of Matteo Ricci.* New York: Penguin Books, 1984.

St. Clair Segurado, Eva María. "Difusión en América de la polémica Europa en torno a la Compañía de Jesús: Literatura propagandística pro y antijesuita en Nueva España, 1754–1767." *Dimensión antropológica* 27 (2003): 7–45.

———. *Expulsión y exilio de la provincia jesuita mexicana (1767–1820).* Alicante: Universidad de Alicante, 2009.

Steedman, Carolyn, *Dust: The Archive and Cultural History.* New Brunswick, NJ: Rutgers University Press, 2002.

Stewart, Susan. *The Ruins Lesson: Meaning and Material in Western Culture.* Chicago: University of Chicago Press, 2020.

Stock, Brian. *Augustine, the Reader: Meditation, Self-Knowledge and the Ethics of Interpretation.* Cambridge, MA: Harvard University Press, 1998.

Stoler, Ann Laura. "Colonial Archives and the Arts of Governance." *Archival Science* 2 (2002): 87–109.

Stolley, Karen. "East of Eden: Domesticating Exile in Jesuit Accounts of Their 1767 Expulsion from Spanish America." In *Jesuit Accounts of the Colonial Americas: Intercultural Transfers, Intellectual Disputes, and Textualities,* ed. Marc André Bernier, Clorinda Donato, and Hans-Jürgen Lüsebrink, 243–62. Toronto: University of Toronto Press, 2014.

Strasser, Ulrike. "Copies with Souls: The Late Seventeenth Century Marianas Martyrs and the Question of Clerical Reproduction." *Journal of Jesuit Studies* 2 (2015): 558–85.

———. "The First Form and Grace: Ignatius of Loyola and the Reformation of Masculinity." In *Masculinity in the Reformation Era,* ed. Scott H. Hendrix and Susan C. Karant-Nunn, 45–70. Kirksville, MO: Truman State University Press, 2008.

———. *Missionary Men in the Early Modern World: German Jesuits and Pacific Journeys.* Amsterdam: Amsterdam University Press, 2020.

Sweet, David G. "Black Robes and 'Black Destiny': Jesuit Views of African Slavery in 17th Century Latin America." *Revista de historia de América* 86 (1978): 87–133.
Tanner, Kathryn. *Economy of Grace*. Minneapolis: Augsburg Fortress, 2005.
Taylor, Diana. *The Archive and the Repertoire: Performing Cultural Memory in the Americas*. Durham, NC: Duke University Press, 2003.
Taylor, William B. *Magistrates of the Sacred: Priests and Parishioners in Eighteenth-Century Mexico*. Palo Alto, CA: Stanford University Press, 1996.
———. *Theater of a Thousand Wonders: A History of Miraculous Images and Shrines in New Spain*. Cambridge: Cambridge University Press, 2016.
Thjülen, Lorenzo Ignazio. *Dialoghi nel regno de'morti*. Bologna: Nella Tipografia Arcivescovile, 1815–1819.
Torales Pacheco, María Cristina. "Del nacimiento a la muerte en las familias de la élite novohispana del siglo VXIII." In *Familia y vida privada en la historia de Iberoamérica*, ed. Pilar Gonzalbo Aizpuru and Cecilia Rabell Romero, 423–36. Mexico City: El Colegio de México, Instituto de Investigaciones Sociales de la Universidad Nacional Autónoma de México, 1996.
Trouillot, Michel-Rolph. *Silencing the Past: Power and the Production of History*. Boston: Beacon Press, 1995.
Untitled. Legajo 150. Fondo jesuitas. Fondo Antiguo, Biblioteca Histórica José María Lafragua de la BUAP.
Untitled miscellaneous letters. Vitae 1006. Archivum Romanum Societatis Iesu (ARSI).
Valdés, Dennis N. "The Decline of Slavery in Mexico." *The Americas* 75, no. 1 (2018): 167–94.
Van Kley, Dale. *Reform Catholicism and the International Suppression of the Jesuits in Enlightenment Europe*. New Haven, CT: Yale University Press, 2018.
Vargas Alquicira, Silvia. *La singularidad novohispana en los jesuitas del siglo XVIII*. Mexico City: UNAM, 1989.
Velez, Karin. *The Miraculous Flying House of Loreto: Spreading Catholicism in the Early Modern World*. Princeton, NJ: Princeton University Press, 2019.
Venegas, Miguel. *Vida y virtudes de Juan Bautista Zappa de la Compañía de Jesús*. Barcelona: Pablo Nadal, 1754.
Vizuete Mendoza, J. Carlos. "En las fronteras de la ortodoxia: La devoción a la Virgen de la Luz (Madre Santísima de la Luz) en Nueva España." In *Religión y heterodoxia en el mundo hispánico, siglos XIV–XVIII*, ed. Ricard Izquierdo Benito and Fernando Martínez Gil, 255–79. Madrid: Sílex, 2011.
Voekel, Pamela. *Alone Before God: The Religious Origins of Modernity in Mexico*. Durham, NC: Duke University Press, 2002.
———. *For God and Liberty: Catholicism and Revolution in the Atlantic World, 1790–1861*. Oxford: Oxford University Press, 2022.

Wandel, Lee Palmer . *The Eucharist in the Reformation: Incarnation and Liturgy*. Cambridge: Cambridge University Press, 2006.
Watkins, Daniel J. *Berruyer's Bible: Public Opinion and the Politics of Enlightenment Catholicism*. Montreal: McGill-Queen's University Press, 2021.
Watson, B. M. "Please Stop Calling Things Archives: An Archivist's Plea." *Perspectives* 59, no. 1 (2021).
Watts, William. "Seneca on Slavery." *The Downside Review* 90, no. 300 (1972): 183–95.
Weaver, Brendan J. M. "Rethinking the Political Economy of Slavery: The Hacienda Aesthetic at the Jesuit Vineyards of Nasca, Peru." *Post-Medieval Archaeology* 52, no. 1 (2018): 117–33.
Winchell, Mareike. "Alterable Geographies: In/Humanity, Emancipation, and the Spatial Poetics of *Lo Abigarrado* in Bolivia." *Critical Times* 6, no. 2 (2023): 271–88.
Woloch, Alex. *The One Vs. The Many: Minor Characters and the Space of the Protagonist in the Novel*. Princeton, NJ: Princeton University Press, 2004.
Xavier, Angela Barreto, and Ines Županov. *Catholic Orientalism: Portuguese Empire, Indian Knowledge (16th–18th Centuries)*. Oxford: Oxford University Press, 2014.
Zahino Peñafort, Luisa. *Iglesia y sociedad en México, 1765–1800: Tradición, reforma y reacciones*. Mexico City: UNAM, 1996.
Zárate Toscano, Verónica. *Los nobles ante la muerte en México: Actitudes, ceremonias, y memoria, 1750–1850*. Mexico City: El Colegio de México, 2005.
Zelís, Rafael de. *Catálogo de los sugetos de la Compañía de Jesús que formaron la provincia de México el día del arresto, 25 de junio de 1767*. Mexico City: I. Escalante, 1871.
———. "Viajes en su destierro." In *Tesoros documentales de México: Siglo XVIII*, ed. Mariano Cuevas, 1–405.1785. Mexico City: Editorial Galatea, 1944.
Županov, Ines. *Disputed Mission: Jesuit Experiments and Brahmanical Knowledge in Seventeenth Century India*. Oxford: Oxford University Press, 1999.
Županov, Ines, and Pierre Antoine Fabre. "The Rites Controversies in the Early Modern World: An Introduction." In *The Rites Controversies in the Early Modern World*, ed. Ines Županov and Pierre Antoine Fabre, 1–26. Leiden: Brill, 2018.

Index

accommodation, Jesuit modes of, 7, 52–53. *See also* laity, Jesuit relations with
affect theory, 100
affective inventory, 90, 113
Alarcón, Alma Montero, 210n14
altars: centrality of for colonial power, 14–15, 25, 29, 48, 61, 87–88, 92–93; centrality of for Jesuit haciendas, 75–76, 78–80; Christ's/God's presence on, 14, 62–63, 93–94. *See also* silver altarware
Ananias of Damascus, 105–6, 121
anchorites, 178, 182–84, 191
anti-Jesuitism, 5–8
Aramburu, Francisco de, 40, 50–51, 53, 56, 58–59, 152
Aranda, Conde de, 31, 33, 62
archives, 3–5, 8, 94, 204n7
Arenas, Pedro, 136, 139, 144
Arriola, Juan de, 39, 47
Auslander, Leora, 43
Ayer 1128, 11, 14, 64

baptism, 75, 84, 153
Bargellini, Clara, 209n14
Bellarmine, Robert, 6, 84–85, 117
Benfumea, Miguel de, 41, 150
Berlant, Lauren, 19, 100
Bernard, Jean Frédéric, 102–3
Berruyer, Isaac, 51–53, 117
Bologna, experiences of expelled Jesuits in, 161–66
books, centrality of for Jesuit practice, 9–11, 26, 35, 40, 57, 114–18, 124
Bourdieu, Pierre, 22
Braun, Bartholome, 154
Breve de Abolición, 159. *See also* Society of Jesus, abolition of; Society of Jesus, suppression of

Brewer-Garcia, Larissa, 91
Bucareli y Ursúa, Antonio María, 117
burials of Jesuits, 139–45, 153–54, 161, 172–73, 182. *See also* death
Burns, Kathryn, 27
Bynum, Caroline Walker, 22, 59, 71

Cabranes-Grant, Leo, 9, 65
Cabrera, Miguel, 55
Cádiz, experiences of expelled Jesuits in, 108, 116
Carruthers, Mary, 16
Casa de Ejercícios, 35–38, 151–52
Castillo, José, 35, 40
Castillo, Manuel del, 27, 31–35, 37–38, 45–47, 56, 62, 190
Chinese Rites controversy, 7
Christ, body of, 13–15, 30, 48, 64, 66, 72, 85, 91, 94–95, 194–95; material, 29; mystical, 25, 28, 60–62, 65, 94
church-state conflict. *See* sovereignty
Cid, Antonio, 40, 47
Clavigero, Francisco Javier, 148
Clement XIII (pope), 1
Clement XIV (pope), 159
Colegio de Espíritu Santo, 11, 25–27, 89, 144, 163, 165, 181; inventory of items at the, 31–32, 63, 67–68, 75, 88, 92
Coleman, Charly, 29
colleges, Jesuit, 24–28, 30, 163–69; safekeeping of lay community property in, 28, 33–35, 38–43 (*see also* laity, Jesuit relations with). *See also* haciendas, Jesuit
colonialism, 25, 62, 87, 94
communion, centrality and frequency of for Jesuits, 6, 13, 30, 44, 49–50, 80–82, 92, 222n166. *See also* Eucharist

Comte de Narbonne Pelet-Fritzlar, 123–24
confession, 6, 30, 44, 49, 119, 151, 151. *See also* penance
Congregación de la Escalvitud de Nuestra Señora la Virgen Santísima de la Anunciata, 89
Congregación de la Santísima Virgen de Morenos y Pardos, 89–90
Congregación del Pópulo, 34, 56, 150
consolation (concept in Jesuit spirituality), 118–19
contemplatives in action, Jesuits as, 118, 147, 158, 182, 191
conversion narratives, 1, 3, 15–17, 99–100, 105, 107, 118, 125, 132, 193. *See also* inventories of self
corporales, 64, 74, 78. *See also* altars; Eucharist
Council of Trent, 60
Counterreformation, 48
Croix, Marquis de, 31

death: good, 134–36, 140, 145, 172, 181, 192; unaccompanied by rituals, 139–40, 178–79. *See also* burial; inventories of the dead
Deleuze, Gilles, 101
Delgado, Jessica, 83
Devil, the, 114, 120
Diamond, Elin, 20–21, 193
Doctrina Cristiana, 81–84, 117, 124
Ducrue, Benito, 110
Durkheim, Emile, 65. *See also mana* (Durkheimian concept)

Enlightenment, 7, 16, 98–99, 102, 119, 130–31, 190
enslaved persons, 26, 76–77, 79–91
Ethics (work by Baruch Spinoza), 100
Eucharist, 29–30, 48–50, 60–61, 64, 71, 75, 82, 91, 94, 178. *See also* communion
Extreme Unction, 179

Fernández, Eligio, 42, 164, 181–83
fictive kinship, 79, 82–86, 119–20, 126, 157
Figueora, Manrique, 209n14
Fourth Mexican Council (1771), 58

France, opposition to Jesuits in, 5–6
Francis (pope), 3
Franciscans, 116, 139, 161, 180–81
free will, 6, 49

Gallicanism, 5–6, 8
Gell, Alfred, 13, 194
Genovese, Giuseppi Maria, 54
genre, 3–4
Gentry, James, 43
Greenblatt, Stephen, 8
Guaraní revolt, 7
Guasti, Niccolò, 203n4
Guerro, Joseph, 145

haciendas, Jesuit, 25–27, 34, 72–87, 167–68; administrators of, 75–77, 79–85, 167–69, 192; economics of, 85–87; racialization in, 25, 75–76, 85–88, 90–91. *See also* colleges, Jesuit
Hanks, William, 22
Havana, experiences of expelled Jesuits in, 15, 51, 117, 145, 152
hermanos (temporal coadjutors), 76, 81, 86, 141, 155–56, 168
Hills, Helen, 62
Histoire du peuple de Dieu (work by Isaac Berruyer), 51–53
holy water, 77
Hovland, Ingie, 87
Hughes, Jennifer Scheper, 61

Iberia, opposition to Jesuits in, 6–8. *See also* Cádiz, experiences of expelled Jesuits in
Ignatius of Loyola, 1, 34, 52, 66, 69, 127, 130, 212n49, 222n166
images, 54–59, 69, 90, 191. *See also* Madre Santísima de la Luz
imprisonment of Jesuits, 45, 143–45, 152–52, 159, 163, 180–81
incarnational theology, 13–14, 29, 66, 72, 194
indigenous peoples in Jesuit missions, 26, 61, 79, 81–82, 86, 91, 151–52, 158, 170
"Instructions That the Brothers Administrators of the Haciendas Must Observe," 75–79, 81–82, 86–87, 167. *See also* haciendas, Jesuit

inventories and inventorying, 1, 3–4, 11, 14–20, 94, 193–95
inventories of self, 1, 15–16, 18–19, 86, 99, 109, 113. *See also* conversion narratives
inventories of the dead, 1, 17–18, 134–35, 138–39, 191–92
inventories of things/notarial lists, 1, 3, 9–11, 14, 27–28, 44–45, 62–63, 75–76, 86, 93–95, 189
Iturriaga, Manuel, 16, 99, 101, 105–7, 112–15, 118–24, 126, 128–30, 190

Jansenism, 5–8, 49, 53
José I (king of Portugal), 7

Kennedy, David, 135
Kieckhefer, Richard, 60–61, 94

labor systems, Jesuit, 75–76, 79, 82, 85, 87
laity, Jesuit relations with, 44, 75, 151, 167. *See also* accommodation
Laqueur, Thomas, 162, 172, 186
Larkin, Brian, 61
last rites, 75, 182
Latour, Bruno, 22–23, 30, 48, 65, 72, 132, 189, 194
Leone, Massimo, 194
lists and listmaking, 3, 10–11, 64, 179
liturgy. *See* Mass
locational anxieties (of Jesuits), 4, 8–10, 14, 22–23
López de Priego, Antonio, 109, 111–14
Lorenzana, Francisco Antonio de, 58
Luengo, Manuel, 161
Luther, Martin, 48, 105, 112, 122
Lutherans and Lutheranism, 98–99, 102, 104, 107, 111–12, 119, 122, 124, 126, 130
Luz de verdades católicas y explicación de la doctrina christiana (work by Juan Martínez de la Parra), 79

Machado, Francis Xavier, 31–33, 37, 45
Madre Santísima de la Luz, 53–59, 84, 88, 152, 191, 239n106. *See also* Virgin Mary
Malabar Rites controversy, 7

mana (Durkheimian concept), 13, 29–30, 66, 71, 87–88, 91–93, 96, 191
Marder, Michael, 45
Mariana, Juan de, 6
marriage, 75, 83–84, 103, 129
martyrdom, 136, 143–46, 174, 176, 179
Mass, 30, 75, 77–78, 80–85, 110–12, 178
Mazzarella, William, 65–66
McAllister, Carlota, 29, 44, 72
McGreevy, John, 203n4
meditative practices, Jesuit, 16, 36, 52, 118, 130, 191. *See also* Spiritual Exercises, Ignatian
Memorias de los padres y hermanos de la Compañía de Jesús de la Provincia de Nueva España (work by José Felix de Sebastián), 18, 134–38, 147, 155, 159, 169, 173, 175, 179, 181, 184, 192
mental illness: Jesuit care for people with, 42, 47, 140, 144; Jesuits with, 136, 144–46, 177–78, 239n105
mimesis, 20
Mittermaier, Amira, 14
mobility, Jesuit, 4, 8, 15, 45, 76, 101, 113–14, 147–49, 183
Molina, Luís, 6, 49
Moore, Brenna, 119
moral laxity, accusations of against Jesuits, 6, 48–49, 51, 53, 58, 92
mourning, 135, 155, 172–82
Mozarabe, Ignacio, 35, 38
Muñoz, Juan Josef, 34, 41, 48, 178, 184, 239n106

Nadal, Jerónimo, 118
Napolitano, Valentina, 29, 44, 72
naturales (born in the New World), 9
Nelles, Paul, 57
networks, Jesuit, 3, 24–30, 63–66, 78, 115, 132, 163, 166, 180–82, 191
networks, sacramental, 14, 26, 30, 65–66, 71–72, 91, 95, 191, 194
Nieremberg, Juan Eusebio, 84–85
Nobili, Roberto de, 53
notaries, 1, 10–14, 27, 31–33, 71, 93–94, 190
novices and novitiates, 128–29, 169, 171. *See also* Tepotzotlán
Nuestra Señora de Dolores, 69–70. *See also* Virgin Mary

Och, Joseph, 37, 110–11, 115–17
Olivier, Laurent, 23, 189, 193
O'Malley, John, 186
"On the Obligations of Masters and Slaves" (work by Juan Martínez de la Parra), 86
Orsi, Robert, 13
Oyarzún, Manuel Joseph, 140, 144

Palafox, Juan de, 6
Papal States, 123–24, 135, 147, 166, 180, 190
Parmentier, Richard, 194
Parra, Juan Martínez de la, 79, 84–86
penance (sacrament of), 30, 44, 48–49, 75, 222n166. *See also* confession
Pérez, Tomás, 12, 173–74, 176
performance and performativity, 5, 8, 11, 21–22, 146–49
Picart, Bernard, 102–3
Pickering, Andrew, 64, 95
pláticas, 80, 84. *See also* sermons
power: colonial, 11, 13–15, 22, 25, 28–31, 87, 190; Jesuit, 1–3, 9–11, 14, 24–30, 33, 48, 190, 194; objects of, 43–44, 72, 88–89, 93; religious, 3, 7, 9, 13, 18, 25, 95; sacramental, 15, 25, 45, 66, 69, 76–78, 87–93, 95; secular, 29; state/Crown, 10–11, 14, 24, 27, 29, 37, 42, 90, 94–95
Priego, López de, 228n29
purificadores, 64, 74, 78. *See also* altars

racialization, 75–76, 85–91
Reales, Pedro, 141
Reason, 15, 98–99, 104, 106, 113–15, 119, 121, 126, 130
Reformation, the, 48–49, 60, 122
Reform Catholicism, 5
religion, 15, 25, 44, 71, 95, 98, 102, 104, 114, 191, 194
Religious Ceremonies of the World (work by Bernard Picart and Jean Frédéric Bernard), 102–3
Ricci, Lorenzo, 101, 130, 161
Ricci, Matteo, 53
Rincón, Luis, 54
Ríos, Vicente Antonio de los, 58
ropa blanca, 41, 74, 78. *See also* altars

rosary, praying the, 80, 82, 85, 97, 110, 121, 125, 131, 173
Rubio y Salinas, Manuel, 154
Russo, Alessandra, 10, 219n126

sacramentality, 13, 25, 62, 65, 72, 76, 78, 92, 94–95
sacramental logics, 13–14, 22, 29–30, 42–45, 87, 90, 93–95, 194
sacramental networks, 14, 26, 30, 65–66, 71–72, 91, 95, 191, 194
Sacred Heart of Jesus, Jesuit devotion to, 59, 69, 191
salvation, 44–45, 48–50, 57–58, 62–63, 88, 146
Santa María, experiences of expelled Jesuits in, 110–11, 142–44, 152, 180
Santevas, Miguel, 34
Sarmiento, Bernardino, 48, 236n61
Schneider, Rebecca, 1, 5, 22
scurvy, 143, 176
Sebastián, José Felix de, 17–18, 23, 134–86, 191–92
secularism, 29, 95, 156
secularized Jesuits, 132, 162–64, 193, 229n41, 236n61
self: formation of, 16, 99, 110, 191–92; inventories of, 1, 15–16, 18–19, 86, 99, 109, 113; sense of, 15–16, 23, 99–100, 119, 131
self-fashioning, spiritual, 79
sermons, 35–36, 40, 79, 80, 112, 117, 122, 150
Silva, Josef Vicente de, 40, 51
Silva, Pablo, 89–90
silver: sacramental, 64–65, 72–78, 94, 190; significance of in Catholic institutions, 62–64, 72–75, 78, 84, 88–89
silver altarware, 13–14, 28, 43, 60, 62–72, 75–78, 88, 91, 194; contact of with the Eucharist/body of Christ, 13, 60, 62, 64–69, 71–72, 78, 89–90, 94, 194–95. *See also* altars
slaves. *See* enslaved persons
slavery, spiritual, 89
Society of Jesus: abolition of, 1–2, 5, 17, 135, 159–60, 166, 169, 183, 190; expulsions of, 1–3, 5, 7–9, 18, 24, 58, 108–9, 115, 146; Restoration of, 3,

186, 191, 238n90; suppression of, 2, 138, 159, 166, 175, 177, 238n90
sovereignties, 30, 43, 94; colonial, 94; competing, 10, 13–14, 25, 27–28, 60, 92, 95, 194; ekklesial, 25; Jesuit, 14, 26, 29, 92; scaffolding of, 14, 43, 60, 72
Spain, opposition to Jesuits in, 6–8. *See also* Cádiz, experiences of expelled Jesuits in
Spinoza, Baruch, 23, 100–1, 107
Spiritual Exercises, Ignatian, 16, 36–37, 52, 86, 127–28, 130, 151–52, 169, 191
spirituality, Ignatian, 49
St. Clair Segurado, Eva María, 8
Stewart, Susan, 134, 137, 146, 160–61, 184, 186
Stoler, Ann, 94
suicide, 136–37, 146, 163, 173, 239n105
surgeons, 174–77
Sweet, David, 85

Taylor, Diana, 204n7
temporal coadjutors (*hermanos*), 76, 81, 86, 141, 155–56, 168
Tepotzotlán, 116, 169–72. *See also* novices and novitiates
theopolitics, 28–30, 43–44, 48–50, 60, 87, 89, 91–92, 95, 191
Thjülen, Lars Birger (Lorenzo Ignazio), 15–19, 98, 101–5, 110–13, 118–21, 126–33, 190, 193; conversion of, 98–100, 105–8, 113–14, 121–26, 131

transubstantiation, 29, 60, 71, 93
Tridentine reforms, 60
Triduum, 127
typhus, 157, 175

Van Kley, Dale, 5–6, 8, 51
Venegas, Miguel, 163
Veracruz, experiences of expelled Jesuits in, 15, 108, 116–17, 140–41, 159
verdadero Jesuits, 149–58, 174, 182–84, 192
Viaticum, 179. *See also* death
Virgin of Guadalupe, 112, 122, 190
Virgin Mary, 54, 58–59, 84, 90, 121–22, 126. *See also* Madre Santísima de la Luz; Nuestra Señora de Dolores
Voekel, Pamela, 50, 205n20
Voltaire, 98, 102–3

Watkins, Daniel, 51
Wild, Christopher, 125
Williams, Tennessee, 22
Winchell, Mareike, 87
The Work of the Dead (work by Thomas Laqueur), 172

Xavier, Francis, 153–54, 212n49

yellow fever, 108, 140–41, 173

Zelís, Rafael de, 109, 116, 228n29, 229n41

J. MICHELLE MOLINA is Associate Professor of Religious Studies at Northwestern University. Her most recent book is *To Overcome Oneself: The Jesuit Ethic and the Spirit of Global Expansion, 1542–1767.*

CATHOLIC PRACTICE IN THE AMERICAS

James T. Fisher and Margaret M. McGuinness (eds.),
    The Catholic Studies Reader
Jeremy Bonner, Christopher D. Denny, and Mary Beth Fraser
    Connolly (eds.), *Empowering the People of God: Catholic Action
    before and after Vatican II*
Christine Firer Hinze and J. Patrick Hornbeck II (eds.), *More than a
    Monologue: Sexual Diversity and the Catholic Church. Volume I:
    Voices of Our Times*
J. Patrick Hornbeck II and Michael A. Norko (eds.), *More than a
    Monologue: Sexual Diversity and the Catholic Church. Volume II:
    Inquiry, Thought, and Expression*
Jack Lee Downey, *The Bread of the Strong:* Lacouturisme *and the Folly
    of the Cross, 1910–1985*
Michael McGregor, *Pure Act: The Uncommon Life of Robert Lax*
Mary Dunn, *The Cruelest of All Mothers: Marie de l'Incarnation,
    Motherhood, and Christian Tradition*
Dorothy Day and the Catholic Worker: The Miracle of Our Continuance.
    Photographs by Vivian Cherry, Text by Dorothy Day, Edited,
    with an Introduction and Additional Text by Kate Hennessy
Nicholas K. Rademacher, *Paul Hanly Furfey: Priest, Scientist, Social
    Reformer*
Margaret M. McGuinness and James T. Fisher (eds.), *Roman
    Catholicism in the United States: A Thematic History*
Gary J. Adler Jr., Tricia C. Bruce, and Brian Starks (eds.), *American
    Parishes: Remaking Local Catholicism*
Stephanie N. Brehm, *America's Most Famous Catholic (According to
    Himself): Stephen Colbert and American Religion in the Twenty-First
    Century*
Matthew T. Eggemeier and Peter Joseph Fritz, *Send Lazarus:
    Catholicism and the Crises of Liberalism*
John C. Seitz and Christine Firer Hinze (eds.), *Working Alternatives:
    American and Catholic Experiments in Work and Economy*

Gerald J. Beyer, *Just Universities: Catholic Social Teaching Confronts Corporatized Higher Education*

Brandon Bayne, *Missions Begin with Blood: Suffering and Salvation in the Borderlands of New Spain*

Susan Bigelow Reynolds, *People Get Ready: Ritual, Solidarity, and Lived Ecclesiology in Catholic Roxbury*

Katherine Dugan and Karen E. Park (eds.), *American Patroness: Marian Shrines and the Making of U.S. Catholicism*

Sandra Yocum and Nicholas Rademacher (eds.), *Recovering Their Stories: US Catholic Women in the Twentieth Century*

Maya Mayblin, *Vote of Faith: Democracy, Desire, and the Turbulent Lives of Priest Politicians*

Cristóbal Gnecco and Adriana Schmidt Dias (eds.), *Heritage and Its Missions: Contested Meanings and Constructive Appropriations*

J. Michelle Molina, *Inventories of Ruin: The Demise of the Mexican Jesuits, in Three Acts*

www.ingramcontent.com/pod-product-compliance
Lightning Source LLC
Chambersburg PA
CBHW020400080526
44584CB00014B/1106